# ARKANSAS VALLEY MOUNTAIN BIKING

## Leadville to Salida
## (Including South Park)

Mark Wolff

Barking Dog Guides

The opinions expressed in this publication are solely those of the author and do not represent the opinions or thoughts of the publisher. The author represents and warrants that he either owns or has the legal right to publish all material in this book.

Arkansas Valley Mountain Biking:
Leadville to Salida (Including South Park)
Second Edition
All Rights Reserved.
Copyright 2008, 2009, and 2010 Mark Wolff
Third Edition, November 2010.

This book may not be reproduced, transmitted, or stored, either in whole or in part, by any means, including graphic, electronic, or mechanical, without the express written consent of the publisher.

Published by:
Barking Dog Guides Press
PO Box 1486, Lyons, CO 80540
info@arkvalleymtb.com

ISBN: 978-0-578-07408-5

PRINTED IN THE UNITED STATES OF AMERICA

Cover photo: Sterling Mudge and Luna, the World's Greatest Trail Dog. Courtesy of Eric Wanless, Copyright 2010.

# Contents

Disclaimer..................................................................................6
Acknowledgements.................................................................7
About the author......................................................................7
Area map....................................................................................8
Classic rides index....................................................................9
Welcome to the Arkansas Valley..........................................10
    History lesson....................................................................10
    How to use this guide......................................................11
    Maps.....................................................................................11
    Mileage information.........................................................11
    Riding time.........................................................................12
    Surface.................................................................................12
    Elevation data and profiles.............................................12
    Ride difficulty ratings......................................................12
    Season..................................................................................13
    Trailhead GPS coordinates..............................................13
    Getting there......................................................................14
    Trailhead/trail amenities................................................14
    Alternate route options....................................................14
    What to expect...................................................................14
    Weather...............................................................................15
    Sun........................................................................................16
    Equipment..........................................................................16
    Safety...................................................................................17
    Water...................................................................................18
    Altitude...............................................................................18
    More rides!.........................................................................19
IMBA Rules of the Trail.........................................................20
Leadville...................................................................................21
    Ride 1: Camp Hale to Tennessee Pass..........................22
    Ride 2: Mitchell Creek Loop...........................................25
    Ride 3: Sugarloaf-Turquoise Lake Loop......................28

Ride 4: Hagerman Pass......................................................................................31
Ride 5: Sugarloaf-Power Line Loop....................................................................35
Ride 6: Ball Mountain Pass................................................................................38
Ride 7: 100 Scouting Route................................................................................41
Ride 8: 50 Scouting Route..................................................................................44
Ride 9: Mineral Belt Trail...................................................................................48
Ride 10: Lake County Singletrack......................................................................51

Twin Lakes.................................................................................................................54
Ride 11: Twin Lakes to Mount Massive Trailhead............................................55
Ride 12: Interlaken Loop....................................................................................58
Ride 13: Twin Lakes to Clear Creek...................................................................61
Ride 14: Cache Creek Loop................................................................................64

Granite.......................................................................................................................67
Ride 15: Lost Canyon Road to Twin Lakes Loop..............................................68
Ride 16: Lost Canyon Road (Columbine Climb)...............................................71
Ride 17: Spring Creek Loop...............................................................................74

Buena Vista...............................................................................................................77
Ride 18: Castle Rock Gulch Loop......................................................................78
Ride 19: Bald Mountain Gulch Loop.................................................................81
Ride 20: Davis Meadow Loop............................................................................84
Ride 21: FSR 373 (Natural Arch) Loop..............................................................88
Ride 22: Fourmile Cutoff Loop..........................................................................91
Ride 23: Lenhardy Cutoff...................................................................................94
Ride 24: Midland Bike Trail...............................................................................97
Ride 25: Midland Railroad Grade....................................................................100
Ride 26: Gentlemen's Loop...............................................................................103
Ride 27: Fourmile Recreation Area Loop........................................................106
Ride 28: Buena Vista River Park......................................................................111
Ride 29: Trout Creek Pass to Buena Vista.......................................................113
Ride 30: Fourmile Road – Buena Vista Overlook...........................................116
Ride 31: Buena Vista River Road.....................................................................119

Nathrop...................................................................................................................121
Ride 32: Frontier Ranch to South Cottonwood Creek....................................122

Ride 33: Mt. Princeton Road..................................................................125
Ride 34: Raspberry Gulch Loop............................................................128
Ride 35: Cascade Railroad Grade..........................................................131
St. Elmo.........................................................................................................134
Ride 36: Alpine Tunnel..............................................................................135
Ride 37: Alpine Tunnel to Tin Cup Pass Road Loop.........................138
Poncha Springs............................................................................................142
Ride 38: Colorado Trail: US 50 to Chalk Creek..................................143
Ride 39: Marshall Pass to Silver Creek Loop.....................................147
Ride 40: Silver Creek Loop......................................................................151
Monarch Crest.............................................................................................154
Ride 41: Monarch Crest Trail..................................................................155
Ride 42: Descending Marshall Pass Road..........................................158
Ride 43: Descending Starvation Creek Trail......................................161
Ride 44: Descending Silver Creek Trail...............................................164
Ride 45: Descending South Fooses Creek Trail................................168
Ride 46: Descending Agate Creek Trail...............................................171
Salida..............................................................................................................174
Ride 47: Bear Creek to Methodist Mountain Loop..........................175
Ride 48: Spiral Drive/Tenderfoot Mountain......................................179
Ride 49: Ute Trail Loop.............................................................................182
Ride 50: The Crater....................................................................................185
Ride 51: Upper Bighorn Sheep Canyon...............................................188
South Park....................................................................................................191
Ride 52: Salt Creek-McQuaid Loop.......................................................192
Ride 53: Tumble Creek Trail...................................................................195
Ride 54: Weston Pass.................................................................................198
Ride 55: Sheep Creek Trail......................................................................201
Ride 56: Mosquito Pass.............................................................................204
Ride 57: Boreas Pass-Gold Dust Trail..................................................207
One more ride.............................................................................................211
Ride 58: River Park to River Park- Buena Vista to Salida............211
Local resources...........................................................................................217

# Disclaimer

**Warning! Ride at your own risk!**

Mountain biking is inherently dangerous and there is no way to eliminate all risks. Using this book indicates a user's acceptance of all potential risks.

This book tells you where to do it, not how. Therefore, any information provided by is strictly informational and not instructional. You should not attempt these routes unless you have sufficient experience to manage the potential hazards of backcountry travel. Every rider is solely accountable for his or her own abilities to ride in a safe and responsible manner.

Documenting current trail conditions is beyond the scope of this book. Changes in routes, whether attributed to human efforts, natural events, or property closures, are possible. Such changes could impact the technical and aerobic difficulty of a route.

The information in this book is based upon the experiences of the author and may not be perceived as accurate by others. There are no warranties, either perceived or actual, that the information contained in this book is accurate. The technical and aerobic ratings for each ride reflect the experiences of the author and may not be agreed upon by others. In addition, all mileage and elevation data included with the route descriptions are estimates.

Getting lost is possible whenever you venture into the wilderness. Always be prepared. No book serves as a substitute for sound judgment. Know your limits and be safe. You alone are responsible for your fate.

The author, publisher, or any other persons or organizations mentioned in this book are not responsible or liable in any way for incidents, property damage, accidents, injuries, or deaths that may result from attempting the routes described in this guide.

# Acknowledgements

Many people helped make this book possible, but I'd especially like to thank the following:

Keith and Evelyn Baker of Buena Vista for giving me a place to plant my feet as I explored the Valley. Sterling Mudge, Eric Wanless, and all of the Cloud City Wheelers for trail information, photos, and great trail advocacy work. And Jody and Brian Stack for photos.

Andy Applegate of Carmichael Training Systems for continually inspiring me to keep my old butt moving (however slowly I go these days).

And I especially want to thank my wife for her great patience, enduring faith, and steadfast support. Without her, none of this would have been possible.

All Maps and elevation profiles created with TOPO! (© National Geographic Maps) http://www.nationalgeographic.org/maps

In addition, thanks to the International Mountain Biking Association for their great advocacy work with the Continental Divide Trail and for permission to reprint their "Rules of the Trail." (http://www.imba.com)

# About the author

With more than twenty years of experience in the saddle, Mark currently splits his time between Laguna Niguel, CA and Lyons, Colorado. Over the years he has aggressively explored numerous trails in Washington, Utah, Pennsylvania, Kansas, California, Oregon, and Hawaii. In addition to mountain biking, he has snowboarded throughout the U.S. and Europe, including a couple epic descents in Alaska's Chugach Range. He enjoys mountaineering and has climbed in Africa and South America (in addition to reaching many summits at home in the U.S.). He wasted his youth surfing along the west and east coasts of the U.S.

*San Mateo Trails, San Clemente, CA (May 2010)*

8 • *Arkansas Valley Mountain Biking*

# Area map

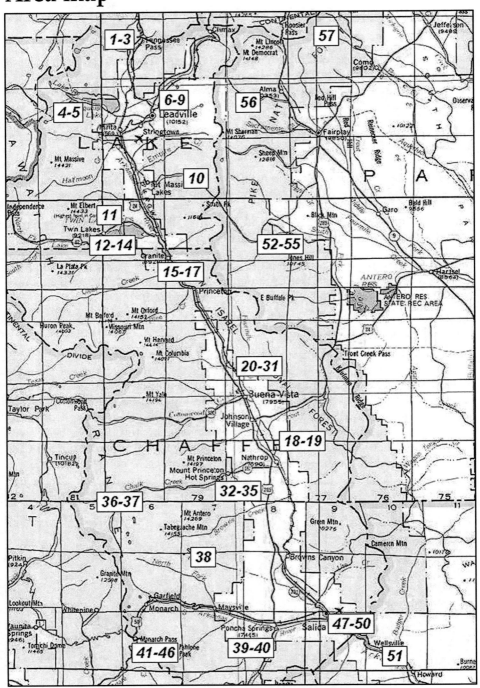

Ride locations by route number (© National Geographic)

# Classic rides index

These are the best rides in the Valley (listed with book ride number):

**Colorado Trail single-track**
Camp Hale to Tennessee Pass (1)
Mitchell Creek Loop (2)
Sugarloaf-Turquoise Lake Loop (3)
Twin Lakes to Mt Massive (11)
Interlaken Loop (12)
Twin Lakes to Clear Creek (13)
Cache Creek Loop (14)
Lost Canyon to Twin Lakes Loop (15)
Frontier Ranch to S Cottonwood (32)
Raspberry Gulch Loop (34)
US 50 to Chalk Creek (38)
Monarch Crest/S. Fooses (45)

**All Monarch Crest routes** (41-46)

**More amazing single-track**
Alpine Tunnel to Tin Cup Pass (37)
Marshall Pass to Silver Creek (39)
Silver Creek Loop (40)
Bear Creek to Methodist Mt. (47)
Salt Creek-McQuaid Loop (52)
Boreas Pass-Gold Dust Trail (57)

**Monster climbs**
Hagerman Pass (4)
Twin Lakes to Mt Massive (11)
Twin Lakes to Clear Creek (13)
Lost Canyon Road (16)
Davis Meadow Loop (20)
Fourmile Recreation Area Loop (27)
Mt Princeton Road (33)
Marshall Pass to Silver Creek (39)
Bear Creek to Methodist Mt (47)
Ute Trail Loop (49)
The Crater (50)
Weston Pass (54)
Mosquito Pass (56)
River Park to River Park (58)

**Experts only**
Davis Meadow Loop (20)
Alpine Tunnel to Tin Cup Pass (37)
US 50 to Chalk Creek (38)

Marshall Pass to Silver Creek (39)
Monarch Crest/Silver Creek (44)
Monarch Crest/Agate Creek (46)
Ute Trail Loop (49)

**Epics**
100 Scouting Route (7)
50 Scouting Route (8)
Fourmile Recreation Area Loop (27)
US 50 to Chalk Creek (38)
Marshall Pass to Silver Creek (39)
River Park to River Park (58)

**Novice-friendly**
Mitchell Creek Loop (2)
Interlaken Loop (12)
Lenhardy Cutoff (23)
Midland Bike Trail routes (24-26)
Trout Creek Pass to Buena Vista (29)
Raspberry Gulch Loop (34)
Alpine Tunnel (36)

**Family-friendly**
Mineral Belt (9)
Castle Rock Gulch Loop (18)
Buena Vista River Road (31)
Cascade Railroad Grade (35)
Spiral Drive (48)
Upper Bighorn Sheep Canyon (51)

**Historically interesting (ghost towns, mine sites, etc.)**
Hagerman Pass (4)
Ball Mountain Pass (6)
50 Scouting Route (8)
Mineral Belt Trail (9)
Weston Pass (54)
Interlaken Loop (12)
Midland Bike Trail routes (24-26)
Alpine Tunnel (36)
Weston Pass (54)

# Welcome to the Arkansas Valley

Imagine a region central to the some of the best sections of the Colorado Trail, the Rainbow Trail, and the Continental Divide Trail. Next, surround that area with the greatest concentration of mountains exceeding fourteen thousand feet in the contiguous United States. Finish that dreamscape with an ideal climate of moderate summer temperatures and brilliant sunny skies.

That's what you will find in Colorado's Arkansas Valley.

Running more than sixty miles from Leadville to Salida, the region is as of yet a little-known fat tire Nirvana. An advanced cyclist can literally spend an entire summer riding and exploring the area without repeating a single route. With rides ranging in difficulty from beginner to expert, however, there is enough varied terrain to cater to every skill level.

While the Monarch Crest Trail is perhaps the best-known ride in the region, the other major trail systems that thread the Valley offer miles of superb riding. In addition, there are countless miles of old mining routes and rugged jeep trails, all prime for fat tire exploration. Whether you seek the sublime single-track of Salida, the screaming jeep trails of Buena Vista, or the celestial lung-busters of Leadville, this guide will lead you to the best rides in Colorado's Arkansas Valley.

Stomp on those pedals and let it rip!

# History lesson

Long before the discovery of gold near Leadville sparked widespread settlement of the area, Native Americans of the Ute Nation sought winter refuge in the mild climate of the southern Valley. In addition to the Ute, other native nations, such as the Comanche, Kiowa, Sioux, and Cheyenne, utilized the Arkansas River Valley as a gateway to the buffalo hunting grounds of South Park.

The first recorded visit of U.S. citizens to the area did not occur until the Pike expedition of 1806. Sent to find the headwaters of the Arkansas River, Zebulon Pike's group entered the region in mid-December. By December 22, Pike and some of his men almost reached the river's headwaters near Leadville, but snow forced them to retreat south where they spent Christmas Day camped along the river near Poncha Springs. There's a plaque posted on US Highway 285 (near CR 165) to memorialize this event.

In 1860, the discovery of gold in California Gulch, a small valley just outside of Leadville, changed everything. Within months, a rough and tumble settlement of tents and cabins dubbed Oro City housed thousands of miners and prospectors, all drawn to the area with hopes of striking it rich.

Just as the gold yields ebbed, bountiful silver strikes in the same vicinity created a second boom. By 1880, Leadville blossomed into a city of more than 30,000, becoming one of Colorado's largest cities of the time. The city was so vibrant that some people considered naming Leadville the capitol of the newly formed state of Colorado.

The repeal of the Sherman Silver Act in 1893 brought an end to the boom. Many of the region's aristocrats lost their fortunes and abandoned their mines. The most famous tragedy to emerge from the sudden economic downturn is the legend of Baby Doe Tabor. The once young and beautiful widow of Horace Tabor froze to death in her one-room shack on the grounds of the Matchless Silver Mine as she waited in vain for silver prices to return to their boom-time highs.

To support the mining enterprises of the northern Valley, the southern towns became important rail centers. Buena Vista, established in 1879, started as a railroad town with three lines: the Denver & Rio Grande, South Park & Pacific, and Colorado Midland. Founded in 1880, Salida was a significant link in the Denver & Rio Grande railroads.

The legacy of this rich heritage becomes apparent as you explore the area by mountain bike. Many of the routes in this guide either exploit old railroad grades, access abandoned mine sites, or pass through ghost towns and vacant homesteads. Even though the once bountiful mines are now depleted, the mountains surrounding the Arkansas Valley still hold many treasures awaiting your discovery.

# How to use this guide
Understanding a few conventions will help you use this guide.

## Maps
The maps provided give you a general perspective and orient you to the nature of a route. Unless you are already familiar with the area, you should carry additional maps. Good quality, highly detailed topographic maps provide a better interpretation of the terrain than any guidebook can. While many maps do not include some of the trails included in this guide, you stand a much better chance of staying oriented if you have a map.

In addition to USGS quadrangles, National Geographic's Trails Illustrated regional maps are excellent resources.

## Mileage information
It's probably worth taking a few words to discuss mileage. While great pains were taken to record accurate mileage readings, the final work can only serve as an estimate. As anyone who has spent a fair amount of time in the backcountry already knows, all cycling computers, global positioning systems, computer software, and maps contain a certain margin of error. Compiling data using a combination of all of these tools results in compounded, albeit small, errors. It's an unavoidable fact of life.

I used to scoff when I encountered discrepancies of 0.1 miles (or greater) between my cycling computer readings and those recorded in a guide. After gaining a great deal of experience working with GPS units and multiple mapping tools, however, I found that if I repeated a route ten times, the result would yield ten unique mileage readings. While the differences were often miniscule, they were there nonetheless. Go figure.

Forewarned with this information, be aware that all mileage data are estimates and serve only to give you a frame of reference for where you are in relation to other relative data points.

## Riding time

The riding time estimates provided give a general idea of the time needed to complete the ride. Obviously, more experienced riders may find these times very generous while others may find them too tight. In general, the estimates are based on what most recreational bikers will find to be a relaxed, steady pace. Since these estimates do not include breaks taken along the trail, you may want to budget a little extra time.

## Surface

The surface describes the riding surface of the route: paved road, dirt road, jeep track, double-track, single-track, etc.

## Elevation data and profiles

The elevation data and profiles provide elevation statistics and a visual depiction of the climbing and descending nature of the route. Once again, all data are estimates based on GPS and USGS 7.5-minute map values.

## Ride difficulty ratings

Two criteria determine a route's rating: the aerobic level of the route and the technical difficulty of the terrain.

### Aerobic level

The aerobic rating describes the physical fitness demand of a route. There are three primary levels: easy, moderate, and strenuous. Altitude plays a significant role; if you aren't acclimatized, expect the rides to feel a little tougher than the rating.

**Easy** rides generally involve little climbing or brief climbs on easy terrain.

**Moderate** rides typically involve some climbing. The climbs may be steep but relatively short, or sustained at a gradual grade. The technical difficulty also plays a factor. For example, a gentle grade may be physically moderate due to rocks or sand. Most recreational cyclists will be able to complete moderate rides with minimal walking.

**Strenuous** rides demand a high level of physical fitness. Steep climbs can be sustained and littered with technical obstacles. Riders without significant endurance and the power gained through many hours of training are likely to find these routes exceedingly difficult. Less fit riders may encounter long stretches where they must either take breaks or walk the bike.

## Technical difficulty

The quantity and nature of the obstacles encountered along a route determine the technical difficulty of a ride. Technical ratings are divided into five levels from 1 to 5, with 1 being the easiest.

**Level 1** rides have few obstacles and do not require any special bicycle handling skills. The riding surface is generally smooth and descents are gentle.

**Level 2** rides may have some rocks or patches of loose gravel or sand, but novice mountain bikers should have little problem riding through these obstacles.

**Level 3** rides are technically moderate and typically on single-track or jeep trails. Riders may encounter rocks, roots, erosion damage, or other obstacles that require specific cycling techniques. Line selection, or the ability to direct a bicycle along a specific, narrow path, becomes important at this level. Some intermediate and most novice riders will encounter short sections of hike-a-bike.

**Level 4** rides have combined obstacles and fewer line choices than Level 3 rides. Riders may encounter sections of trail that are both loose and rocky. Laterally eroded single-tracks may also be steep. Some intermediate riders may have to push their bikes through extended portions of these routes, increasing the time it takes to complete the ride.

**Level 5** rides typically feature very steep sections that are frequently littered with many obstacles. Intermediate riders will struggle and find themselves at an increased risk for sustaining serious injury on these routes. As such, only expert riders should attempt these rides.

## Season

Each route has an optimal riding season listed. Late or early snowfall will affect this range. Please refrain from riding on snowy or muddy trails as doing so damages the trail surface. Call a local bike shop or Forest Service office for current conditions.

## Trailhead GPS coordinates

Provided with each route are the GPS coordinates for the trailhead. These will assist GPS-equipped riders with finding a route's starting point. In addition, GPS route files (.gpx format) for all the rides in this guide are available free on the Internet at: *www.arkvalleymtb.com*.

## Getting there

Directions to the trailhead originate from distinct locations in the closest town and follow major thoroughfares. If you are already familiar with the area, you may know shortcuts or alternate ways of getting to a trailhead. If a route has alternate riding options or multiple access points, directions to those locations are also included.

## Trailhead/trail amenities

A list of amenities (restrooms, etc) available at the trailhead or along the trail.

## Alternate route options

Most routes have interesting, alternate ways of riding them. The alternate options provided are suggestions that some riders may wish to explore. There are many ways to do these routes and as you become more familiar with the area you are bound to find variations better suited to your taste.

# What to expect

The Arkansas Valley is predominantly high desert where one can expect dry weather and sunny skies throughout the year. The Sawatch Mountain Range bounds the Valley to the west, the Sangre de Cristo Mountains to the south, and the Mosquito Range to the east. The northern end of the Valley is bounded by the Continental Divide, which runs east to west above Leadville.

Coursing the entire length of the Valley is its namesake river, the Arkansas. Well-known to whitewater enthusiasts, the river crashes nearly one vertical mile down from its headwaters just below the Continental Divide at Fremont Pass north of Leadville to the Royal Gorge east of Salida.

When surveying the area, one cannot ignore the fact that in some places the valley floor is more than six thousand feet below the highest peaks surrounding it. The net result is three distinct climate zones, each with unique characteristics.

Routes at elevations of less than nine thousand feet typically run through sage and stands of scraggly pinon. The single-track and jeep/ATV trails in this zone are typically comprised of crushed granite and may be sandy in summer. Many of these trails remain dry and snow-free for much of the winter, and in some years several of these routes can be ridden year-round. Since this zone can get uncomfortably hot in summer, it's best to ride in the early morning or late afternoon. The Arkansas Hills north of Salida and the Fourmile Recreation Area east of Buena Vista are good examples of this zone.

Higher up, the landscape slowly changes to classic Colorado sub-alpine forests of pine and aspen. It's in this zone where trails are frequently loamy and fat tire knobs are at their best. You'll sail over trail-beds that are at once soft and fast. Furthermore, these forested areas offer relief from the summer sun and higher temperatures of the lower valley. Trails through here are typically dry and snow-free from mid-May through October. Much of the Colorado and Rainbow Trails run through this zone.

Routes accessing terrain above the trees, at elevations of twelve thousand feet or more, slice through alpine meadows of brightly blooming wildflowers and fragile grasses. Without the shelter of trees, you are likely to encounter higher winds, cooler temperatures, and intensely strong ultraviolet rays. This is also the last place you want to be in the event of a storm. Trails here have the shortest season: July through October. Much of the Monarch Crest Trail, some sections of the Continental Divide Trail, and many of the rides in the Leadville area access this zone.

There are a few other things to consider when visiting the area. Summer daytime temperatures in Salida average in the mid-eighties, but can reach into the nineties on some days. Leadville, due to its high altitude, is typically ten or fifteen degrees cooler than Salida. Nighttime temperatures may be up to forty degrees cooler than day, so if you plan to camp, pack accordingly.

Hunting season begins in fall (check with the Colorado Division of Wildlife for more information). This is also an ideal time to ride because the aspens are at peak color and the weather is great. If you plan to ride after the start of hunting season, be sure to wear bright clothing and avoid popular hunting areas.

Try to avoid riding when trails are muddy or remain covered with large areas of snow. Riding in mud damages trails and may affect the quality of the riding surface for a long time. If you encounter a small mud patch, ride or, better yet, push your bike directly through the center of the trail. Bypassing mud damages a trail by making it wider and potentially increasing the effects of erosion.

In addition, resist the temptation to ride on trails closed to mountain bikes and don't ride illegal (rogue or social) trails. This is a serious problem in some places and jeopardizes bike access to the region. If in doubt, don't do it. If you find a trail that interests you but are uncertain of its status, contact a local bike shop or the proper land management agency to learn more before riding it.

## Weather

In general, the weather in the Arkansas River Valley is exceptional. Mountain weather, however, is notoriously fickle and requires some preparation. Summer storms are usually fast moving and can be fierce. With little warning, perfect crystal-blue skies turn gray, the temperatures plunge, and thunder shakes the Valley as lightning dances across the sky. If caught by surprise, cherry-sized raindrops, hail, or even snow could fall on you.

Fortunately, these storms often pass as quickly as they arrive.

If you see a storm forming, it's best to turn back and head for the car. If caught in a storm, here are a few things you can do to reduce your risk of injury. First, be prepared. Always carry rain gear. If you get wet, your chance of developing hypothermia (the cooling of your body's core to dangerously low levels) increases exponentially. This potentially life-threatening condition is possible even when temperatures are in the low 50's. Altitude, dehydration, and fatigue all contribute to your susceptibility. A light, waterproof/breathable shell tucked into your pack can literally be a lifesaver. If you are going high, you should also bring extra insulating layers.

If you hear thunder, you are within the striking range of lightning. If caught in an exposed area, ditch the bike and look for a gully or low spot where you can crouch or sit on your pack. Do not lie down and avoid all puddles and running water. Do not take shelter under lone trees or close to isolated rock outcroppings. If you are in a forested area, descend as much as possible and take shelter in a dense stand of uniformly tall trees. If you are part of a group, spread out to decrease the risk of a single strike disabling everyone.

Though the day may be warm and balmy, be prepared for as much as a forty-degree drop in temperature when the sun goes down. This may be fine as you slip into your sleeping bag at camp, but if you underestimate the time it takes to complete a ride it could mean trouble. So if you are attempting an epic be sure to pack extra clothes, extra food, and a headlamp.

## Sun

Don't underestimate the sun. Most of the rides in this guide are in excess of eight thousand feet where there is little atmosphere to protect your eyes and skin from powerful ultraviolet rays. Even though the air may feel cool, the sun quickly burns unprotected, exposed skin. Always wear sun block with a minimum SPF of 30 and wear protective sunglasses. If you are riding with small children in tow, be sure to take measures to protect their eyes and skin as well.

## Equipment

How much stuff to bring? It depends on you. Your standard gear should include a helmet, gloves, sport sunglasses, and a cycling computer. A helmet is a no-brainer, or at least it will help prevent you from becoming a no-brainer in the event of a crash. Gloves add comfort to your ride and help protect your hands if you fall. Sunglasses shade your eyes from ultraviolet rays and protect them from bugs and trail debris kicked-up by tires. A cycling computer/odometer is essential because you won't know where you are if you don't know how far you've gone.

One of the most versatile yet least expensive pieces of gear I own is a urethane-coated nylon rain poncho. Costing less than thirty dollars, I have used it for everything from an emergency camping shelter to a highly effective rain garment. It packs small, weighs about twenty ounces, and fits easily into my hydration pack. While it isn't practical to wear it while riding, when caught in a shower I simply throw it over my head and find a comfy place to sit until the storm passes. I stay dry. My pack stays dry. Perfect!

*At a minimum, you should also bring:*
- this trail guide
- bicycle multi-tool
- spare tube(s)
- chain tool
- tire levers
- wrist watch
- patch kit
- pump
- small first aid kit
- sun block
- rain gear
- trail food
- extra layers if going high
- cigarette lighter

*Other wise things to include:*
- chain repair links
- spare derailleur hanger
- area map and compass
- spoke tool
- extra pedal cleat bolts
- headlamp

*If you attempt a longer ride, consider taking:*
- sports drink with electrolytes
- spare cables
- 2 extra spokes and nipples
- water treatment tablets

*Super gear-heads may also want:*
- global positioning system (GPS)
- CO2 inflation tool and cartridges
- heart rate monitor

Always give your bike a quick checkup before you ride. Visually inspect your wheel skewers, rims, brakes, cables, headset, and cranks to be sure everything is in good condition. Check your tire pressure and your tires (healthy tread, no sidewall cracks, etc.). Take a quick spin around the parking area to check seat height, pedal cleats, and brakes.

One mistake many riders make is that they never check or change their chains. A dirty or dry chain quickly wears out, and a worn chain has a greater chance of breaking on the trail. Additionally, a stretched chain will silently ruin the components of your drive train, a costly repair. Do yourself a favor and check, clean, and lube your chain frequently, or take it to a shop to have it done professionally.

## Safety

Chaffee, Lake and Park Counties are predominantly rural and sparsely populated. Many of these routes, therefore, go deep into remote wilderness. Help may not be expedient or readily available in the event of an emergency. Use common sense and always ride well within your ability.

At best, cellular telephone reception is spotty in the backcountry. In addition, some providers either do not offer service or have limited coverage in some parts of the Valley. If possible, however, always carry a cell phone. Signals frequently improve as you gain altitude, especially when riding in areas adjacent to the larger towns. The number of places you have service may astonish you.

In addition, consider purchasing a Colorado Search and Rescue (COSAR) card. For a nominal cost this card will cover search and rescue fees incurred if you get in a jam. You can find them at many retailers throughout the Valley.

## Water

You'd be surprised how quickly you can dehydrate while riding. The dry climate and high altitude conspire to desiccate you even on easy rides. While a single bottle may be more than adequate for your single-track outings at home, you will need to carry more when you venture into the high country of the Arkansas Valley.

Hydration packs work well and are available in sizes of 20 to 100 ounces. On longer rides, you should also carry a bike bottle or two of electrolyte-replenishing sports drinks. One trick is to mix the sports drink in your bottles a little "thick" so that it is slightly more concentrated than the recommended serving. This gives you a few extra calories with each gulp and works to prevent hyponatremia, a dangerous depletion of your body's electrolytes. If you super-concentrate your sports drink, however, be sure to also drink plenty of water to ease digestion and offset the potential dehydrating effect of the concentrate.

If you run dry on the trail, your best bet is to bum water from your friends or others on the trail. If that doesn't work, filter or treat water from streams following the directions of your water treatment system or tablets. Unless it is an extreme emergency, DO NOT DRINK UNTREATED WATER FROM STREAMS. Giardia cysts are common in the Arkansas Valley and ensure that you, or at least your bottom, will never forget the time you sipped from that sparkling Rocky Mountain stream.

## Altitude

Locals are acclimatized to the high elevation and won't have any problems with altitude. If you are visiting from a lower elevation, however, there are a few precautions to take to reduce your risk of developing Acute Mountain Sickness (AMS). First, give your body a day or two to rest and acclimatize. Take it easy and don't hammer on your first few rides. Drink plenty of fluids, but try to avoid heavy consumption of caffeine and alcohol.

You might experience mild symptoms of AMS, such as faint headaches, light-headedness, and slight fatigue during your first couple of days. If symptoms intensify or don't subside within a few days, however, consider moving to a lower altitude. Descending as little as one thousand feet may be enough to make you feel much better.

If you experience two or more severe symptoms, such as aspirin resistant headaches, irregular breathing, a rapid resting pulse rate, nausea, dizziness, or difficulty sleeping, descend immediately. Though uncommon in Colorado, it is possible for these symptoms to develop into a life-threatening build-up of fluids in the lungs and brain.

Welcome • 19

# More rides!

This guide is a companion to the free, on-line e-Guide: *www.arkvalleymtb.com*. On this site you will find free GPX files (GPS routes) for every route in this guide. These files can be downloaded and imported into most recreational mapping software packages, such as National Geographic's TOPO!, and loaded into your GPS unit.

In addition, you will find more area rides (those that didn't make the editorial cut for this printed edition) and other useful area information to help you get the most from your visit to the Arkansas Valley. Check it out and tell your friends!

**Interlaken Loop**

# IMBA Rules of the Trail

The way we ride today shapes mountain bike trail access tomorrow. Do your part to preserve and enhance our sport's access and image by observing the following rules of the trail, formulated by IMBA, the International Mountain Bicycling Association. These rules are recognized around the world as the standard code of conduct for mountain bikers. IMBA's mission is to promote mountain bicycling that is environmentally sound and socially responsible.

### 1. Ride On Open Trails Only

Respect trail and road closures (ask if uncertain); avoid trespassing on private land; obtain permits or other authorization as may be required. Federal and state Wilderness areas are closed to cycling. The way you ride will influence trail management decisions and policies.

### 2. Leave No Trace

Be sensitive to the dirt beneath you. Recognize different types of soils and trail construction; practice low-impact cycling. Wet and muddy trails are more vulnerable to damage. When the trailbed is soft, consider other riding options. This also means staying on existing trails and not creating new ones. Don't cut switchbacks. Be sure to pack out at least as much as you pack in.

### 3. Control Your Bicycle!

Inattention for even a second can cause problems. Obey all bicycle speed regulations and recommendations.

### 4. Always Yield Trail

Let your fellow trail users know you're coming. A friendly greeting or bell is considerate and works well; don't startle others. Show your respect when passing by slowing to a walking pace or even stopping. Anticipate other trail users around corners or in blind spots. Yielding means slow down, establish communication, be prepared to stop if necessary and pass safely.

### 5. Never Scare Animals

All animals are startled by an unannounced approach, a sudden movement, or a loud noise. This can be dangerous for you, others, and the animals. Give animals extra room and time to adjust to you. When passing horses use special care and follow directions from the horseback riders (ask if uncertain). Running cattle and disturbing wildlife is a serious offense. Leave gates as you found them, or as marked.

### 6. Plan Ahead

*Know your equipment, your ability, and the area in which you are riding -- and prepare accordingly. Be self-sufficient at all times, keep your equipment in good repair, and carry necessary supplies for changes in weather or other conditions. A well-executed trip is a satisfaction to you and not a burden to others. Always wear a helmet and appropriate safety gear.*

**Keep trails open by setting a good example of environmentally sound and socially responsible off-road cycling.**

---

**Reprinted with permission from the International Mountain Biking Association.**

# Leadville

While Leadville was once the bustling epicenter of the Arkansas Valley, nearly a century of economic downturns dealt a series of blows to the town. Despite these adversities, however, the town has not only survived but managed to thrive against all odds.

Borne of this hardscrabble spirit is America's highest altitude ultra cycling event: the Leadville Trail 100. In recent years the race garnered international attention by attracting elite competitors. But to solely focus on the superstars at the head of the pack misses a crucial aspect of the event. Each year hundreds of average cyclists take on the challenge of competing not against each other, but against the course and clock as they push their limits to finish before the cutoff.

No other city in the United States provides as much easy access to high altitude terrain. Before setting out, please bear in mind the unique demands of this environment. First, you will want to get an early start to avoid potentially dangerous afternoon storms. Many of the local routes access terrain above tree line, the last place you want to experience a storm. Next, visitors to Colorado from lower altitudes may want to take a few days to acclimatize before going nuts in the saddle.

Since a number of these rides start at the center of town, they offer easy access to post-ride amenities. (Support local merchants; things are changing for the better and your contribution makes a difference!) If you need any gear or have questions, there is a great, full-service bike shop in the center of town. While visiting, take a tour of the Matchless Mine or ride the Leadville, Colorado and Southern Railroad. The National Mining Hall of Fame and Museum, and the Tabor Opera House provide interesting diversions if you need time to acclimatize or rest your weary legs. Discover why Leadville is one of Colorado's greatest treasures.

# 22 • *Arkansas Valley Mountain Biking*

# Ride 1: Camp Hale to Tennessee Pass

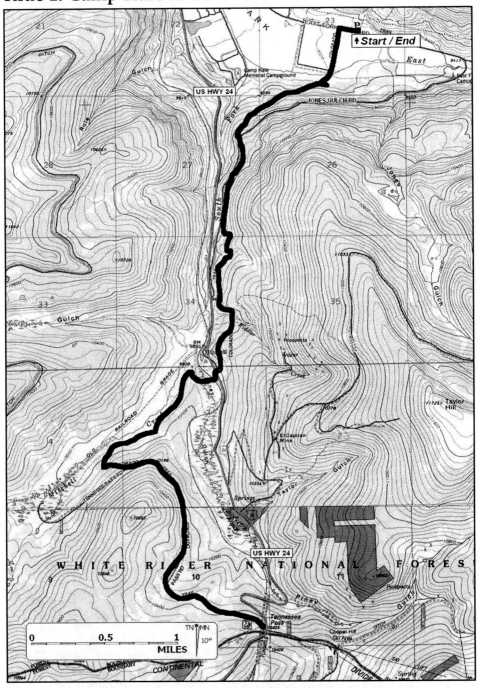

*Map 1: Camp Hale to Tennessee Pass (© National Geographic)*

During World War II, Minnie Dole, father of the National Ski Patrol, convinced the War Department of the need for a specialized division trained in skiing and winter survival skills. Following initial training trials in Paradise, Washington, Camp Hale was built to serve as the base for this unit. Nicknamed by some as "Camp Hell" for the dense cooking and heating smoke that filled the basin in winter, the area provided the perfect place for troops to hone their skiing and climbing skills. After two years of rigorous training, the Tenth Mountain Division deployed to Europe where they played a key role in the liberation of northern Italy.

As for the ride, this is one of the best in the Leadville area. Most of the grade is mild enough to crank in your middle ring and the technical obstacles are just challenging enough to test your skills without slowing you down. The icing on the cake, however, is the return trip from the pass. It is so much fun that you may not be able to stop smiling when you're done.

**Ride length:** 12.9 miles
**Ride type:** out-and-back
**Riding time:** 2 hours
**Surface:** dirt road/jeep track (5.0 miles); single-track (7.9 miles)
**Elevations:** start/end 9,360'; max 10,440'; min 9,330'
**Total climbing:** gain/loss 1,410'

**Aerobic level:** moderate (on the easy side of moderate; some climbing on single-track)
**Technical level:** 3 (a few tricky spots, but mostly smooth trail)
**Season:** June through October
**USGS Quadrangles:** Leadville North, Pando

**Trailhead GPS coordinates:** 39° 25.446' N; 106° 17.919' W

**Elevation profile:**

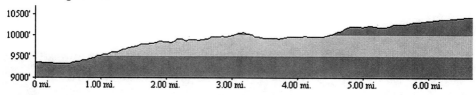

**Getting there:** from the stoplight at 6th St. and Harrison Ave. (US 24) in downtown Leadville, drive 15.8 miles north on US 24 to the Camp Hale Forest Service Campground exit. Turn right to exit and drive 0.1 miles to the intersection. Turn right and continue east for 0.5 miles, crossing the bridge over the Eagle River East Fork. At the "T" intersection with Road #714, turn right and drive about 1.5 miles to the trailhead and parking lot on the left.

**Trailhead/trail amenities:** pit toilet at mile 6.5.

**The ride:**
0.0    Start at the parking lot of the Camp Hale trailhead of the Colorado Trail. Turn right (west) onto Road #714.
0.1    Turn left (south) onto Road #7141C, following the Colorado/Continental Divide trail markers.

## 24 • *Arkansas Valley Mountain Biking*

- **0.5** Turn left and cross the bridge. Trail markers help you find the route.
- **1.2** Pop-out on a dirt road. Head left, pass through a gate, then immediately turn right and continue on the single-track. Trail markers lead the way.
- **1.5** Pass an overlook with a bench.
- **2.2** Cross a gnarled jeep track and continue riding the sweet line on the other side.
- **3.0** Cross the highway. Watch for traffic! Head left, dropping down and around the gate. At the bottom, bunny-hop the train tracks (or walk your bike across as I do) and continue riding the fine line ahead.
- **3.1** Cross the water on tricky bridges. Ride them if you don't mind swimming if you don't clean them.
- **4.5** Intersect a well-maintained dirt road and continue riding left (east) toward the pass.
- **5.3** Continue straight on the double-track after crossing a bridge.
- **5.4** Enter a clearing. Look left to see the slopes of Ski Cooper.
- **6.5** Arrive at the Tennessee Pass trailhead. Return the way you came. What a blast!

**Options:** extend this ride by incorporating the **Mitchell Creek Loop**, turning the ride into a lollipop-loop (clockwise) of approximately 18 miles. Or shuttle it from Tennessee Pass for a short, fun ride into Camp Hale.

*Camp Hale cantonments.*

# Ride 2: Mitchell Creek Loop

Leadville • 25

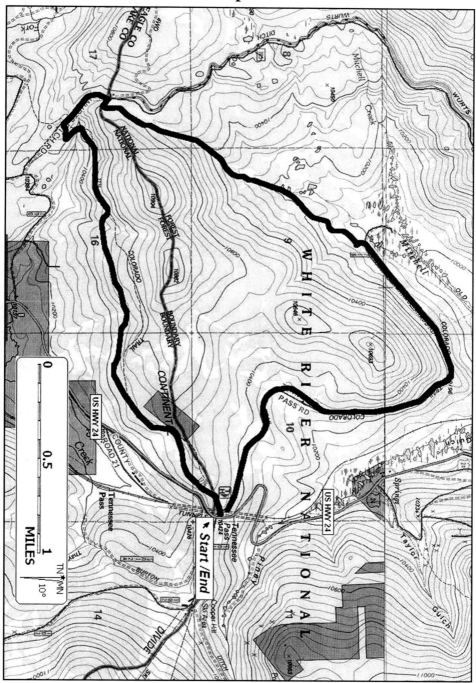

Map 2: Mitchell Creek Loop (© National Geographic)

# 26 • *Arkansas Valley Mountain Biking*

This ride is a perfect way to start the day. The single-track is manageable for beginners yet interesting enough to satisfy more experienced riders. Strong riders can probably blast through two laps in under two hours.

The route starts on pleasant single-track through a pine forest. Next, you'll ride a short stretch on dirt road followed by a smooth and effortless single-track descent into the Mitchell Creek basin. The ride ends on an easy-graded double-track along the route's only sustained climb.

**Ride length:** 7.1 miles
**Ride type:** loop (clockwise)
**Riding time:** 1 hour
**Surface:** single-track (4.1 miles); double-track (2.6 miles); dirt road (0.4 miles)
**Elevations:** start/end 10,440'; max 10,630'; min 10,060'
**Total climbing:** gain/loss 900'
**Aerobic level:** easy (but the entire ride is over 10,000')
**Technical level:** 2+ (easy overall with a couple short rocky sections)
**Season:** June through October
**USGS Quadrangles:** Leadville North, Pando

**Trailhead GPS coordinates:** 39° 21.761' N; 106° 18.675' W

**Elevation profile:**

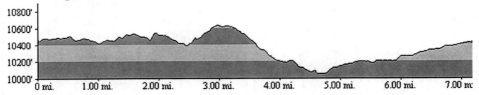

**Getting there:** from the stoplight at 6th St. and Harrison Ave. (US 24) in downtown Leadville, drive 10.0 miles north on US 24 to Tennessee Pass. Park in the parking area on the west side of the highway. The ride begins at the trailhead adjacent to the highway at the southeast corner of the parking lot.

**Trailhead/trail amenities:** pit toilet at trailhead.

**The ride:**
0.0   Start at the Colorado Trail trailhead adjacent to the highway at the southeast corner of the parking lot. Get ready to roll on some nice single-track.

0.9   Pass a trail sign for the Colorado Trail and "Tree line." Continue straight on the Colorado Trail.

2.4   Cross the bridge and continue straight on the single-track. Cross another bridge in 50 yards. Follow the sign directing you to the "10th Mountain Division Hut." (Pass the spur on the left that leads to Crane Park.)

2.5   Turn right at the intersection with the dirt road and ride uphill. *Note- the Colorado Trail continues for approximately 3.5 miles before entering a wilderness area where mountain bikes are prohibited. Add miles by riding this section of the Colorado Trail as an out-and-back.*

2.9 Turn right onto FSR 705, Wurts Ditch Road. Ride about 10 yards then turn right again at the trailhead sign. Continue riding past the sign, bearing right onto the obvious trail. (The faint left spur leads to a campsite.)

4.5 After a very fun and easy downhill, the trail enters an open meadow in a boggy area. The trail gets a little hard to follow, but stay left and ride along the southern edge of the meadow. As you ride through the Mitchell Creek basin, be sure to either ride or walk your bike through the center of any muddy spots; riding around the mud damages the trail.

4.7 The trail widens to a double-track and starts to climb.

5.3 Continue straight on the road as the Colorado Trail intersects on the left.

7.1 Arrive back at the parking lot. Do it again?

**Options:** ride to the end of Wurts Ditch Road for a pleasant out-and-back spur. Return to the trailhead by resuming the Mitchell Creek Loop.

*Sunset over Leadville and Turquoise Lake from the historic Mining District*

## 28 • Arkansas Valley Mountain Biking
# Ride 3: Sugarloaf-Turquoise Lake Loop

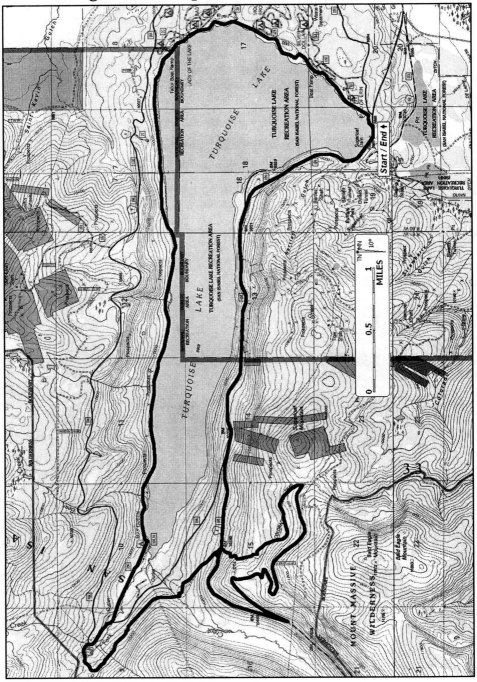

*Map 3: Sugarloaf-Turquoise Lake Loop (© National Geographic)*

# Leadville • 29

This ride explores the best single-track in the Turquoise Lake Recreation Area. Start with a relatively easy climb to the top of Sugarloaf Pass. From the top, drop into a sublime single-track descent on the Colorado Trail. Work your way through the rock gardens to the Timberline Trailhead, then finish on the fast single-track of the Turquoise Lake Trail.

**Ride length:** 17.5 miles
**Ride type:** 8-loop (clockwise)
**Riding time:** 3-4 hours
**Surface:** paved road (4.3 miles); dirt road (4.2 miles); single-track (9.0 miles)
**Elevations:** start/end 9,860'; max 11,145'; min 9,850'
**Total climbing:** gain/loss 1,630'
**Aerobic level:** moderate (climbing)
**Technical level:** 4 (numerous rock gardens)
**Season:** June through October
**USGS Quadrangle:** Leadville North, Homestake Reservoir

**Trailhead GPS coordinates:** 39° 15.125' N; 106° 22.146' W

**Elevation profile:**

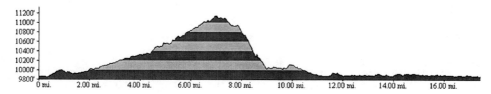

**Getting there:** from the traffic light at the intersection of 6th St. and Harrison Ave. (US 24) in downtown Leadville, drive 0.8 miles west on W. 6th St. Turn right at the intersection with McWethy Drive (becomes CR 4), following the signs to Turquoise Lake. Drive 3.6 miles west on CR 4, until you reach the parking area on the south side of the road just east of the dam. Park here and the ride starts at your car.

**Trailhead/trail amenities:** pit toilet at mile 11.2 and at several campgrounds along the lake; water spigot at mile 11.2.

**The ride:**
0.0   From the parking area, turn left on CR 4 to ride west over the dam.
1.4   Pass the Abe Lee fishing access area on the right.
3.3   Turn left to remain on CR 4 (toward Hagerman Pass) as it turns to dirt.
      *Note- to skip the climb on Sugarloaf and just ride the Turquoise Lake Trail, Continue downhill to the Mayqueen Campground (it will be on the right). Jump to mile 10.7 in this log.*
4.2   Pass the intersection with the Colorado Trail. You will see this intersection again.
5.2   Turn left to begin the climb to Sugarloaf Pass and the ride's highpoint.

| | |
|---|---|
| 7.2 | Continue straight on the main road (FSR 105A) as you pass an unmarked road on your right. |
| 7.4 | Turn left at the Colorado Trail marker to begin your single-track descent. |
| 8.6 | Cross CR 4. Look left to find the next section of Colorado Trail. **Note-** *the next stretch of trail is much tougher than the section you just finished. If you want to skip it, turn right, descend on CR 4, then turn left on CR 9 to descend on paved road to the Turquoise Lake Trail. From here, jump to mile 10.7 in this log.* |
| 10.2 | Turn right and descend along the Colorado Trail. |
| 10.3 | Turn left and ride over the bridge. |
| 10.4 | Enter the Timberline Lake Trailhead parking area. Ride downhill to paved CR 9. Turn right and descend along CR 9. |
| 10.7 | Turn left into the May Queen Campground. |
| 11.2 | Bear left at the fork as you pass a pit toilet. |
| 11.4 | Continue straight toward the lake as you pass a pit toilet on the right. Ride around the loop until you reach the Turquoise Lake Trailhead. Enter the trail and enjoy the single-track line around the lake. |
| 11.7 | Cross the bridge then continue straight and uphill along the main trail. |
| 15.5 | Cross the paved Tabor Boat Ramp. From this point forward the trail gets difficult to follow. Just ride the most obvious line that parallels the shore as you pedal your way around the lake and back to the dam. |
| 16.9 | Cross a paved parking lot, ride past the toilets on the left, then cross the boat launch access road to resume riding on single-track. |
| 17.4 | Watch for a faint fork in the trail. Bear right to stay along the lake shore. |
| 17.5 | Arrive at CR 4. Carefully cross the road to return to your vehicle. |

**Options:** if you prefer to skip the climb to Sugarloaf Pass and just ride the Turquoise Lake Trail around the lake, continue straight to the May Queen Campground along paved CR 9 at mile 3.3. After turning into the campground, skip to mile 10.7 in the mileage log.

## Ride 4: Hagerman Pass (with Colorado Centennial Midland Trail)

*Leadville • 31*

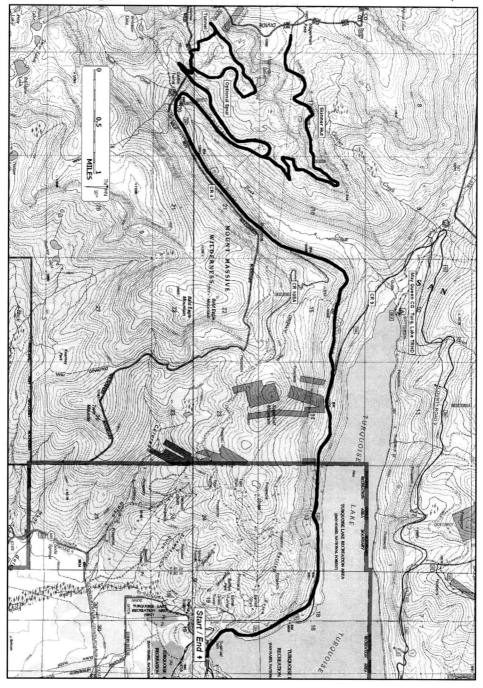

*Map 4: Hagerman Pass (© National Geographic)*

## 32 • *Arkansas Valley Mountain Biking*

The majority of this route follows the Colorado Centennial Midland Railroad grade. Beyond the grade, the road continues to Hagerman Pass, the high pass between the Turquoise Lake Recreation Area and the Hunter-Frying Pan Wilderness Area. The push to the summit is relatively easy (when compared to other alpine passes), and along the way you'll pass Skinner Hut, part of the 10th Mountain Division hut route between Leadville and Aspen.

One highlight is the optional spur loop that leads to the east portal of the Hagerman Tunnel of the Colorado Centennial Midland Railroad. This fun, 5.6-mile single-track/double-track spur is well worth the extra time it takes to complete. Along the way, you'll pass Hagerman Lake and enter the historic Douglass City site.

**Ride length:** 22.4 miles (Colorado Centennial Midland Trail: 5.6 miles)
**Ride type:** out-and-back (Colorado Centennial Midland Trail: lollipop-loop)
**Riding time:** 2.5-3 hours (Colorado Centennial Midland Trail: 1 hour)
**Surface:** paved road (6.6 miles); dirt road (17.8 miles)
**Elevations:** start/end 9,860'; max 12,000'; min 9,850'
**Total climbing:** gain/loss 2,630'

**Aerobic level:** strenuous (climbing on rough road, altitude; the Colorado Centennial Midland Trail is moderate/easy)
**Technical level:** 3+ (a few steeps with rocks; the Colorado Centennial Midland Trail has short sections of technical 5)
**Season:** July through October
**USGS Quadrangles:** Leadville North, Homestake Reservoir, Mount Massive

**Trailhead GPS coordinates:** 39° 15.125' N; 106° 22.146' W

**Elevation profile:**

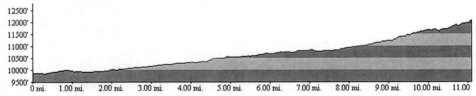

**Getting there:** from the traffic light at the intersection of 6th St. and Harrison Ave. (US 24) in downtown Leadville, drive 0.8 miles west on W. 6th St. Turn right at the intersection with McWethy Drive (becomes CR 4), following the signs to Turquoise Lake. Drive 3.6 miles west on CR 4 until you reach the parking area on the south side of the road just east of the dam. Park here and the ride starts at your car.

**Trailhead/trail amenities:** none.

# Leadville • 33

**The ride:**

- **0.0** Start the ride by crossing CR 4 and riding west over the dam.
- **1.3** Continue on CR 4 as you pass the Abe Lee fishing access on your right.
- **3.3** Bear left to stay on CR 4 as the riding surface changes to dirt.
- **4.2** Pass the intersection with the Colorado Trail and Continental Divide Trail. ***Note-*** *this section of the CDT/COT is open to bikes, but it is somewhat technical and relatively short.*
- **5.1** Continue riding on CR 4 as you pass the unmarked intersection with FSR 105A on your left. ***Note-*** *fans of the Leadville Trail 100 Mountain Bike Race know this road as the Sugarloaf Mountain climb to the infamous Power Line descent.*
- **6.9** Pass the Highline Trailhead on the left. No bikes allowed.
- **7.0** Pass the east portal of the Ivanhoe (Carlton) Tunnel on your left as the road makes a sharp bend right and gets steeper.
- **8.0** Pass the Colorado Centennial Midland Trail trailhead on your left. ***Note-*** *this is an interesting and fun 5.6-mile diversion that leads to the Hagerman Tunnel's east portal. Detailed information follows this log.*
- **8.1** Continue climbing on the main road as CR 4 ends and becomes FSR 105.
- **9.6** Keep climbing past a campsite spur on the right.
- **9.8** Keep climbing as you pass the Skinner Hut (10th Mountain Division Hut) on your right. Very nice.
- **11.2** Summit! Keep going a little past the summit for spectacular views of Ivanhoe Lake on the west slope. Turn around and return along the same route.

**Colorado Centennial Midland Trail**

- **0.0** From CR 4, enter at the sign that describes the history of the trail. Ride in the wide railroad grade cut on your right. The first 0.25 miles can be very wet and may resemble a stream more than a trail.
- **1.4** Turn right to ride the single-track that climbs through a slightly technical rock garden.
- **1.6** Turn right to start the loop. Ride on the railroad grade for 10 yards then descend left to cross a stream. Your feet will get very wet. ***Note-*** *riding the loop counter-clockwise results in a longer climb to the tunnel; riding clockwise provides a longer downhill, but some might have to walk a good chunk of the 0.6 miles to the tunnel. Your choice.*
- **1.9** Stay left as the trail narrows and enters a railroad cut.
- **2.4** Turn left to ride the single-track as the railroad grade ends.
- **2.5** After a brief, steep climb on skinny single-track, return to the railroad grade as it skirts Hagerman Lake.

3.4 Arrive at the east portal of the Hagerman Tunnel. After getting your fill of tunnel gazing, turn around and ride 0.1 miles back the way you came. Look for the single-track drop to the lake that is just past the telegraph pole on the right. This is a very technical descent, but it is easy to take on foot. *Do not descend along the very step and loose erosion (false) trail south of the telegraph pole.*

3.9 After some bumpy terrain, enter the Douglass site. Read the sign and ponder the fun the rail workers must have had in their day.

4.0 Close the loop by riding straight.

5.6 Arrive back at the trailhead.

**Options:** return to your car via the Turquoise Lake Trail that starts in the May Queen Campground on the western edge of the lake. This single-track route is a mountain biking "must-do" in the Leadville area. It's a flat but fun romp along the northern shore of Turquoise Lake.

Eliminate all of the pavement spinning by starting at the intersection of CR 9 and CR 4 (mile 3.3). Park in the pullout on the right, just beyond the start of the dirt on CR 4.

***Descending from the Hagerman Tunnel***

# Ride 5: Sugarloaf-Power Line Loop

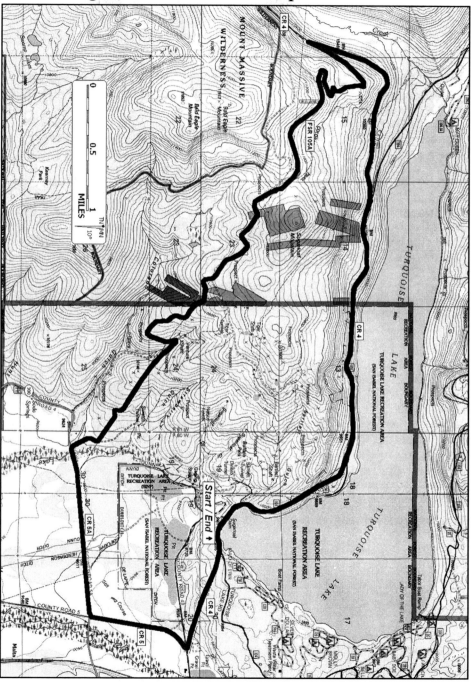

*Map 5: Sugarloaf-Power Line Loop (© National Geographic)*

## 36 • Arkansas Valley Mountain Biking

Fans of the Leadville 100-mile mountain bike Race already know of this infrmous section of the course. The Power Line cut is steep, deeply rutted, and probably the most technical section of the race. During the race, the return trip up this grade is a place of absolute torture, pushing more than a few racers as close as they will get to their breaking point.

When ridden solely as a descent outside the pressures of the race, however, the Power Line is downright fun. It's so much fun that it would be one of my regular rides if I lived closer to Leadville.

**Ride length:** 13.9 miles
**Ride type:** loop
**Riding time:** 2 hours
**Surface:** paved road (6.4 miles); jeep road (7.5 miles)
**Elevations:** start/end 9,860'; max 11,145'; min 9,565'
**Total climbing:** gain/loss 1,750'

**Aerobic level:** moderate (those not acclimatized or used to climbing might find it tougher)
**Technical level:** 4+ (critical line selection on the descent)
**Season:** June through October
**USGS Quadrangles:** Leadville North, Homestake Reservoir, Mount Massive, Leadville South

**Trailhead GPS coordinates:** 39° 15.125' N; 106° 22.146' W

**Elevation profile:**

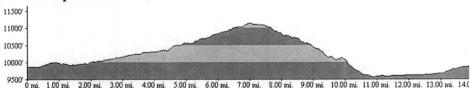

**Getting there:** from the traffic light at the intersection of 6th St. and Harrison Ave. (US 24) in downtown Leadville, drive 0.8 miles west on W. 6th St. Turn right at the intersection with McWethy Drive (becomes CR 4), following the signs to Turquoise Lake. Drive 3.6 miles west on CR 4, until you reach the parking area on the south side of the road just east of the dam. Park here and the ride starts at your car.

**Trailhead/trail amenities:** none.

**The ride:**
0.0    From the parking area, turn left onto CR 4 to ride west over the dam.
1.3    Pass the Abe Lee fishing access area on the right.
3.3    Bear left to remain on CR 4 (toward Hagerman Pass) as it turns to dirt. *Note-* *if you are scouting the racecourse, consider starting your ride at the pullout on CR 4 (dirt) just west of this intersection. Ride it as an out-and-back, turning around when you hit the pavement.*
4.2    Pass the intersection with the Colorado Trail. *Note-* *this short section of the trail is open to bikes.*

| | |
|---|---|
| 5.1 | Turn left on FSR 105A (unmarked) to begin the assault on the Sugarloaf climb. The road surface is rougher and the grade steeper. |
| 7.2 | Continue straight on FSR 105A past an unmarked spur on your right. |
| 7.5 | As you begin the descent, bear right to cross under the power lines. (Pass the unmarked spur that climbs parallel to the power lines on the left.) Look ahead to draw your line as you rip the descent. |
| 10.7 | Water crossing. Look left to where the stream narrows; there may be a plank to help you cross. |
| 10.8 | Turn left onto paved CR 5A. |
| 12.2 | Turn left onto CR 5 and ride north toward the golf course. |
| 12.9 | Turn left (west) onto CR 4 and ride toward Turquoise Lake. |
| 13.8 | Continue on CR 4 past the intersection with CR 9C on the right. |
| 13.9 | You are back at the car. Test your hardiness by turning around and riding the same route in reverse. Or not. |

**Options:** if you are training or scouting the course for the race, consider riding this as an out-and-back with your turn-around point at the intersection with CR 5A (the pavement). The return trip is so difficult that some racers consider the top of Power Line as the "half-way" point of the race; imagine how it feels to climb this after you've completed the Columbine climb and all the miles between them!

*Leadville locals getting it done (photo courtesy of Jody Stack, 2009)*

# 38 • *Arkansas Valley Mountain Biking*
# Ride 6: Ball Mountain Pass

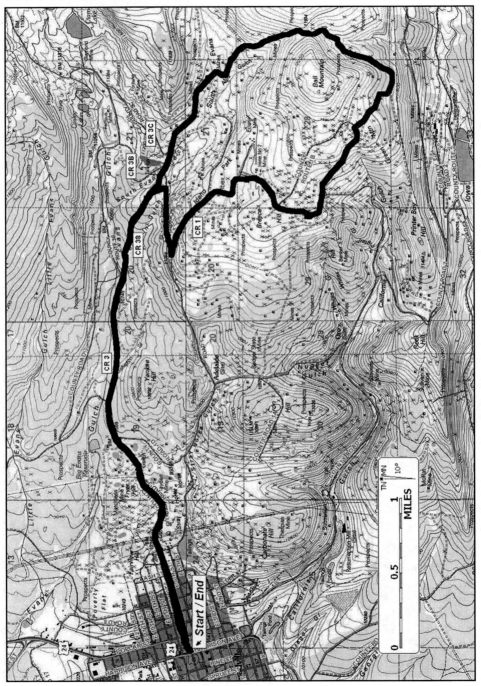

*Map 6: Ball Mountain Pass (© National Geographic)*

Along this route you'll pass more abandoned mines and prospect sites than you can count, including the famous Matchless Mine just outside of town. You'll see numerous collapsed structures and ride right next to sulfurous tailings that emit the faint scent of rotten eggs. It's the kind of place you might have dreamed about if you played with toy trucks as a kid. The ride itself is a lot of fun. Sure, you'll work a little for that fun, but that only makes the reward so much sweeter.

Ride this one in the morning, before the afternoon storms roll in. Because mining was so active in this area, finding your way might be challenging. So many unmapped and unmarked roads zigzag across the route that a wrong turn or two may prove inevitable. If you don't have a GPS (get the GPX file for the route free at *www.arkvalleymtb.com*), consider carrying quality maps and a compass as a supplement to this guide.

**Ride length:** 12.2 miles
**Ride type:** lollipop-loop (counter-clockwise)
**Riding time:** 2 hours
**Surface:** paved road (3.0 miles); dirt road/jeep trails (9.2 miles)
**Elevations:** start/end 10,160'; max 11,990'; min 10,160'

**Total climbing:** gain/loss 2,325'
**Aerobic level:** strenuous (sustained climbs at high altitude)
**Technical level:** 4 (the descent from the pass is loose, steep and fast)
**Season:** July through October
**USGS Quadrangles:** Leadville North, Climax, Mount Sherman

**Trailhead GPS coordinates:** 39° 14.976' N; 106° 17.52' W

**Elevation profile:**

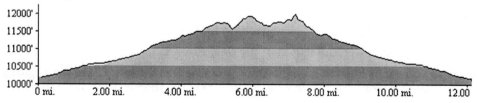

**Getting there:** park anywhere in downtown Leadville. From the stoplight at 6th St. and Harrison Ave. (US 24) in downtown Leadville, ride one block north to E. 7th St. The ride starts at the intersection of Harrison and E. 7th.

**Trailhead/trail amenities:** ride starts/ends in town.

### The ride:
- **0.0** From the intersection of E. 7th St. and Harrison Ave., ride east (uphill) on E. 7th.
- **0.7** E. 7th St. becomes CR 3. Continue on CR 3 toward the Matchless Mine.
- **1.2** Pass the entrance to the Matchless Mine. *Note- the bridge you are about to pass under is the Mineral Belt Trail; an entrance to it is just past the bridge.*
- **1.5** Stay on CR 3 as it changes to dirt.
- **1.6** Continue on CR 3, passing a spur on your right.

| | |
|---|---|
| 1.8 | Continue straight on CR 3, past the intersection with CR 3A on the left. |
| 2.7 | Bear right onto CR 38 and continue riding uphill. (CR 3 heads left.) |
| 2.9 | Continue climbing on the main road past a short spur on your right. |
| 3.3 | Approach a 3-way intersection at the top of the climb. Take the middle fork that climbs between two mines (the left fork is a short spur). Turn right after a couple hundred yards and continue to climb. |
| 3.9 | At the top of another climb, take the hard left and continue climbing on the well-maintained road. This unmarked road is CR 1 (E. 5th St.). |
| 4.4 | Continue straight on the main road as it levels. (Don't take the right that heads up to a mine site.) Ride for another 50 yards to the fork and bear right (uphill), away from CR 38. |
| 4.6 | Turn right onto CR 1A and continue climbing. |
| 4.9 | Pass some yellow-tinted (sulfurous) tailings and take in the scent. ***Note**—when rain hits the tailings, the sulfur reacts with the water to create sulfuric acid. This acidic runoff has the potential to contaminate ground water and streams, adversely affecting plant and animal life in the area.* |
| 5.0 | Top out and continue straight on the main road past an unmarked intersection on the right. |
| 5.2 | Take the left-most fork at the 3-way split. You'll soon approach a mine site with a tremendous overlook of Leadville and Turquoise Lake. Take only pictures; leave only tread marks. |
| 5.5 | After a quick dip, turn left at the fork and climb through a rough section. |
| 6.0 | After topping out on a literally breathtaking climb, turn right at a 4-way intersection. You will now descend toward the power lines. |
| 7.0 | Stay left at the fork and start the final climb to the pass. |
| 7.3 | You made it! (Is that single-track you smell on the left?) Take the obvious descent into Alps Gulch. Get ready for some speed. |
| 8.0 | After the hairy descent, cross a stream on a plank bridge. |
| 8.2 | Take the left fork of the double-track after a small climb; ride downhill toward some mine sites. |
| 8.6 | Pass CR 3C on the right and continue straight downhill. |
| 8.8 | Continue straight and downhill, passing CR 3B on the right as you go. |
| 9.2 | Close the loop by staying right at the intersection while descending on CR 38. |
| 9.6 | Rejoin CR 3. Fly downhill on CR 3/E. 7th St. all the way back to town. |
| 12.2 | The end. Grab a tasty beverage at one of the town's fine watering holes. Life is good. |

## Ride 7: 100 Scouting Route

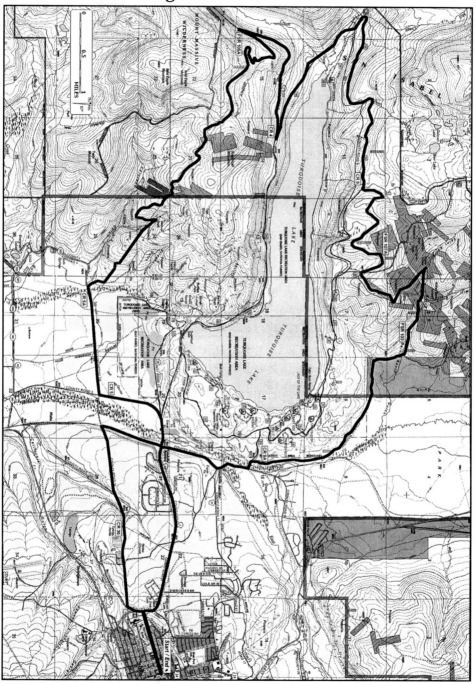

*Map 7: 100 Scouting Route (© National Geographic)*

## 42 • Arkansas Valley Mountain Biking

This loop incorporates the first two sustained climbs of the 100-mile mountain bike race course. Start at the race's Start/Finish line, then follow the course up St. Kevins and over Sugarloaf. After descending along the infamous Power Line, you'll return to the start along the Boulevard. Reversing the loop will give you a taste of the return climbs up Power Line and along Turquoise Lake.

**Ride length:** 30.2 miles
**Ride type:** loop (counter-clockwise)
**Riding time:** 2-5 hours
**Surface:** paved road (12.6 miles); dirt road (17.6 miles)
**Elevations:** start/end 10,145'; max 11,145'; min 9,565'
**Total climbing:** gain/loss 3,250'

**Aerobic level:** moderate (clockwise is tougher)
**Technical level:** 3 (the Power Line descent is 4)
**Season:** June through October
**USGS Quadrangles:** Homestake Reservoir, Mount Massive, Leadville North, Leadville South

**Trailhead GPS coordinates:** 39° 14.922' N; 106° 17.524' W

**Elevation profile:**

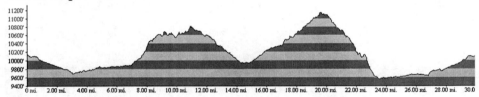

**Getting there:** park anywhere in downtown Leadville. This ride starts at the stoplight at 6th St. and Harrison Ave. (US 24) in downtown Leadville.

**Trailhead/trail amenities:** ride starts/ends in town.

**The ride:**

| | |
|---|---|
| 0.0 | From the intersection of W. 6th Street and Harrison Avenue, ride west (downhill) on W. 6th Street. |
| 0.8 | Turn right onto McWethy Drive. |
| 0.9 | Continue straight and downhill as McWethy Drive becomes CR 4. |
| 3.0 | Shy of the railroad tracks at Leadville Junction, turn right onto CR 9D. |
| 3.8 | Bear left to continue riding on CR 9/99. |
| 4.2 | Turn left onto CR 9. |
| 4.3 | Turn right onto unpaved CR 9A. This is where the lead-out escort ends and the race begins. |
| 7.0 | Turn left onto FSR 103. The first significant climb of the race will soon begin. *Note- the pack is typically heavy and split into two lanes through here; this makes passing very difficult. When scouting, try to determine which side, left or right, has the cleanest overall line.* |
| 7.6 | Continue climbing on the main road past private drives on the right. |
| 8.2 | Turn left and enjoy a quick break from climbing. |

## Leadville • 43

**8.7** Continue uphill past an unmarked intersection on your right.

**8.8** Bear right past a private drive on the left. You will pass another unmarked road on the right in about 100 yards.

**9.3** After a quick descent, diagonally cross FSR 107 and continue riding on the double-track (FSR 107A; unmarked) beyond the gate. Ride around the gate if it is closed.

**11.1** Ride around the gate to continue descending to CR 9.

**11.4** Turn right (downhill) on paved CR 9. Stay on this road for about 4.6 miles as you wind your way around the lake. *Warning - watch for traffic as you rocket downhill.*

**16.0** Turn right onto dirt CR 4 (FSR 105).

**17.8** Turn left onto unmarked FSR 105A to begin the assault on Sugarloaf Pass.

**20.0** Stay left on FSR 105A as you pass an unmarked road on your right.

**20.2** Turn right to cross under the power lines as you begin the steep, technical Power Line descent.

**23.3** Turn right and ride away from the power lines at the bottom.

**23.6** Turn left onto paved CR 5A. *Note- this is an ideal spot to turn around if you riding this an out-and-back; scout "The Boulevard" by jumping to mile 26.1 of this log when you return to Leadville Junction.*

**24.9** Turn left onto CR 5.

**25.8** Merge right onto CR 4.

**26.1** At Leadville Junction, turn right onto a public road through private property. *Please respect property owners in this area by not littering, wandering off the road, or stopping for nature calls. If asked to leave by residents, please turn around and return to Leadville via CR 4.*

**26.7** Bear right at the fork.

**26.9** Turn left to begin a steep, rocky ascent. *Note- the private road ends and becomes CR 36 at the top of this climb.*

**29.2** Turn left and ride toward the high school athletic field on CR 31.

**29.3** Turn left onto paved McWethy Drive.

**29.4** Turn right and climb back to the start on W 6th Street.

**30.2** Finish. Are you ready?

## 44 • *Arkansas Valley Mountain Biking*
# Ride 8: 50 Scouting Route

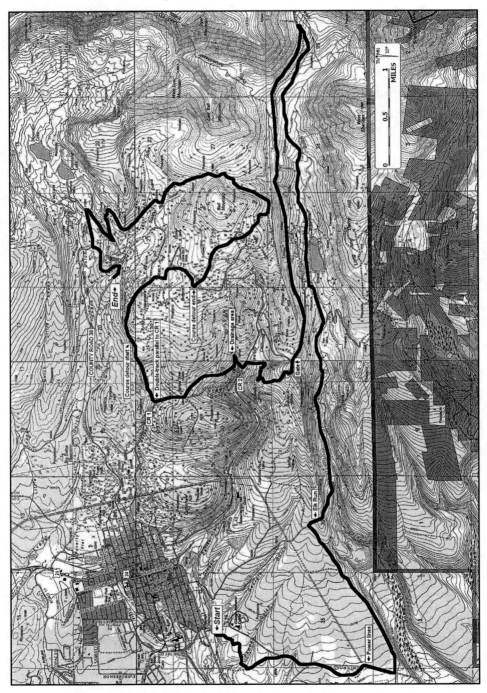

*Map 8: 50 Scouting Route (© National Geographic)*

# Leadville • 45

Take a grueling tour of Leadville's historic mining district as you scout the 50-mile race course. Don't get frustrated while riding if you begin to feel like a rat trapped in a maze. Without the benefit of course marshals and flagging, you will probably have a very tough time following this route.

Because the course tends to weave through a web of rugged, unmarked, and unmapped roads, your best bet is to load the .gpx file (*download it free at www.arkvalleymtb.com*) into a GPS and refer to this guidebook when in doubt (*expect variances between your GPS mileage readings and the elevation-corrected values presented here*). No GPS? Visit the official race web site and download the course map; be prepared to calibrate the mileage difference between your cycling computer and the values presented here.

**Ride length:** 46.2 miles
**Ride type:** out-and-back
**Riding time:** 5-10 hours
**Surface:** paved road (0.8 miles); dirt road (45.4 miles)
**Elevations:** start/end 9,950'; max 12,020'; min 9,950'

**Total climbing:** gain/loss 7,715'
**Aerobic level:** strenuous
**Technical level:** 3+ (some descents are more difficult)
**Season:** June through October
**USGS Quadrangles:** Leadville South, Climax, Mount Sherman

**Trailhead GPS coordinates:** 39° 14.305' N; 106° 18.219' W

**Elevation profile:**

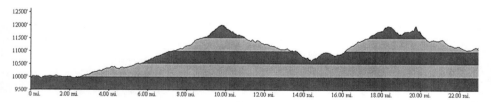

**Getting there:** from the traffic signal at the intersection of 6th Street and Harrison Avenue, drive or ride 1.2 miles south on US 24 (Harrison Ave.). Turn left into the Mineral Belt trailhead parking lot. The ride begins on the east side of the Cloud City Ski Club building 100 yards east of the parking area.

**Trailhead/trail amenities:** seasonal Porta-pot at start.

**The ride:**
0.0 From the east side of the Cloud City Ski Club, ride up the steep access road immediately north of the hill. At the top, turn right, ride 25 yards, then turn left and ride another 25 yards. Once you reach the dirt road, turn right to ride away from the college campus.
0.2 Continue straight past the unmarked road on the right.
0.3 Continue straight past an unmarked road on the left.
0.4 Enter a clearing then turn left onto a double-track. This may be difficult to find.

| | |
|---|---|
| 0.5 | Turn right onto the paved Mineral Belt Trail, ride 50 feet, then turn left to climb on a single-track. |
| 0.6 | Cross the Mineral Belt Trail and continue climbing on a double-track. |
| 0.75 | Cross the Mineral Belt Trail to continue on the double-track. |
| 0.8 | Continue straight past an unmarked, merging road on the right. The road gets wider here. |
| 1.0 | Continue straight past a couple unmarked roads on your left. |
| 1.3 | Continue straight on CR 45 past the intersection with the Rocky Mountain Bowmen Archery Range. |
| 1.8 | Pass an unmarked road on the right. |
| 1.9 | Turn right onto a gradual descent under the power lines. |
| 2.1 | Continue descending under the power lines. |
| 2.3 | Turn left and ride away from the power lines. |
| 3.4 | Continue straight past an unmarked road on the right. |
| 3.5 | Continue straight through an unmarked intersection. |
| 3.8 | Continue straight through intersections with the single-track trail system. Climb a short hill. |
| 4.1 | Turn right onto the road. |
| 4.2 | Ride straight past the intersection with Elk Run trail. |
| 4.8 | Stay left to continue climbing on the main road past an unmarked road on the right. |
| 5.6 | Continue straight past an unmarked road on your right. |
| 5.7 | Continue straight on the main road. |
| 6.1 | Pass an unmarked road on the right. |
| 6.4 | Turn right to ride under the utility lines. |
| 7.1 | Bear left at the fork to ride uphill. |
| 9.7 | Climb up to maintained CR 2B (unmarked) and the highpoint of the course. Turn left to descend. Continue descending on the main road past all intersections for the next 3.3 miles. |
| 13.0 | Merge right and climb on paved CR 2. |
| 13.4 | Bear left to leave the pavement. Ride up to and around a gate to access a double-track. |
| 13.5 | Turn right (north) onto a double-track. |
| 13.7 | Continue straight and downhill past a road on the left. |
| 14.0 | Continue descending on the main road. |
| 14.4 | Turn left, away from the Oro City sign. Descend 50 yards then turn right and cross paved CR 2. Bear right and climb on an unmarked road distinguished by a large tailings pile on your left. |

| | |
|---|---|
| 14.6 | Make a hard left just shy of the first cement drainage diversion. *Note- this one requires a little faith as there's a hidden road about 20 yards uphill from the main road. Look for bike tracks on the ground to help you find it.* |
| 14.8 | Bear right to continue climbing past an unmarked road on the left. |
| 15.0 | Turn left onto a wide road. |
| 15.3 | Descend past an unmarked road on the right. |
| 15.4 | Turn right to descend along a well-maintained road (CR 2A). |
| 15.7 | Just shy of the "T" intersection with CR 1 turn right to drop onto a double-track that parallels CR 1. |
| 16.4 | Bear left to continue climbing on CR 1. *Note- this is where the training route departs from the actual race course for approximately 1.4 miles.* **Please follow the route described here and respect land rights by not trespassing on private property.** |
| 17.2 | Continue straight past CR 38 on your left. |
| 17.4 | Turn right onto CR 1A. |
| 17.8 | Turn left, cross a rocky runoff diversion, then rejoin the official race course on a double-track. |
| 18.2 | Turn right. |
| 18.5 | Bear right at the fork. |
| 18.6 | Ride straight through the unmarked intersection. |
| 19.5 | Stay left past an unmarked double-track on your right. |
| 19.8 | Cross the saddle to begin a steep, technical descent into Alps Gulch. |
| 20.7 | Climb straight through an unmarked intersection. |
| 21.6 | Turn right at a "T" intersection to descend past an old mine structure. |
| 22.1 | Turn left to descend on CR 3. |
| 22.5 | Turn left onto CR 3B. |
| 23.0 | Turn right onto CR 38. |
| 23.1 | Enter a large clearing where 4 unmarked roads converge. This is the site of the Stumphtown Aid Station/race turn-around. Back-track this route to the start or return to town by descending CR 38 away from the mining district to CR 3, then descend to Leadville via CR 3/7th Street. |

**Options:** ride it as a loop, either clockwise or counter-clockwise, by using East 7th Street/CR 3 and CR 38 to connect Leadville to Stumphtown.

## Ride 9: Mineral Belt Trail

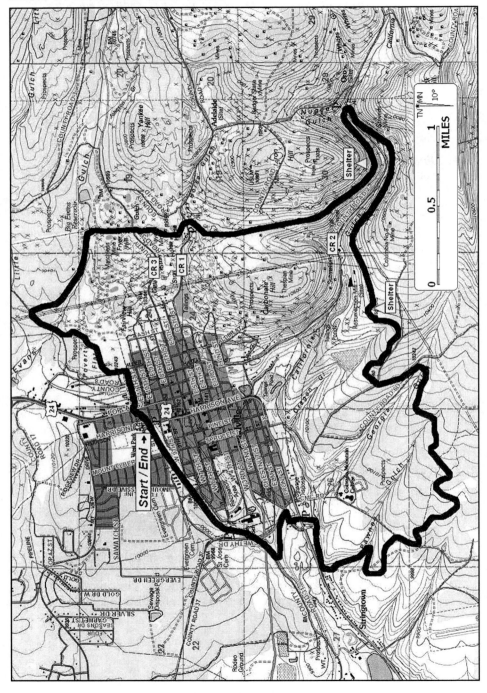

*Map 9: Mineral Belt Trail (© National Geographic)*

# Leadville • 49

Take a journey through the pages of history as you ramble along this fascinating and exquisite trail. Appropriate for everyone, this trail is both well planned and well built. Interpretive signs and plaques scattered throughout give one a matchless appreciation for the town's rich heritage.

As the plaque says, "Built in the Leadville spirit through the cooperation of many for the enjoyment of all."

**Ride length:** 11.6 miles
**Ride type:** loop (counter-clockwise)
**Riding time:** 1-2 hours
**Surface:** paved multi-use path
**Elevations:** start/end 10,200'; max 10,630'; min 9,910'

**Total climbing:** gain/loss 800'
**Aerobic level:** easy
**Technical level:** 1
**Season:** May through October
**USGS Quadrangles:** Leadville South, Leadville North

**Trailhead GPS coordinates:** 39° 15.173' N; 106° 17.614' W

**Elevation profile:**

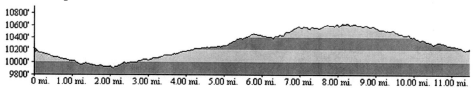

**Getting there:** park anywhere in downtown Leadville. From the stoplight at the intersection of Harrison Ave. (US 24) and 6th St. in downtown Leadville, ride about 0.20 miles north on Harrison Ave. to Ice Palace Park (behind the National Mining Hall of Fame and Museum). The ride starts at the intersection of the trail and Harrison Ave.

**Trailhead/trail amenities:** ride starts/ends in town.

**The ride:**
For the sake of convenience, this route description and elevation profile start in the center of town and proceed counter-clockwise. There are, however, several other trailheads and parking areas; choose the one that suits you best.

The trail itself is extremely well marked and a mileage log isn't necessary. Having said that, it is highly suggested that you stop at the visitor center between 8th and 9th Sts. on Harrison Ave. to pick up an official map and guide to the trail before setting out on your ride.

While slightly more difficult than riding the loop clockwise, starting at the Ice Palace Park and riding counter-clockwise gives the route a nice flow. You'll begin with a swift descent (southwest) through modern Leadville. After crossing US 24 at the southwest edge of town (approx. 1.6 miles), you'll pass a parking area and trailhead, and then pass some historical buildings. Next, you'll ascend into a peaceful, forested stretch that gives you a sense of what the area may have been like prior to development.

## 50 • *Arkansas Valley Mountain Biking*

After passing the first shelter at the Leadville Overlook (approx. 5.6 miles), you'll enter California Gulch (approx. 6.2 miles), the site of the area's first major mining development. It was here that they first discovered placer gold in 1860. The adjoining camp, dubbed "Oro City," drew more than 8,000 hopeful prospectors to a rough-and-tumble assortment of tents and shacks.

At approximately mile 7.2, pass another trailhead and parking area at CR 2.

Pedaling the leg of trail between California Gulch to the Matchless Mine is like riding through a museum exhibit. The path weaves between interpretive signs, old mining carts, and heaps of mining waste tailings.

At the Matchless Mine (approx. 9.3 miles) just past E. 7th St./CR 3, Baby Doe Tabor's last home, nothing more than a weather-beaten, one-room shack, still stands less than 100 feet from the trail. Nearly forty years after the repeal of the Sherman Silver Act in 1893, she froze to death in that hovel as she waited for the return of silver's boom days.

The rest of the route is almost a coast all the way back to town. At the intersection of E. 12th and Alder Sts., the route runs down E. 12th St. for about 265 yards. You are less than 0.25 miles from the Ice Palace Park after crossing US 24 at the north end of town.

**Options:** if you are riding with small children, people not acclimatized to the altitude, or if bad weather rolls in, there are several shortcuts back to town: descend CR 2/Hazel St. through California Gulch (at approx. 7.2 miles); descend CR 1/E. 5th St. (at approx 9.0 miles) at the bridge just north of the infamous red pond (no swimming!); or descend CR 3/E. 7th St. (at approx 9.3 miles) at the bridge just south of Tabor's Matchless Mine.

*Along the Mineral Belt Trail*

# Ride 10: Lake County Singletrack

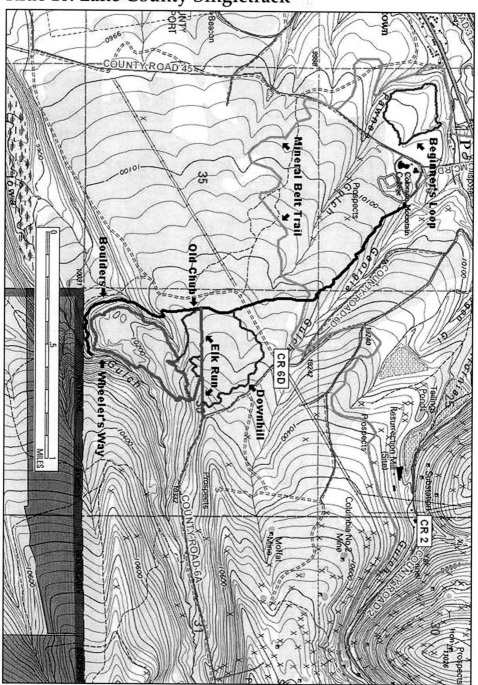

Map 10: Lake County Singletrack (© National Geographic)

# 52 • *Arkansas Valley Mountain Biking*

To meet the demand for more, high-quality single-track easily accessed from Leadville, local cyclists stepped up with amazing results. Summer 2010 efforts resulted in the opening of the first stage of what will eventually be an elaborate stacked-loop trail system providing superb riding opportunities for cyclists of all abilities.

> The Cloud City Wheelers Bike Club was formed in 2007 to promote and expand the sport of cycling in and around Lake County. Since its formation, the club worked hard to build the local bike park (located at 500 West 4th St.), complete with a huge pump track, dirt jumps, and wood skills features.
>
> The club also sponsors Trips for Kids Leadville, a program promoting the involvement of local youth in the sport of cycling. During the winter the club hosts the Leadville Winter Mountain Bike Series.
>
> Starting in May 2010 the Cloud City Wheelers began construction of new mountain bike trails with plenty of more trails to come in the near future, including flow trails and a jump trail, all within a mile of downtown Leadville.
>
> Check out our website: **www.cloudcitywheelers.org**.
>
> **Sterling Mudge, September 2010**

Trailbuilding is active in this area and new segments will be opening soon. For more information on trail status, riding suggestions, and better maps, stop by Cycles of Life on Harrison Avenue in Leadville.

**Ride length:** Various
**Ride type:** stacked-loop system
**Riding time:** 1-? hours
**Surface:** single-track
**Elevations:** start/end 10,380'
**Total climbing:** it's up to you

**Aerobic level:** moderate
**Technical level:** system trails individually rated
**Season:** June through October
**USGS Quadrangles:** Leadville South

**Trailhead GPS coordinates:** 39° 13.' N; 106° 16.862' W

**Getting there:** because of limited parking at the trailhead, you'll want to ride your bike to the trails. From the traffic signal at the intersection of 6th Street and Harrison Avenue, ride 0.6 miles south on US 24 (Harrison Ave.). Turn left (south-east) onto CR 6 then ride uphill for approximately 0.5 miles. Turn right onto CR 6D and ride about 1.4 miles uphill to the signed Elk Run trailhead on your right. The trail begins with a descent.

Another option is to ride up the Colorado Mountain College road and veer far left at the top of the hill; you'll see a sign for Boulders, Elk Run, and Wheelers Way.

**Trailhead/trail amenities:** none

## Trail segments completed in 2010

**Boulders:** More difficult, 1.95 miles (connects CMC to the Creek; some fast rocky sections and tight trees)

**Old Chub:** Easiest, 1500' (fast trail, rides great both ways; connects Wheelers Way with Boulders)

**Elk Run:** More difficult, 0.5 miles (best climbed in conjunction with Upper Deck)

**Upper Deck:** Easiest, 1,000' (best ridden as a climbing route to the Deck, Elk Run, and Wheelers Way)

**Wheeler's Way:** More difficult with optional diversions rated most difficult, 1.6 miles (flowy trail with an exciting mix of sage, pine, and aspen)

*Wheeler's Way Opening (Photo courtesy of Sterling Mudge, 2010)*

# Twin Lakes

Roadies and summer tourists already know Twin Lakes as the gateway to Independence Pass, the high mountain pass that separates the Arkansas Valley from Aspen and the Roaring Fork Valley. What they may not know, however, is that this quiet and scenic village is also the gateway to some of the best single-track in the northern Arkansas Valley.

Most of the action happens on the two major trail systems that intersect the town, the Colorado Trail (COT) and the Continental Divide Trail (CDT). North of town, the COT surfs the eastern shoulder of Mount Elbert (14,433'), Colorado's tallest peak, providing a single-track line that extends all the way to Halfmoon Road and Mt. Massive, Colorado's second tallest peak.

South of CO Highway 82, the COT skirts the lakes then continues all the way to Clear Creek, offering several tasty single-track riding options along the way. The trail is skinny, smooth, and fast, but seldom ridden, and the only crowd you are likely to encounter is the one you bring.

The most notable section is the COT descent to Clear Creek. In summer 2007, trail crews re-directed the trail, the effort resulting in a sweet and fast downhill. Best of all, the new route won't leave you stranded at the bottom; the trail climbs almost as well as it descends!

The town's centerpiece trail, the Interlaken Loop, is a relatively easy but spectacular single-track that circumnavigates the lake and provides access to the historic Interlaken Resort Restoration Project. Initially established in 1879 as a small hotel along the shores of the lake, by 1890 the Interlaken Resort was transformed into one of Colorado's premier mountain destinations. Today, it is widely regarded as the one of the best historic sites in the state, and the only way to reach it is by trail or by boat.

While visiting, stop by the visitor center (once the site of the notorious Red Rooster Tavern and Brothel) and have lunch or coffee at a charming cafe.

# Ride 11: Twin Lakes to Mount Massive Trailhead

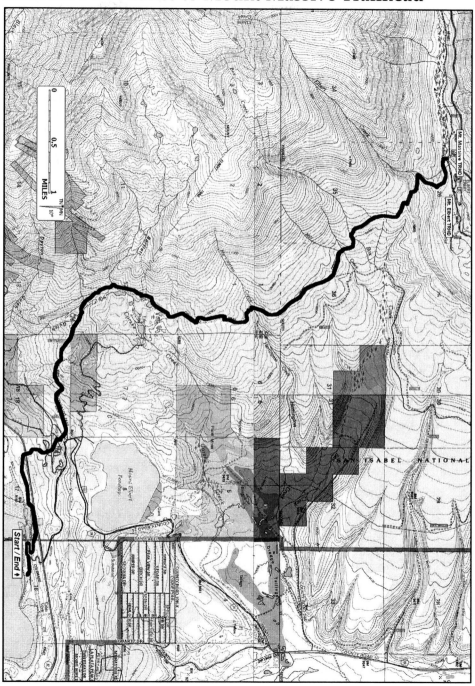

*Map 11: Twin Lakes to Mt. Massive Trailhead (© National Geographic)*

## Arkansas Valley Mountain Biking

This route, a beautiful section of the Colorado Trail, reminds me of riding in the densely forested hills back East. After the initial lung-searing climb, the ride is a fast and smooth spin through thick stands of aspen. The big descent to Halfmoon Road is less technical than steep, but it will challenge even advanced riders.

**Ride length:** 17.0 miles
**Ride type:** out-and-back
**Riding time:** 3.5 hours
**Surface:** single-track (13.2 miles); jeep road (3.8 miles)
**Elevations:** start/end 9,220'; max 10,670'; min 9,220'
**Total climbing:** gain/loss 3,320'
**Aerobic level:** strenuous (climbing)
**Technical level:** 3 (one very steep section is a 4, but it can be easily walked)
**Season:** June through October
**USGS Quadrangles:** Granite, Mt. Elbert, Mt. Massive

**Trailhead GPS coordinates:** 39° 5.647' N; 106° 20.572' W

**Elevation profile:**

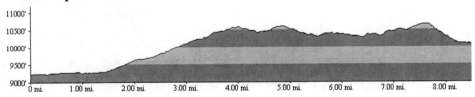

**Getting there:** from the intersection of US 24 and CO 82, drive 3.9 miles west on CO 82 to the intersection with CR 24C. Turn left onto CR 24C and drive 0.5 miles. Turn left at the "T" intersection and continue on CR 24C for 0.3 miles. Turn right and park in the "Mnt. Elbert" picnic area.

**Trailhead/trail amenities:** pit toilets at trailhead and near mile 8.5

**The ride:**

| | |
|---|---|
| 0.0 | From the restrooms at the parking area, ride back to CR 24C and turn left. |
| 0.3 | Turn right up the paved road. |
| 0.5 | Look left for the entrance to the Colorado Trail. Turn left and start riding west on the single-track. |
| 0.9 | Cross the paved entrance to the power plant. Look for the Colorado Trail marker to help you find the next segment of the trail. |
| 1.5 | Stay left at the fork and head down through the tunnel under CO 82. The climb on the north side of the tunnel is slightly technical. |
| 1.7 | Cross another trail. Look for a marker on the right. |
| 1.8 | Cross a dirt road. The trail resumes on the other side of the road adjacent to the gate. 100 yards later, cross another dirt road and ride up a short climb. The trail may be a little difficult to follow. Look slightly northwest and you'll notice a faint path in the pine needles leading the way. |
| 1.9 | Cross another dirt road. |

## Twin Lakes • 57

**2.0** Continue straight on the main trail. (The trail on your right leads to the South Elbert Trail parking area.) Ride until you reach another dirt road in about 50 yards. Turn left onto the road then stay on this road past all spurs for the next 1.7 miles.

**2.2** Continue straight, passing a spur on the left.

**2.4** Bear right and pass a spur on the left.

**2.8** Stay left, passing a spur on the right.

**3.3** Stream crossing.

**3.7** Turn right at the fork. Look for the Colorado Trail marker. A second post is visible on the right side of the road about 50 feet from the intersection.

**3.9** Cross a bridge and resume riding on single-track. About 50 yards after the bridge bear left at the fork marked by the Mount Elbert trail sign. Look for the Colorado Trail marker to confirm your route.

**4.1** Bear right at the fork. (Left is the South Mount Elbert Trail.) 100 yards later, switchback to the left, following the Colorado Trail marker.

**4.3** After passing above and to the left of what could arguably be the biggest beaver pond I've ever seen, the trail may get faint. Stay right and sniff out the path on the forest floor.

**5.8** Stream crossing. There are several stream crossings in the next 0.6 miles (some may be seasonal).

**7.3** Continue straight through the intersection with the Mount Elbert Trail. (The Mount Elbert trail switches back to your left.)

**8.2** Stream crossing after the raging downhill. Fifty yards after crossing the stream, the Mount Elbert trail departs to your right; turn left to stay on the Colorado Trail.

**8.5** Intersect the road. The Mount Massive trailhead is across the road on the left. Turn around and return the way you came.

**Options:** some people prefer to ride this as a one-way with shuttles. As to which way is better, you decide. North-to-south has a greater net downhill, but starts with a short, fiendish climb. South-to-north starts with a 2.5-mile grunt uphill, but the downhill at the end is a whole lot of fun.

To get to the Mount Massive trailhead: from the intersection of US 24/CO 82, drive 11 miles north on US 24. Turn left (west) on CO 300 and drive 0.8 miles to CR 11. Turn left (south) on CR 11 and drive 1.3 miles. Turn right (following the signs for Halfmoon Creek) and drive 5.5 miles to the Mount Massive trailhead parking area on the right (north) side of the road. The road is a little rough in sections, but should be okay for most passenger cars.

**58** • *Arkansas Valley Mountain Biking*

# Ride 12: Interlaken Loop

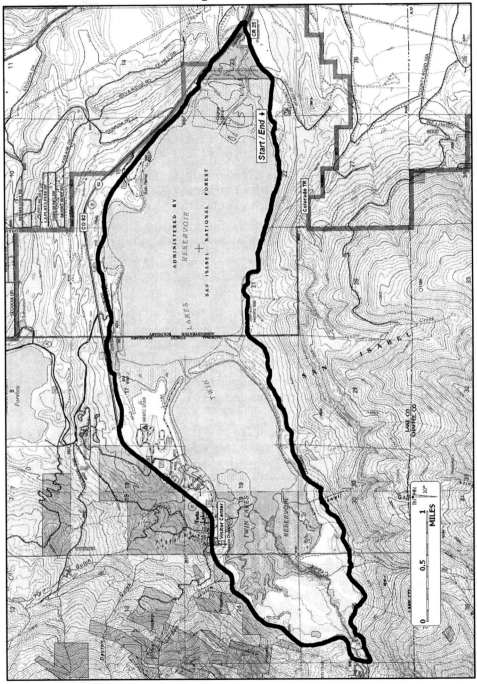

*Map 12: Interlaken Loop (© National Geographic)*

## Twin Lakes

This beautiful trail is a local favorite. The terrain is moderate, just easy enough for you to enjoy the magnificent scenery as you make your way around the lake. The trail also provides access to the historic Interlaken Resort—the only other way to get there is by boat!

Start with some easy/moderate single-track that skirts the lake until you arrive at the Interlaken Restoration Project. A few difficult, short, technical climbs come next, but before you know it, you're flying like a demon through Twin Lakes on CO 82. A fun stretch of easy single-track drops you less than a mile from the parking area and trailhead.

*Note-* crossing the dam may not be possible due to Homeland Security concerns. If the dam is open to bikes, no signs will be present. If it's closed, prominent signs will be posted. Just follow any posted instructions and use your best judgement.

**Ride length:** 14.3 miles
**Ride type:** loop (clockwise)
**Riding time:** 2 hours
**Surface:** single-track (8.6 miles); pavement (3.8 miles); dirt road (1.9 miles)
**Elevations:** start/end 9,250'; max 9,410'; min 9,190'

**Total climbing:** gain/loss 640'
**Aerobic level:** easy
**Technical level:** 3 (a few sections may be 4, but they are easily walked)
**Season:** May through October
**USGS Quadrangles:** Granite, Mt. Elbert

**Trailhead GPS coordinates:** 39° 4.454' N; 106° 18.637' W

**Elevation profile:**

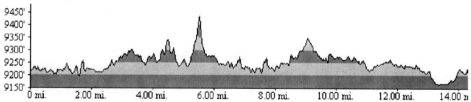

**Getting there:** from the intersection of US 24 and CO 82, drive 1.8 miles west on CO 82 to the intersection with CR 25. Turn left onto CR 25 and drive 0.5 miles. Turn left at the "T" intersection and continue on CR 25, avoiding all spurs until you reach the trailhead parking area in 0.5 miles. The road is a tad rough, but should be okay for most passenger cars.

This ride has many potential starting points, but the trailhead on CR 25 gives you easy access to the lake, a great place to kickback after the ride.

**Trailhead/trail amenities:** restrooms, café, general store around mile 7.5.

**The ride:**
0.0    Start at the trailhead sign/maps at the entrance to the single-track.
0.25   Continue straight past the trail intersection on your left.

| | |
|---|---|
| 1.2 | Continue straight along the lake. At this intersection you'll pass a post on your left with a CDT/Colorado Trail marker. |
| 1.9 | Enter the historic Interlaken Restoration Project. *Note- this project is sponsored by the US Forest Service with a number of partners and provides an interesting diversion. Take some time to read the interpretive signs along the way.* |
| 3.7 | Stream crossing. Use good judgment and caution when crossing. If water levels are high and the stream turbulent, consider turning back. |
| 4.3 | Cross a wide trail and continue on the single-track. You'll see a small log bridge ahead marking the way. Several more small stream crossings await you. Use the log bridges when possible and be careful. |
| 4.8 | Nice, tough little climb. Things get a little rougher for the next 0.4 miles or so. Even though some of the crux moves are more advanced, intermediate riders should have few problems riding most of it. Do your best. |
| 5.0 | Pass the "Big and Little Willis" trail on your left. |
| 5.4 | Turn right at the "T" intersection with a wide, unmarked trail. Continue for approximately 75 yards and cross the bridge over Lake Creek. Turn right after the bridge and ride to CO 82. Turn right onto CO 82 and ride downhill to the town of Twin Lakes. *Note- some people prefer to turn around here and return to the trailhead along the same route.* |
| 7.5 | Enter Twin Lakes. Stop, have a look around, and treat yourself to some refreshments. There is a public restroom at the Visitor Center. |
| 9.1 | Cross a small bridge over the Colorado Trail and look right for the small, single-track connector to the Colorado Trail. Take that connector then turn left (east) on the single-track. This provides a nice alternative to riding on CO 82 and the single-track is fast and smooth. |
| 9.7 | Cross the driveway to the Mt. Elbert Pumped Storage Power Plant. |
| 10.3 | Cross CR 24C (unmarked, paved). |
| 12.9 | Turn right to cross the dam. *Note- the dam crossing has a history of closing due to Homeland Security concerns. Just follow posted security warnings and use your best judgement.* |
| 13.3 | Turn right onto CR 25 and stay on CR 25 until you return to your vehicle. *Note- there is a new single-track segment from the dam to mi. 0.25 of this ride. Explore it to add more fun. Turn right at the end to return to the trailhead.* |
| 14.3 | End at your car. Breakout the grill and beers, and spend the rest of the day relaxing lakeside. |

**Options:** start the ride from the town of Twin Lakes; plenty of parking is available at the Visitor Center across from the general store. If you stay at one of several Forest Service campgrounds or at one of the town's inns, start the loop from there.

Or, do this ride as an out-and-back by turning around at mile 5.4.

# Ride 13: Twin Lakes to Clear Creek

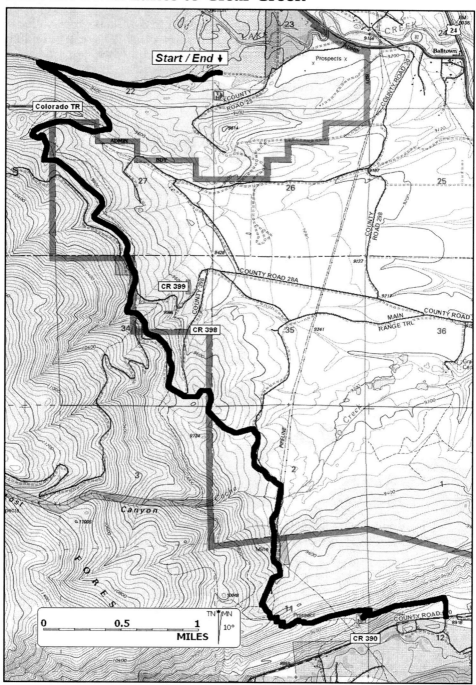

*Map 13: Twin Lakes to Clear Creek (© National Geographic)*

# Arkansas Valley Mountain Biking

Here's another tasty slice of Colorado Trail, and this section offers some of the best mountain biking in the Arkansas Valley. The single-track is narrow, well maintained, and very fast in sections. The descent into the Clear Creek valley is breathtaking and the new re-route of the trail is first-class. This gem is seldom ridden, but it won't remain overlooked for long: it's simply too good.

**Ride length:** 17.2 miles
**Ride type:** out-and-back
**Riding time:** 3 hours
**Surface:** single-track (13.2 miles); dirt road (4.0 miles)
**Elevations:** start/end 9,250'; max 9,950'; min 8,950'
**Total climbing:** gain/loss 3,230'
**Aerobic level:** strenuous (climbing)
**Technical level:** 3 (a few fast descents)
**Season:** May through October
**USGS Quadrangle:** Granite

**Trailhead GPS coordinates:** 39° 4.451' N; 106° 18.622' W

**Elevation profile:**

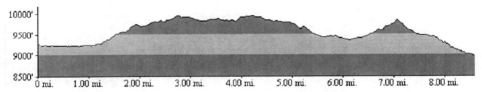

**Getting there:** from the intersection of US 24 and CO 82, drive 1.8 miles west on CO 82 to the intersection with CR 25. Turn left onto CR 25 and drive 0.5 miles. Turn left at the "T" intersection and continue on CR 25 until you reach the trailhead and parking area in 0.5 miles. The road is a tad rough, but should be okay for most passenger cars.

**Trailhead/trail amenities:** none.

**The ride:**

| | |
|---|---|
| 0.0 | Start at the trailhead sign/maps at the entrance to the single-track. |
| 0.25 | Continue straight past the trail intersection on your left. |
| 1.2 | Turn left at the CDT/Colorado Trail post marker. This starts the first major climb of the ride. |
| 2.0 | At the bottom of a slightly rocky descent, turn right onto a jeep track. A large cairn on your left marks the intersection. |
| 2.4 | Turn left at the cairn. The single-track resumes. |
| 3.8 | A small climb will bring you up to CR 399. Cross the road and resume climbing on the single-track. Look for the old log structures on your right and left. |
| 4.6 | Intersect CR 398 (Lost Canyon Road) and turn left (downhill). *Note-* don't cross the road and continue on the faded single-track leading into the forest (the trail dead-ends after a lot of tree fall). |

| | |
|---|---|
| 4.8 | Turn right onto a small road leading into a clearing. Your speed will be up, but look for the Colorado Trail marker. Once on the road, look left for the next marker; it's about six feet up on a tree. Next, look left for the faint single-track heading left (east) into the grass. A couple trail markers help you find your way. Let it rip, but watch for tree fall. |
| 5.3 | Cross a funky bridge and head left. |
| 5.5 | Intersect a faint jeep trail at a "T" and turn right, continuing downhill. |
| 5.6 | Continue straight as you cross another, even lighter jeep track. Look for the Colorado Trail marker on the fat tree to your left. |
| 5.8 | Continue straight. Look for a trail marker to guide you. |
| 6.0 | Turn right at the intersection with the power line road and drop down to cross Cache Creek. A Colorado Trail marker tells you where to go. |
| 6.3 | Bear right onto the double track and veer slightly away from the power lines. Several tracks intersect at this point, but you can't go wrong by staying on the most prominent line. |
| 6.5 | Bear right at the fork as the Colorado Trail and the power line road diverge. A trail marker leads the way. |
| 6.8 | Bear left and start your assault on the final ridge. A trail post marker and a tree marker let you know that you're on the right track. |
| 7.1 | The top. Wow!!! Check out that view! Get ready for some speed, but watch the switchbacks. You will descend almost 900' in a little over 1.5 miles. Don't let thoughts of climbing back up discourage you: because it's so well built and in such good condition, moderately strong riders will be able fly back up with little difficulty (yeah, right). *Note- if you're beat, turn around here and return along the same route.* |
| 8.6 | Cross the road and take a seat on the boulders. Have a snack then return along the same route. Remember as you gaze back up at the ridge: pondering a task is often more daunting than the task itself! |

**Options:** ride it as a one-way with shuttles. Leave a car at the intersection of the Colorado Trail and CR 390. From the intersection of CR 390 and US 24, drive about 2.1 miles west on CR 390. Look for the clearly marked trailhead designating the junction of segments 11 and 12 of the Colorado Trail.

**64** • *Arkansas Valley Mountain Biking*

# Ride 14: Cache Creek Loop

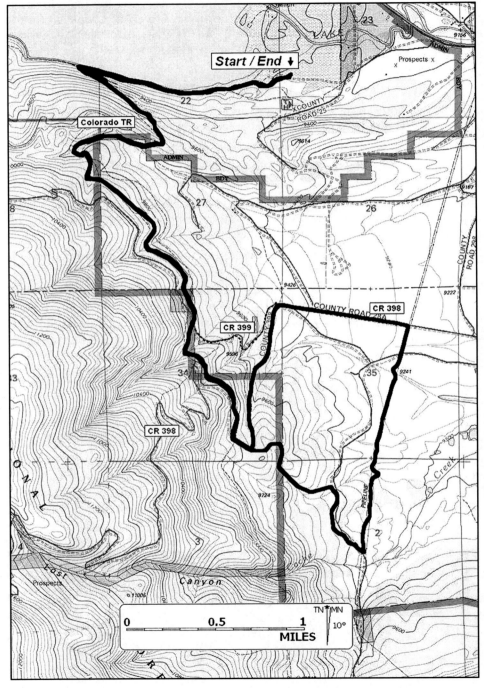

*Map 14: Cache Creek Loop (© National Geographic)*

## Twin Lakes

Here's another route on the superb stretch of the Colorado Trail single-track between Twin Lakes and Clear Creek. The trail is rarely level and you will either be flying downhill or cranking up hills. The climbing grades are somewhat steep but never sustained, and the constant transitions will keep you firing on all cylinders.

**Ride length:** 14.1 miles
**Ride type:** lollipop-loop (counter-clockwise)
**Riding time:** 2 hours
**Surface:** single-track (10.0 miles); dirt road (4.1 miles)
**Elevations:** start/end 9,250'; max 9,950'; min 9,190'

**Total climbing:** gain/loss 1,890'
**Aerobic level:** moderate (short, but steep climbs throughout)
**Technical level:** 3 (a steep descent on an eroded slope)
**Season:** May through October
**USGS Quadrangle:** Granite

**Trailhead GPS coordinates:** 39° 4.451' N; 106° 18.622' W

**Elevation profile:**

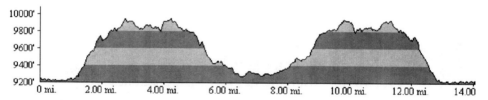

**Getting there:** from the intersection of US 24 and CO 82, drive 1.8 miles west on CO 82 to the intersection with CR 25. Turn left onto CR 25 and drive 0.5 miles. Turn left at the "T" intersection and continue on CR 25 until you reach the trailhead parking area in about 0.5 miles. The road is a tad rough, but should be okay for most passenger cars.

**Trailhead/trail amenities:** none.

**The ride:**

- **0.0** Start at the trailhead sign/maps at the entrance to the single-track.
- **0.25** Continue straight past the trail intersection on your left.
- **1.2** Turn left at the CDT/Colorado Trail post marker. This starts the first major climb of the ride.
- **2.0** At the bottom of a slightly rocky descent, turn right onto a jeep track. A large cairn on your left marks the intersection.
- **2.4** Turn left at the cairn. The single-track resumes.
- **3.8** A small but steep climb will bring you up to CR 399. Cross the road and resume climbing on the single-track. Look for the remnants of old log structures on your right and left as you climb.

## 66 • Arkansas Valley Mountain Biking

**4.6** Intersect CR 398 (Lost Canyon Road) and turn left (downhill). **Note-** *don't cross the road and continue on the faded single-track leading into the forest (the trail dead-ends after much tree fall).*

**4.8** Turn right onto a small road leading into a clearing. Your speed will be up, but look for the Colorado Trail marker. After turning, look left for the next marker; it's about 6 feet up on a tree. Next, look left for the faint single-track heading left (east). There are some trail markers to help you find your way. Let it rip, but watch for tree fall.

**5.3** Cross a funky bridge and head left.

**5.5** Intersect a faint jeep trail at a "T" and turn right, continuing downhill.

**5.6** Continue straight as you cross another, even lighter jeep track. Look for the Colorado Trail marker on the fat tree to your left.

**5.8** Continue straight. Look for a trail marker to guide you. Continue straight through the rock barrier.

**6.0** Turn left at the intersection with the power line road. You are now leaving the Colorado Trail.

**6.2** Go around the BLM gate.

**7.2** Pass through another gate.

**7.5** Turn left onto CR 398 and start to climb.

**8.3** Bear left at the fork with CR 398 and CR 399. Continue to climb on CR 398 toward the Gold Basin Mine. **Note-** *to shorten the ride, bear right at this fork and climb on CR 399 for about 0.75 miles. Look for the Colorado Trail marker on the right; turn right onto the Colorado Trail. This cuts nearly a mile and saves about 150' of climbing.*

**9.1** Intersect the Colorado Trail to close the loop. Continue climbing on CR 398.

**9.2** Look for the Colorado Trail marker on your right. Turn right and climb into the forest on the single-track.

**10.1** Diagonally slash CR 399 as you blast downhill on the single-track. (Stop to look for vehicles before crossing the road!).

**11.6** Turn right at the cairn and ride downhill on the jeep track.

**12.0** Bear left at the cairn and climb the single-track. Look for the Colorado Trail marker on your left.

**12.9** Intersect the lake loop and turn right, following the Colorado Trail.

**14.1** Trailhead. Ride back to your car. Ditch the bike and hit the lake.

# Granite

While it was once the Chaffee County seat, Granite is now a humble outpost (ghost town?) on the banks of the Arkansas River. Looking at it now, it's difficult to imagine that this quiet site was once the scene of a notorious scandal. According to local historians, when the citizens of Buena Vista voted in 1880 to make their town the Chaffee County seat, Granite residents refused to relinquish control of county documents. As the legend goes, a group of men from Buena Vista stole a locomotive and drove it to Granite. Once there, they smashed down the door of the courthouse and started removing the records. When the sheriff arrived to investigate the commotion, the men held him at gunpoint until all of the paperwork and furniture was loaded into the hijacked train.

Today, the most prominent landmark is the white public schoolhouse perched on the hillside overlooking the river and highway. Several other old structures and mine sites in the vicinity contribute to the town's ghost vibe.

As for mountain biking, east of town is a network of rarely used jeep trails and true double-track (think parallel single-track separated by tall grass) that border the Buffalo Peaks Wilderness Area. Wildlife abounds and you are likely to see deer, elk, and coyotes. Be aware, however, that this is also mountain lion and bear habitat, and you may want to think twice about riding solo or at dusk and dawn.

On the west side of US 24 you'll have easy access to one of the smoothest sections of the Colorado Trail. Spanning the distance between Twin Lakes and Clear Creek, this single-track segment is fast, fun and seldom ridden.

The trophy ride of the area, however, is the Lost Canyon Road. This test piece serves as the crux climb and turn-around point of the Leadville Trail 100 Mountain Bike Race. If you have the legs and lungs, it is possible to ride it to a communications station located at the top of a 13,000' peak.

68 • *Arkansas Valley Mountain Biking*

# Ride 15: Lost Canyon Road to Twin Lakes Loop

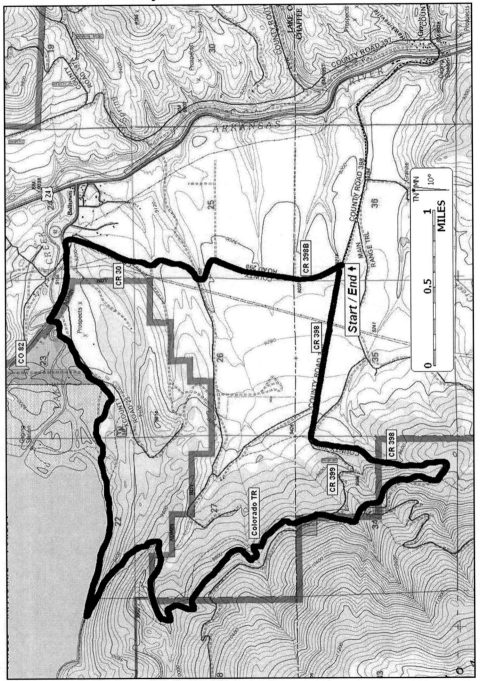

*Map 15: Lost Canyon-Twin Lakes Loop (© National Geographic)*

## Granite • 69

If this ride doesn't make you smile, check your pulse... you may be dead. Though short, the views are spectacular and the single-track sublime. Think of it as "concentrated happiness." While I rarely take breaks while riding, I always stop several times along this route to behold the views, especially when the aspen are in fall color.

The ride begins with a mild climb on roads. Once you get to the Colorado Trail single-track, however, the fun really begins. By the time you reach the lake, the charm of the ride will have you mesmerized. Finish with a fast and easy spin back to the car on mellow-graded county roads.

**Ride length:** 10.1 miles
**Ride type:** loop (clockwise)
**Riding time:** 1.5 hours
**Surface:** dirt road (5.1 miles); single-track (4.6 miles); pavement (0.4 miles)
**Elevations:** start/end 9,250'; max 9,950'; min 9,170'

**Total climbing:** gain/loss 1,060'
**Aerobic level:** moderate (some climbing)
**Technical level:** 3 (the descent to the lake is a little tougher)
**Season:** May through October
**USGS Quadrangle:** Granite

**Trailhead GPS coordinates:** 39° 3.138' N; 106° 17.495' W

**Elevation profile:**

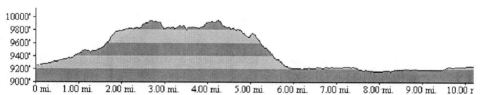

**Getting there:** from the stoplight at the intersection of US 24 and Main St. in Buena Vista, drive 16.6 miles north on US 24. Once in Granite, look for the entrance to Lost Canyon Road on your left. Turn left onto Lost Canyon Road (CR 398) and drive 1.7 miles to the triangular intersection with CR 398B on your right. There is no designated parking area, so park in the small clearing on the south shoulder of CR 398, just west of the intersection with CR 398B.

**Trailhead/trail amenities:** general store/gas station 1.7 miles from trailhead.

**The ride:**
0.0     From the car, ride west (uphill) on CR 398.
0.4     Continue straight on CR 398, passing the power line spur on the left.
1.1     Bear left at the fork to ride west on CR 398. *Note- to shorten the ride, bear right at this fork and climb on CR 399 for about 0.75 miles. Look for the Colorado Trail marker on the right; turn right onto the Colorado Trail. This cuts nearly a mile and saves about 150' of climbing.*

| | |
|---|---|
| 1.9 | Continue on the main road as you pass some campsite spurs on the left and an open meadow to your right. Continue climbing on CR 398 for another 0.2 miles. **Note-** *the Colorado Trail intersects the last campsite spur on your left and descends toward Cache Creek.* |
| 2.1 | Look right for the post and small cairn marking the entrance to the Colorado Trail single-track. |
| 2.8 | Pass the remnants of old log buildings on your left and right. Slow down if you want to see them because you'll be flying down hill. |
| 2.9 | Slow down and look both ways for traffic before diagonally slicing across CR 399 and continuing on the Colorado Trail. |
| 4.2 | Turn right at the "T" intersection and cairn; ride east on the jeep trail. |
| 4.6 | Bear left at the fork with the cairn. The single-track resumes. |
| 5.5 | Intersect the Continental Divide Trail at the bottom of the hill. Turn right to continue along the Colorado Trail as it skirts the south shore of the lake. **Note-** *turn left here to incorporate the* ***Interlaken Loop***. |
| 6.4 | Continue straight past the trail intersection on your right. **Note-** *Turn right here for a nice little single-track segment that ends at the dam on CR 25.* |
| 6.7 | The single-track ends at the trailhead and parking area. Turn right (east) onto CR 25 (unmarked). **Note-** *a hard left leads to a nice beach.* |
| 7.0 | Stay on the main road (CR 25) and follow it to CO 82 |
| 7.7 | Turn right onto paved CO 82. |
| 8.1 | Turn right at the dirt road (CR 30). Cross a cattle guard and turn left. |
| 8.3 | Continue straight on the main road. |
| 9.1 | Bear left, staying on the main road through an unmarked intersection. |
| 9.3 | Bear right, staying on the main road past a driveway on the left. |
| 9.8 | Cross a cattle guard at the Lake/Chaffee County border. CR 30 is now CR 398B. |
| 10.1 | Back at the car! How did that happen? |

**Options:** to add about 3.5 miles and approximately 300' feet of additional climbing, park and start the ride from the river access area across the highway from the Granite store.

Or, incorporate the *Interlaken Loop* at mile 5.5 to add almost 14 miles to this ride.

# Ride 16: Lost Canyon Road (Columbine Climb)

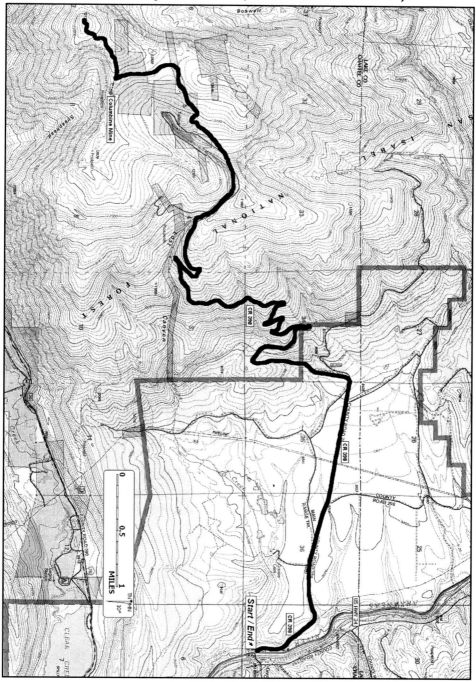

*Map 16: Lost Canyon Road (Columbine Climb) (© National Geographic)*

## 72 • *Arkansas Valley Mountain Biking*

Did you ever wonder if you have what it takes to finish the Leadville Trail 100 Mountain Bike race? Or have you ever wanted to summit a 13'er on your bike? Or are you just a plain, old-fashioned masochist that delights in testing your pain threshold? If any of these apply, you'll want to try this ride.

The ride itself, the crux climb of the Leadville Trail 100 racecourse, is not that bad. The first eight miles are, despite the tremendous gain in altitude, reasonably graded and easy to spin. Once you get above tree line things get a little tougher, but still manageable. The final half-mile push up to Point 13,130' is slightly stupid and some hike-a-bike will be required if you go for it.

If you need any consoling en route, just imagine how fast and fun the downhill return trip will be. 'Nuff said. Get out there!

**Ride length:** 21.4 miles
**Ride type:** out-and-back
**Riding time:** 3.5 hours
**Surface:** dirt road (rough and steep near the top)
**Elevations:** start/end 8,950'; max 13,130'; min 8,950'
**Total climbing:** gain/loss 4,130'

**Aerobic level:** strenuous (lots of climbing and the highpoint is just something silly I rode/hiked for kicks)
**Technical level:** 3- (it's a little rough near the top)
**Season:** July through October
**USGS Quadrangle:** Granite

**Trailhead GPS coordinates:** 39° 2.61' N; 106° 15.985' W

**Elevation profile:**

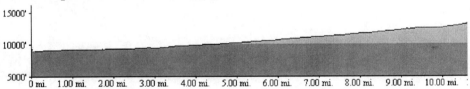

**Getting there:** from the stoplight at the intersection of US 24 and Main St. in Buena Vista, drive 16.6 miles north on US 24. Once in Granite, turn right onto CR 397 and drive over the one-lane bridge. Turn right and park in the boat launch lot between the river and the railroad tracks. From the parking area, ride back across the bridge and carefully cross the highway. The ride starts at the intersection of US 24 and CR 398 (Lost Canyon Road). Use caution when crossing the highway!

**Trailhead/trail amenities:** general store/gas station at start; seasonal porta-pot at parking area.

**The ride:**

**0.0** From the intersection of CR 398 and US 24, start climbing on CR 398. *Note- okay, let's get this out of the way. You won't need this guide until you approach the Gold Basin Mine above tree line. Almost the entire ride is on CR 398. The road is well marked and route finding will not be an issue. If you find you need a break, however, you can use the excuse that you need to check the guide. This will give you a few minutes to catch your breath as you fumble with your pack.*

**1.1** Continue straight on CR 398, passing CR 398D on your left.

**1.7** Bear left at the fork, staying on CR 398 as CR 398B peels away on your right.

**2.1** Continue straight on CR 398, passing the power line road on your left.

**2.8** Bear left, staying on CR 398 as CR 399 heads off to your right.

**3.7** Pass some campsite spurs on your left. *Note- the Colorado Trail intersects the road on your left in about 100 yards.*

**3.9** Pass the Colorado Trail single-track intersection on your right.

**6.6** Continue on the main road as it switches back to the right. Pass the old garage.

**7.7** Stay left on the main road as things get steeper and looser.

**8.1** Continue straight on the main road as you pass a spur leading to the remnants of an old cabin on your right. As you look left up the valley, you will see the Gold Basin Mine.

**8.2** Bear right at the fork. Continue along a steep and rough section for about 30 yards then bear right again at the second fork.

**8.5** Continue straight on the main road, passing a spur on the right.

**9.4** Bear left at the fork as you pedal along a high plateau.

**10.0** Bear right at the fork and start the impossible climb. *Note- if you want to skip this ridiculous final section, head left to explore the Columbine Mine site (the mine site is the halfway/turnaround point of the Leadville 100-mile mountain bike race). Enjoy the views of the 14'ers (Oxford, Belford, Missouri, and Huron) across the valley. Few views anywhere are more spectacular than this!*

**10.7** Whew! That was a bear of a climb. Okay. So, now that you have pushed your bike above 13,000', what's next? Oh yeah, the killer descent along the same route you took to the top!

**Options:** shorten your climb by driving as high as you want along CR 398. The road is passable for most vehicles for the first 7 miles.

74 • *Arkansas Valley Mountain Biking*
# Ride 17: Spring Creek Loop

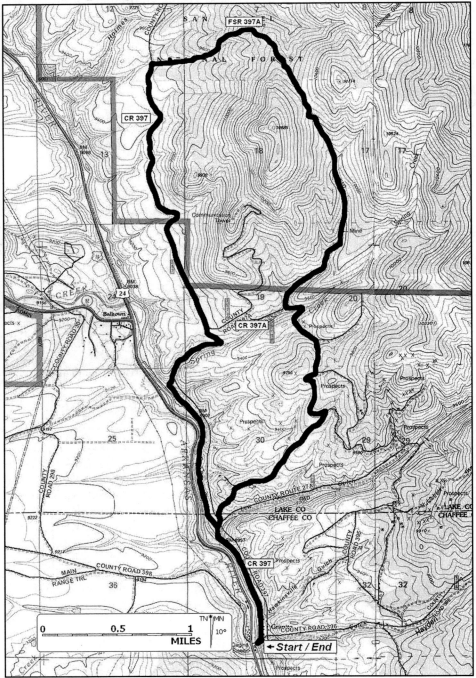

*Map 17: Spring Creek Loop (© National Geographic)*

# Granite • 75

Have you ever ridden in the Fourmile Recreation Area and wished for a more tranquil (fewer ATVs) backcountry experience? This ride, a shorter version of the traditional Spring Creek Loop, is an excellent alternative. Though open to jeeps, motorcycles, and ATVs, the area sees few visitors and you are very unlikely to suck dust and exhaust as you serenely spin this one. The riding surface is refreshingly bereft of tracks and nature is slowly narrowing the lines. Though the eastern side of the loop is technically double-track, the trail is so overgrown that much of it rides like parallel lines of elegant single-track.

Be careful. This is a tricky route to follow and many people have trouble around mile 8.0. In addition, your chances of encountering wildlife on the trail are great (I unwittingly startled a lone coyote as I blasted through a stand of aspen at the start of the descent). This is mountain lion and bear country, so think twice about riding this loop alone or riding at dusk/dawn.

**Ride length:** 11.2 miles
**Ride type:** lollipop-loop (clockwise)
**Riding time:** 1.5-2 hours
**Surface:** dirt road/jeep trails
**Elevations:** start/end 8,950'; max 10,330'; min 8,950'
**Total climbing:** gain/loss 1,880'

**Aerobic level:** moderate (the climb approaching the highpoint is strenuous)
**Technical level:** 3+ (the final descent to CR 397 is intense)
**Season:** May through October
**USGS Quadrangle:** Granite

**Trailhead GPS coordinates:** 39° 2.6' N; 106° 15.917' W

**Elevation profile:**

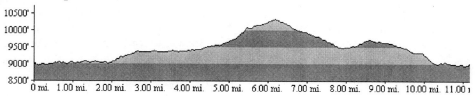

**Getting there:** from the stoplight at the intersection of US 24 and Main St. in Buena Vista, drive 16.6 miles north on US 24. Once in Granite, turn right onto CR 397 and drive over the one-lane bridge. Turn right and park in the boat launch lot between the river and the railroad tracks. The ride starts from the parking area.

**Trailhead/trail amenities:** general store/gas station across from start; seasonal porta-pot at parking area.

**The ride:**
0.0 Turn right (east) from the parking area and cross the railroad tracks. At the intersection with CR 396, turn left (north) and ride parallel to the river on CR 397.

0.9 Continue straight on CR 397. (The spur on the right is at the end of the final descent to this intersection.)

| | |
|---|---|
| 1.9 | Stay left on the main road. |
| 2.6 | Continue left through the forked intersection with CR 397A. |
| 2.7 | Stay left at the fork with CR 397B. Continue riding on CR 397. |
| 3.6 | Continue on the main road as a faint, unmarked jeep track heads right toward the hill. |
| 4.9 | Turn right onto CR 397A. |
| 5.4 | Tough climb, huh. |
| 5.7 | The trail levels a bit as the crux of the killer climb becomes a memory. |
| 6.1 | Continue straight on the main trail through a stand of aspen. Several old and overgrown jeep tracks cross the route. |
| 6.3 | The trail bends right as a drainage line continues straight. The double-track here is sweet and the upcoming downhill is great. The trail gets a little thin; look ahead and ride the most obvious line. |
| 6.6 | Continue descending past an ascending spur on the right. |
| 8.0 | After the descent, you'll approach a thick stand of brush along Spring Creek. Turn left (east) on an overgrown line of double-track that heads upstream. Cross the creek then head toward a stand of pine (south). This is tricky and a wrong turn will most likely return you to mile 2.6. |
| 8.1 | Stay right after crossing the creek. The next section is an ascent into the pines. |
| 8.2 | Crest a small rise and continue straight past a spur on your right. |
| 8.7 | A slightly stiff climb brings you to the top of a small ridge. Descend through a switchback, riding left past a spur on your right inside the turn. Next, descend past an old mine site as the route crosses the tailings. |
| 9.1 | Take the hard right (effectively a switchback) that heads southwest. Get ready for some speed. |
| 10.0 | Things get radical here. Hang on! |
| 10.3 | At the bottom of the white-knuckled descent turn right and head toward the river and US 24. |
| 10.4 | Turn left at the intersection with CR 397. This intersection closes the loop as you coast back into Granite. |
| 11.2 | Arrive back in town and the parking area. |

**Options:** explore the many spurs in the area. Use a map to connect the numerous jeep trails and county roads. *Be sure to respect local land owners and heed all posted private property warnings!*

# Buena Vista

The town's name is Spanish for "good view" and one visit is all it takes to confirm the accuracy of that name. If the founding fathers (and mothers!) had a little foresight, however, they might have also added, "amazing rafting" and "awesome mountain biking" to their list of possible names.

Buena Vista is the geographic hub of the Valley and provides one of the best places to base your visit. Whatever you need, the town has it: restaurants, markets, motels, RV parks, an awesome bike/outdoor gear shop, hot springs, and dozens of primitive campsites (free/no facilities). Best of all, the majority of the routes in this entire guide are within a thirty-minute drive from town.

Most of the rides in the Buena Vista area are in the Fourmile Recreation Area, a vast terrain playground east and south of town. This is also an extremely popular motor sport area, so the routes are loaded with berms and "whoop-de-do" jumps. Because the riding surface is primarily hard-packed, crushed granite, things can get sandy in spots. This is especially true in late summer, after the sun bakes the ground dry and ATV treads stir it up.

If you visit the Fourmile Recreation area, be sure to ride only on trails open to mountain bikes. Local advocacy groups are working hard to open more terrain and riding closed or illegal trails not only damages the area, it hinders their progress.

**Lenhardy Cutoff**

# 78 • *Arkansas Valley Mountain Biking*
# Ride 18: Castle Rock Gulch Loop

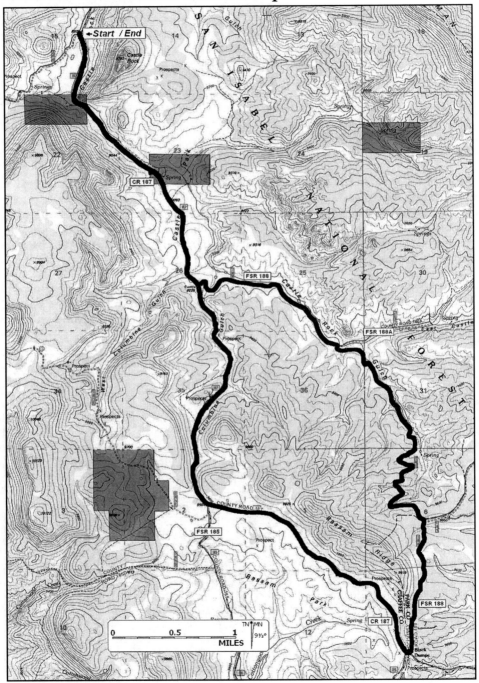

*Map 18: Castle Rock Gulch Loop (© National Geographic)*

Someone once asked me whether a particular route was a "date ride." Well, this one certainly is. Pack a lunch and plan a leisurely outing through some of Colorado's most beautiful country.

The biggest question is whether to ride the loop clockwise or counter-clockwise. The climb is a little longer clockwise, but you'll be in shade for a good chunk of it. Counter-clockwise is a tiny bit steeper, but the road surface is slightly better. One thing to consider: while descending through trees may be more appealing to some, in the heat of summer I'd rather climb in shade. Your choice.

*This ride description is clockwise; reverse the directions for a counter-clockwise ride on the loop.*

**Ride length:** 14.8 miles
**Ride type:** lollipop-loop (clockwise)
**Riding time:** 1.5 hours
**Surface:** dirt road
**Elevations:** start/end 8,900'; max 9,720'; min 8,900'
**Total climbing:** gain/loss 950'

**Aerobic level:** easy (some climbing, but not sustained or steep)
**Technical level:** 1
**Season:** April into November
**USGS Quadrangle:** Castle Rock Gulch

**Trailhead GPS coordinates:** 38° 49.88' N; 105° 59.234' W

**Elevation profile:**

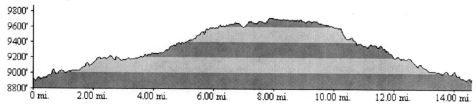

**Getting there:** from the stoplight at the intersection of US 24 and Main St. in Buena Vista, drive 2.4 miles south on US 24 to the intersection with US 24/285. Turn left (east) on US 24/285 and drive 6.4 miles to the intersection with CR 307. Turn right onto CR 307 and drive 1.6 miles to the intersection with CR 187. Turn right onto CR 187 and drive 1.1 miles to the intersection with FSR 300 (not marked). Turn right onto FSR 300 and drive 50 yards to the large parking area. Adjacent to the parking area you'll see a Fourmile sign and a trail marker designating the jeep road (FSR 300) to Bald Mountain Gulch.

**Trailhead/trail amenities:** none.

**The ride:**
0.0   Ride from the parking area back to CR 187. Turn right toward Bassam Park.
2.6   Turn left at the intersection with FSR 188. Drop down a short downhill.
2.9   Look left. What a great spot for a picnic!

| | |
|---|---|
| 4.1 | Continue straight on FSR 188. (FSR 188A heads left.) Rock climbers are bound to drool over the granite formations in the distance. |
| 5.3 | It gets steeper for a little more than a half-mile. |
| 6.6 | Bear right, continuing on FSR 188. (FSR 189 heads left.) |
| 7.2 | Continue straight on FSR 188 through an unmarked intersection. |
| 7.8 | Turn right at the intersection with CR 187. Check out the superb views of Mt. Antero, Mt. Princeton, Mt. Yale, and the Harvard/Columbia group to the west. |
| 10.1 | Continue straight on CR 187 through the intersection with FSR 185. (FSR 185 heads south to Aspen Ridge.) |
| 12.2 | Continue straight on CR 187. Look familiar? FSR 188, the start of this loop, is on your right. |
| 14.8 | End at the intersection with FSR 300. The parking area is uphill on the left. |

**Options:** try it counter-clockwise to determine which direction you like best.

*Castle Rock Gulch*

# Ride 19: Bald Mountain Gulch Loop

Buena Vista • 81

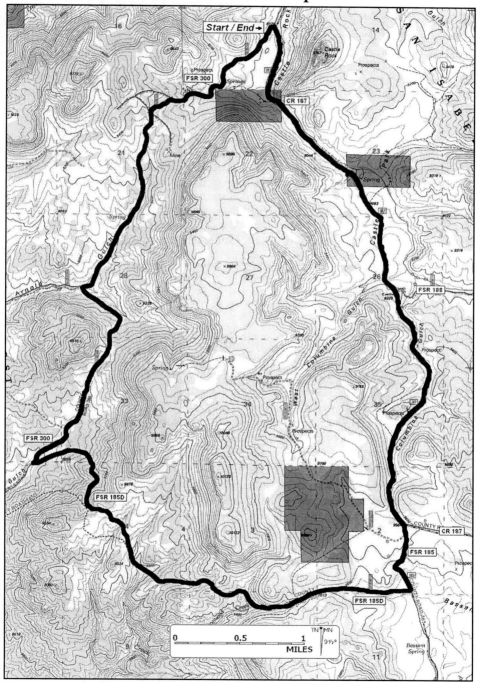

*Map 19: Bald Mountain Gulch Loop (© National Geographic)*

Difficult yet fun. That's about all I can say about this one. The initial uphill grind is mild, but you may want to take it easy so that you have something left when the soup gets thick. Once you hit the jeep track, get ready for some really fun, technical terrain; some of the descents are steep with deep erosion ruts. Finish with a little climbing back to your vehicle on FSR 300.

Route finding gets a little tricky as you approach FSR 300 (between miles 7.0 and 9.2). In addition, this is a popular motor sports area, so watch for motorized traffic on the route.

**Ride length:** 14.0 miles
**Ride type:** loop (clockwise)
**Riding time:** 2.5 hours
**Surface:** dirt road (5.3 miles); jeep trail (8.7 miles)
**Elevations:** start/end 8,930'; max 9,610'; min 8,775'
**Total climbing:** gain/loss 2,130'

**Aerobic level:** strenuous (climbing with some steeps)
**Technical level:** 4 (some of the descents on FSR 185D are steep and rutted)
**Season:** May into November
**USGS Quadrangles:** Castle Rock Gulch, Buena Vista East

**Trailhead GPS coordinates**: 38° 49.877' N; 105° 59.236' W

**Elevation profile:**

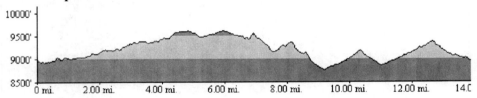

**Getting there:** from the stoplight at the intersection of US 24 and Main St. in Buena Vista, drive 2.4 miles south on US 24 to the intersection with US 24/285. Turn left (east) onto US 24/285 and drive 6.4 miles to the intersection with CR 307. Turn right onto CR 307 and drive 1.6 miles to the intersection with CR 187. Turn right onto CR 187 and drive 1.1 miles to the intersection with FSR 300 (not marked). Turn right onto FSR 300 and drive 50 yards to the large parking area. Adjacent to the parking area you'll see a Fourmile sign and a trail marker designating the jeep road (FSR 300) to Bald Mountain Gulch.

**Trailhead/trail amenities:** none.

**The ride:**
- 0.0   Ride from the parking area back to CR 187 and turn right toward Bassam Park.
- 2.6   Continue straight on CR 187 at the intersection with FSR 188.
- 4.7   Turn right onto FSR 185, following the sign to Aspen Ridge.
- 4.8   Continue on FSR 185 past the intersection with FSR 185E on the right.
- 5.3   Turn right at the intersection with FSR 185D.

| | |
|---|---|
| 5.6 | Pass through the seasonal closure gate. |
| 6.1 | Continue straight, passing an unmarked spur on the left. |
| 6.3 | Continue straight on FSR 185D, passing TR 1434 on the left. |
| 6.5 | Pass through a gate. Be sure to close it. |
| 7.0 | Continue straight on FSR 185D, passing an unmarked spur on the left. |
| 7.5 | Bear right at the unmarked spur. |
| 7.6 | Cross a deep wash and start to climb. |
| 8.4 | Continue straight through the unmarked spur. |
| 9.2 | Pass through the seasonal closure gate and turn right at the intersection with FSR 300. Climb through a short sandy section. |
| 10.4 | Continue straight, passing an unmarked spur on the left. |
| 11.0 | Turn right at the parking area and continue on FSR 300. (FSR 300A is the spur on the far left.) |
| 12.3 | Continue straight (right) on FSR 300, passing TR 1423 on the left. |
| 12.6 | Continue straight through an unmarked intersection; stay on the main road. |
| 13.2 | Bear left at the unmarked intersection. The rock formation in the distance ahead is Castle Rock. |
| 13.3 | Bear right at an unmarked intersection. Continue pedaling toward Castle Rock. |
| 14.0 | Enter the parking area and trailhead. |

**Options:** explore some of the great multi-use trails in the area, but bring a map and compass so you don't get lost!

*Fast descents: Bald Mountain Gulch*

**84** • *Arkansas Valley Mountain Biking*

# Ride 20: Davis Meadow Loop

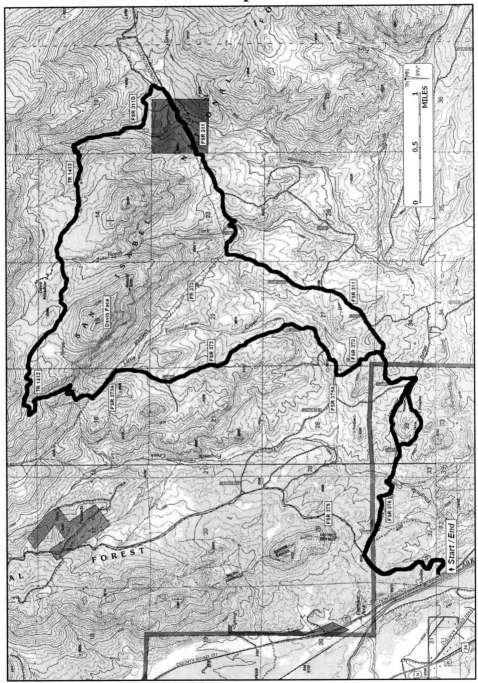

*Map 20: Davis Meadow Loop (© National Geographic)*

As described here, this is one of the most difficult routes in the Buena Vista area. The ride starts by climbing up jeep roads. Then it continues climbing up jeep roads for what seems like an eternity. Eventually you'll reach the faint single-track that leads to the Davis Meadow, but the trail continues climbing until you reach the highpoint of the route.

The single-track descent is steep, stepped and blocky, and good biking skills are needed to ride it cleanly. The jeep tracks back to the start are extremely fun, but several short climbs along the way will remind you that it was a long ride.

**Ride length:** 19.0 miles
**Ride type:** lollipop-loop (counter-clockwise)
**Riding time:** 3.5-4 hours
**Surface:** single-track (4.3 miles); jeep road (14.7 miles)
**Elevations:** start/end 8,130'; max 10,140'; min 8,130'

**Total climbing:** gain/loss 2,725'
**Aerobic level:** strenuous (climbing)
**Technical level:** 4 (steep, technical descents)
**Season:** May through October
**USGS Quadrangles:** Buena Vista West, Harvard Lakes, Marmot Peak

**Trailhead GPS coordinates:** 38° 52.478' N; 106° 8.596' W

**Elevation profile:**

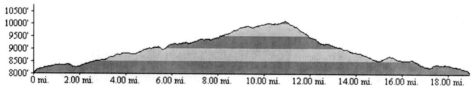

**Getting there:** from the stoplight at the intersection of US 24 and Main St. in Buena Vista, drive 0.2 miles east on E. Main St. Turn left onto N. Colorado Ave. (CR 371) and drive 2.5 miles north to the intersection with CR 375 (just south of the tunnels). Turn right (east) and drive 0.1 miles to the large OHV parking area on your left. The ride starts at the Fourmile sign in the southeast corner of the parking area.

**Trailhead/trail amenities:** seasonal porta-pot at trailhead.

**The ride:**
0.0   Head uphill on CR 375.
0.4   Climb on CR 375 past the intersection with TR 6037 on the right.
0.7   Pass the Turtle Rock camping area on your left. Just beyond the campground, the road becomes FSR 375 as you enter the San Isabel National Forest.
1.0   Turn right onto FSR 376 (**Lenhardy Cutoff**). Stay on FSR 376, passing all trail spurs for the next 1.9 miles.
1.1   Continue riding on FSR 376 as you pass TR 6038 on the right.
1.5   Continue on FSR 376 past TR 6037 (right) and TR 1415 (left).

| | |
|---|---|
| 1.9 | Cross Fourmile Creek. You will get your feet wet. Be prepared for tough sand for approximately 0.4 miles. |
| 2.2 | Ride past the intersections with TR 6029 and TR 6039 as you chug uphill through the sand. |
| 2.9 | Continue straight on FSR 376 as you pass the intersection with TR 6039 on the right. (Spectacular views of Mt. Princeton open to your right.) Ride for another 100 yards, then turn left onto FSR 311. |
| 3.5 | Bear right at the intersection with FSR 373, continuing on FSR 311. |
| 4.0 | Continue straight on FSR 311 past the intersection with FSR 311F on the left. |
| 4.4 | Continue on FSR 311 past the intersection with TR 1414 on the right. |
| 5.4 | Stay right at the intersection with FSR 373; continue riding on FSR 311. |
| 5.8 | Cross a small stream just as your feet were about dry from the last water crossing. |
| 6.1 | Stay on FSR 311 through the intersection with TR 1414 on the right. |
| 6.3 | Continue on FSR 311 past the intersection with FSR 311E on the left. |
| 7.3 | Turn left onto FSR 311D. (Look for a sign that reads "Fuelwood" to help you identify this intersection.) Continue for 100 yards then bear left, passing a short spur on the right. |
| 7.9 | Arrive at the Davis Meadow trailhead (TR 1413). |
| 8.0 | Pass through a gate. A sign designates the start of TR 1413. |
| 8.4 | Cross Sevenmile Creek. This area can get overgrown by late summer. Look for clues to help you follow the trail: cairns, cut branches, etc. |
| 9.6 | Enter a marshy area with several old cabins. Look directly across the marsh to an opening between the buildings; this is where the trail resumes. The trail is marked by a cairn once you pass the cabins. |
| 10.8 | A trail marker lets you know that you are not lost. |
| 11.0 | The trail widens into a very rugged jeep road. |
| 11.1 | Depart right from the jeep road and resume riding on rough single-track. (The road becomes a rutted gully filled with debris.) |
| 11.7 | Another trail marker on the right to reassure you. Enjoy the hard-earned downhill. |
| 12.2 | Arrive at a jeep road (FSR 373A, unmarked) as TR 1413 ends. Pass the aqueduct vent and turn left for a fast descent. |
| 12.6 | Bottom-out from the steep descent and look up at the Davis Face crag on your left. **Note-** *for you climbers out there, the crack up the center is a tasty, 4-pitch, 5.9 trad route with the crux (roof) on the second pitch.* |
| 12.8 | Bear right as FSR 373A ends at a "T" intersection with FSR 373. |
| 15.2 | Deep sand as you enter a seasonal wash. Turn left and climb up FSR 373; look for the sign on your left. (Straight leads to FSR 375A.) |

- **15.7** Turn right onto FSR 311 to close the loop.
- **16.3** Turn right as FSR 311 ends at a "T" intersection with FSR 376. Ride for 100 yards then turn left onto TR 6039. (This is a fun little addition, but if you've had enough stay on FSR 376.)
- **16.7** Continue straight on TR 6039 past TR 6029 on the left.
- **17.0** Rejoin FSR 376 near the top of the sandy section. Turn left and plow through the sand as you descend to Fourmile Creek.
- **17.4** Cross Fourmile Creek and avoid all trail spurs until you reach FSR 375.
- **18.3** Turn left onto FSR/CR 375 (unmarked). Not much left.
- **19.0** Find your car and drive into town for a shower and a malted shake.

**Options:** this is a long ride. Shorten it by starting at the intersection of FSR 311 and FSR 311D. To do this, you'll need to drive to Trout Creek Pass and a high clearance, 4WD vehicle is recommended.

From the intersection of US 24 and Main St. in Buena Vista, drive 2.4 miles south and turn left at the intersection US 24/285. Drive approximately 12.7 miles east/north on US 24/285 to CR 311. Turn left onto CR 311 and continue driving on CR/FSR 311 until you reach the intersection with FSR 311D on your right in approximately 5.7 miles.

Start by riding uphill on FSR 311D (mile 7.3 above). When you get to FSR 311 (mile 15.7 above), turn left and continue riding east on FSR 311 until you return to your vehicle.

*Fourmile TR 6039*

# Ride 21: FSR 373 (Natural Arch) Loop

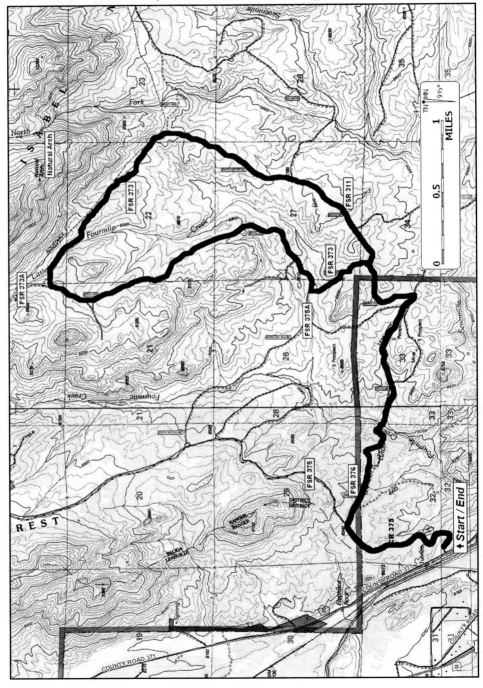

*Map 21: FSR 373 (Natural Arch) Loop (© National Geographic)*

While it's true that discriminating mountain bikers only want single-track, the terrain in this part of the Fourmile Recreation Area is distinguished by fast and steep ATV and jeep trails. There are berms prime for fat tire carving and "whoop-de-do" jumps for getting your share of air time. While it's not single-track, you'll have so much fun riding that you won't care.

This ride starts with an easy but steady climb on dirt roads. A few descents en route break the work and give you a taste of the fun awaiting you on the main downhill. The fun really begins when you reach the second intersection with FSR 373, where the descents are steep and fast. Just before you reach the Davis Face, you get terrific views of a natural arch.

*This is a popular area for jeeps, motorcycles, and ATVs, so stay alert as you bomb the downhills.*

**Ride length:** 12.8 miles
**Ride type:** lollipop-loop
**Riding time:** 2 hours
**Surface:** dirt/jeep roads
**Elevations:** start/end 8,120'; max 9,225'; min 8,120'
**Total climbing:** gain/loss 1,765'

**Aerobic level:** moderate (climbing)
**Technical level:** 3+ (some rutted steeps)
**Season:** April through October
**USGS Quadrangles:** Buena Vista West, Harvard Lakes, Marmot Peak

**Trailhead GPS coordinates:** 38° 52.478' N; 106° 8.596' W

**Elevation profile:**

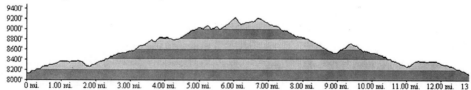

**Getting there:** from the stoplight at the intersection of US 24 and Main St. in Buena Vista, drive 0.2 miles east on E. Main St. Turn left onto N. Colorado Ave (CR 371) and drive 2.5 miles north to the intersection with CR 375 (just south of the tunnels). Turn right (east) and drive 0.1 miles to the large OHV parking area on your left. The ride starts at the Fourmile sign in the southeast corner of the parking area.

**Trailhead/trail amenities:** seasonal porta-pot at trailhead.

**The ride:**
0.0   Ride uphill on CR 375.
0.4   Climb on CR 375 past the intersection with TR 6037 on the right.
0.7   Pass the entrance to the Turtle Rock camping area on the left.
0.8   CR 375 becomes FSR 375 as you enter the San Isabel National Forest.
1.0   Turn right onto FSR 376 (***Lenhardy Cutoff***).

## 90 • *Arkansas Valley Mountain Biking*

**1.1** Continue straight on FSR 376 as you pass TR 6038 on the right.

**1.5** Continue on FSR 376 past TR 6037 (right) and TR 1415 (left).

**1.9** Cross Fourmile Creek. Climb through about 0.4 miles of sand.

**2.2** Continue climbing on FSR 376 as you first pass TR 6029 then TR 6039 on the right.

**2.9** Continue straight on FSR 376 as you pass the intersection with TR 6039 on the right. (Spectacular views of Mt. Princeton open to your right.) Ride for another 100 yards then turn left onto FSR 311.

**3.5** Bear right at the intersection with FSR 373, continuing on FSR 311.

**4.0** Continue straight on FSR 311 past the intersection with FSR 311F on the left.

**4.4** Continue on FSR 311 past the intersection with TR 1414 on the right.

**5.4** Turn left onto FSR 373. Get ready for some steep speed.

**5.8** Approach a turnout on the right with a "NO MOTOR VEHICLES" post. Look slightly left up the rocky hillside to see the natural arch. Trees make it a little tough to see, but it is there. Moab has little on us!

**6.1** Continue straight on FSR 373 as you pass double-track spurs on your left and right.

**6.6** Cross Little Fourmile Creek. After a short uphill, stay on FSR 373 as you pass the intersection with FSR 373A on the right. The next section is a blast. Have fun!

**9.0** Deep sand as you enter a seasonal wash. Turn left and climb up FSR 373; look for the sign on your left. (Straight leads to FSR 375A.)

**9.5** Turn right onto FSR 311 as FSR 373 ends at the intersection. This closes the loop and starts you on your return trip back to FSR 375.

**10.0** Turn right onto FSR 376 as FSR 311 ends at a "T" intersection. Ride for 100 yards then stay right at the forked intersection with TR 6039. ***Note-** TR 6039 is a fun, short OHV trail that parallels FSR 376. Check it out if the mood strikes.*

**10.8** You're back in the sand as you pass TR 6039 and TR 6029 on the left. Continue descending to Fourmile Creek.

**11.1** Cross Fourmile Creek. Stay on FSR 376 until you reach FSR 375.

**11.9** From FSR 376, turn left at the unmarked "T" intersection with FSR 375.

**12.8** Time to end the ride.

**Options:** sample some of the ATV/motorcycle trails that intersect and parallel the route. They are best when ridden on the return trip to FSR/CR 375.

# Ride 22: Fourmile Cutoff Loop

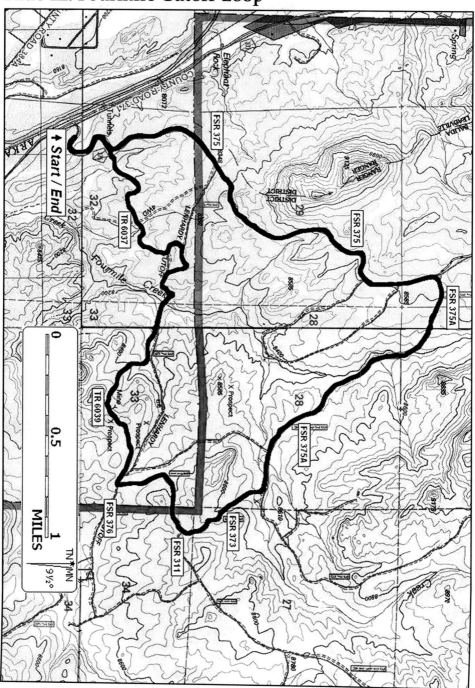

*Map 22: Fourmile Cutoff Loop (© National Geographic)*

## 92 • *Arkansas Valley Mountain Biking*

This short, fun loop is a great morning workout you can sneak in while the others are still stirring in their sleeping bags. Strong riders should be able to close the loop in under an hour, but doing so will require some effort—just enough to make it an extremely satisfying way to start the day.

It starts with a steady climb on a well-maintained dirt road. The drop into FSR 375A is fun and fast with twisting turns. Some short but somewhat steep climbs are spread throughout and serve to keep your heart rate elevated. Several sand traps await you, but most are on downhills and can be ridden with moderate effort and skill.

*This is a popular area for jeeps, trucks and ATVs, and early mornings are best for avoiding motorized traffic.*

**Ride length:** 7.8 miles
**Ride type:** loop
**Riding time:** 1-1.5 hours
**Surface:** jeep/ATV trails
**Elevations:** start/end 8,125'; max 8,720'; min 8,125'
**Total climbing:** gain/loss 940'

**Aerobic level:** moderate (climbing, a few steep sections)
**Technical level:** 4 (sand, ruts, some steeps)
**Season:** April through October
**USGS Quadrangles:** Buena Vista West, Harvard Lakes, Marmot Peak

**Trailhead GPS coordinates:** 38° 52.478' N; 106° 8.596' W

**Elevation profile:**

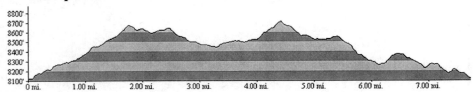

**Getting there:** from the stoplight at the intersection of US 24 and Main St. in Buena Vista, drive 0.2 miles east on E. Main St. Turn left onto N. Colorado Ave (CR 371) and drive 2.5 miles north to the intersection with CR 375 (just south of the tunnels). Turn right (east) and drive 0.1 miles to the large OHV parking area on your left. The ride starts at the Fourmile sign in the southeast corner of the parking area.

**Trailhead/trail amenities:** seasonal porta-pot at trailhead.

**The ride:**
0.0   Ride uphill on CR 375 (Fourmile Road).
0.4   Continue riding uphill on CR 375 as you pass the intersection with TR 6037 on your right.
0.7   Pass the entrance to Turtle Rock camping area on the left.
0.8   CR 375 becomes FSR 375 as you enter the San Isabel National Forest.

*Buena Vista* • 93

| | |
|---|---|
| 1.0 | Continue climbing on FSR 375 past the intersection with FSR 376 (*Lenhardy Cutoff*) on the right. |
| 1.2 | Continue climbing on FSR 375 past the Split Rock area. |
| 2.0 | Continue descending on FSR 375 as it bends right. You will pass the intersection with FSR 375E on the left. |
| 2.3 | Pass the intersection with FSR 375C on your right as you continue climbing on FSR 375. |
| 2.5 | Turn right onto FSR 375A and enjoy the descent. |
| 3.4 | Continue straight on FSR 375A as you pass some campsite spurs leading to the creek on your right. |
| 4.0 | Enter a sandy wash where a shallow runoff stream flows in spring. After about 100 yards in the sand, turn right onto FSR 373 and climb. (This intersection may not be obvious, so keep your eyes open.) The first 100 yards of the climb may be very sandy, but the surface quickly improves. |
| 4.5 | After a quick descent, turn right as FSR 373 ends at a "T" intersection with FSR 311. |
| 5.1 | Turn right as FSR 311 ends at a "T" intersection with FSR 376. Continue riding west on FSR 376 for approximately 100 yards then bear left onto TR 6039 at the fork. |
| 5.6 | After a slightly technical downhill, continue straight on TR 6039 as TR 6029 intersects on your left. *Note- turn left onto 6029 for a more challenging, technical alternative route back to FSR 376; this will add some minutes to your total riding time.* |
| 6.0 | Turn left when you hit the sand and continue riding downhill on FSR 376 (unmarked) toward Fourmile Creek. |
| 6.1 | Continue descending on FSR 376 as you pass the intersection with TR 6029 on the left. |
| 6.2 | Cross Fourmile Creek. |
| 6.6 | Continue on FSR 376 as you pass TR 1415 on your right. |
| 6.7 | Turn left onto TR 6037. |
| 7.4 | Turn left as you pass the intersection with TR 6038 on your right. |
| 7.6 | After some nasty sand and a steep, technical climb, turn left onto CR 375. This closes the loop. |
| 7.8 | The end. Get back to camp and wake the others for breakfast. |

**Options:** plan a longer ride and explore the many riding options available in the Fourmile Area. Free maps are available at many places in Buena Vista and at some of the more popular trailheads.

## 94 • Arkansas Valley Mountain Biking
# Ride 23: Lenhardy Cutoff

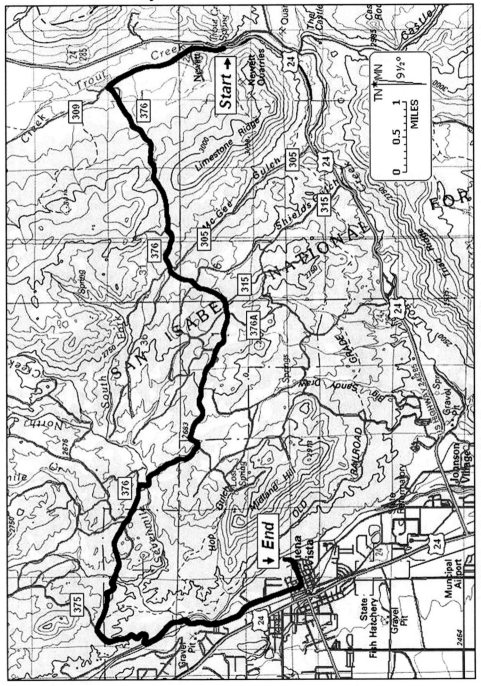

*Map 23: Lenhardy Cutoff (© National Geographic)*

What's Thanksgiving without turkey? Or July 4th without fireworks? The same as a Buena Vista mountain biking guide without the Lenhardy Cutoff!

This legendary ride starts with a brief climb on a county road. It then continues to climb into a pine forest before dropping into a screaming descent through the high desert terrain of the Fourmile Recreation Area. The long descent is especially fun, with fast miles of smooth jumps and bumps. Finish with an easy pedal along the river as you return to town.

*Be careful when you hit the sandy sections!*

**Ride length:** 15.8 miles
**Ride type:** one-way with shuttle
**Riding time:** 2 hours
**Surface:** dirt road/jeep road
**Elevations:** start 9,030'; end 7,960'; max 9,760'; min 7,960'
**Total climbing:** gain 960' - loss 2,050' = total -1,090'

**Aerobic level:** easy (the climb and length make it slightly moderate)
**Technical level:** 3 (short rocky sections; sand on the descent)
**Season:** April into November
**USGS Quadrangles:** Castle Rock Gulch, Antero Reservoir, Marmot Peak, Buena Vista East, Harvard Lakes, Buena Vista West

**Trailhead GPS coordinates:** 38° 51.49' N; 105° 59.182' W

**Elevation profile:**

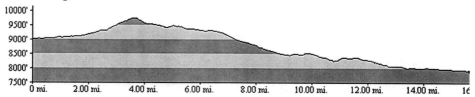

**Getting there:** leave a vehicle at the Buena Vista River Park. From the stoplight at the intersection of US 24 and Main St. in Buena Vista, drive 0.5 miles east to the end of E. Main St. Bear left into the Buena Vista River Park parking lot.

Take the other vehicle, riders and bikes to the trailhead. From the intersection of US 24 and Main St. in Buena Vista, drive approximately 2.4 miles south and turn left (east) at the intersection with US 24/285. Drive approximately 8.6 miles east/north on US 24/285 to the intersection with CR 309. There is a small parking area on the right (east) side of the highway across from CR 309. The ride begins at the start of CR 309. (There is additional parking on CR 307, 0.1 miles further north on US 24/285.)

**Trailhead/trail amenities:** restrooms and water at trail end; seasonal porta-pot at mile 12.7; ends in town.

**The ride:**
**0.0** The ride starts at the start of CR 309. Ride uphill on CR 309.

| | |
|---|---|
| 1.8 | Turn left onto FSR 376. Continue riding on the main road past all campsite spurs for the next 3 miles. *Note- this ride now overlaps the* **Midland Bike Trail** *for approximately 4 miles.* |
| 4.3 | Pass an intersection with an unmarked double-track on your right. |
| 4.8 | Seasonal closure gate. Pass all spurs for the next 100 yards. Continue straight on FSR 376 through the intersection with CR/FSR 305. *Note- there's a sign showing mileage to Buena Vista via this route (10 miles).* |
| 4.9 | Stay on FSR 376 past the intersection with FSR 376B on your right. |
| 5.8 | Stay on FSR 376 past the intersection with CR/FSR 315 on the left. The sign says "BV 9 miles." Stay on the main road past several campsite spurs for the next 0.2 miles. *Note- the* **Midland Bike Trail** *descends CR/FSR 315 (Shields Gulch).* |
| 6.0 | Continue straight on FSR 376, passing the intersection with FSR 376A on your left. The next downhill (2.4 miles) is mucho fun. Go for it! |
| 8.4 | The sand can get thick and loose here. Be careful. |
| 9.5 | Stay on the main route past a spur on the left. |
| 9.9 | Stay on FSR 376 past the intersection with FSR 311 on your right. Ride 100 yards then bear right to stay on FSR 376 at the fork with TR 6039. |
| 10.5 | More sand as you first pass TR 6039 then TR 6029 on your left. |
| 10.9 | Cross Fourmile Creek. Your feet will get wet. |
| 11.3 | Stay on FSR 376 past multi-use trails TR 1415 and TR 6037 on the right and left respectively. |
| 11.7 | Pass TR 6038 on the left. |
| 11.8 | Turn left as FSR 376 ends at a "T" intersection with FSR/CR 375 (unmarked). Enjoy the easy downhill but watch for traffic. |
| 12.8 | Turn left at the intersection with CR 371, the River Road. |
| 15.3 | Turn left at the intersection with E. Main St. in downtown Buena Vista. Continue east on E. Main St. until you reach the River Park. |
| 15.8 | Parking area and end of ride. Now go get your other car. |

**Options:** the Fourmile Recreation Area has so many riding options that one local said, "I've never done the same route twice." One could literally spend a week exploring the area. Take a map and plan before you go.

# Ride 24: Midland Bike Trail

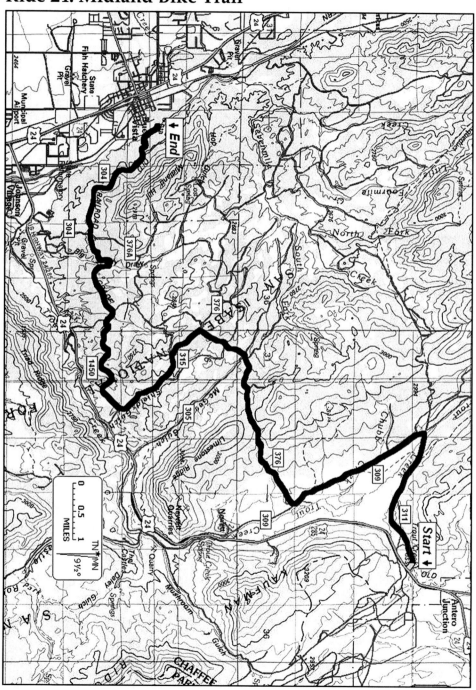

Map 24: Midland Bike Trail (© *National Geographic*)

# 98 • *Arkansas Valley Mountain Biking*

This route provides a pleasant ride with terrific views. Not to be confused with the Midland Railroad Grade, this is the complete route from Trout Creek Pass to Buena Vista.

The ride starts with a gentle descent into the Chubb Park State Wildlife Management Area. You'll next ascend through a pine forest to a ridge with sweeping vistas of the Collegiate Peaks and Arkansas Valley. A fast descent on CR/FSR 315 brings you to the single-track of the Midland Railroad Grade, where technical detours into gullies once spanned by rail trestles put even experienced riders on the edge of their saddles. The last mile returns you to Buena Vista along the serpentine single-track of the Barbara Whipple Trail.

**Ride length:** 18.8 miles
**Ride type:** one-way with shuttle
**Riding time:** 2.5 hours
**Surface:** single-track (4.9 miles); dirt road (13.9 miles)
**Elevations:** start 9,480'; end 7,960'; max 9,750'; min 7,960'
**Total climbing:** gain 840' - loss 2,375' = total -1,535'

**Aerobic level:** easy (some climbing and the length make it somewhat moderate)
**Technical level:** 3 (the few technical sections are easily walked)
**Season:** April into November
**USGS Quadrangles:** Antero Reservoir, Marmot Peak, Buena Vista East

**Trailhead GPS coordinates:** 38° 54.652' N; 105° 58.661' W

**Elevation profile:**

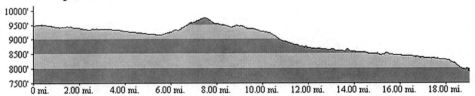

**Getting there:** leave a vehicle at the Buena Vista River Park. From the stoplight at the intersection of US 24 and Main St. in Buena Vista, drive 0.5 miles east to the end of E. Main St. Bear left into the Buena Vista River Park parking lot.

Take the other vehicle, loaded with riders and bikes, to the trailhead. From the intersection of US 24 and Main St. in Buena Vista, drive 2.4 miles south and turn left at the intersection with US 24/285. Drive 12.7 miles east/north on US 24/285 to CR 311. Turn left onto CR 311 and drive approximately 0.2 miles to the parking area and trailhead on the left.

**Trailhead/trail amenities:** restrooms and water at trail end; ends in town.

**The ride:**
0.0  From the trailhead, turn left (west) on CR 311 to start the ride.
1.5  Enter Chubb Park State Wildlife Management Area. Stay on the designated roads through this area.

| | |
|---|---|
| **2.6** | Turn left at the intersection with CR 309. |
| **3.3** | Continue on the main road past all spurs. |
| **4.8** | Cross the cattle guard and stay on CR 309. |
| **5.2** | Turn right onto FSR 376 to start the climb. Continue riding on the main road past all campsite spurs for the next 3 miles. ***Note-*** *from this point this route overlaps the* **Lenhardy Cutoff** *for about 4 miles.* |
| **7.7** | Pass an intersection with an unmarked double-track on your right. |
| **8.2** | Pass through a seasonal closure gate. Avoid all spurs for the next 100 yards. At the intersection with CR/FSR 305, continue straight on FSR 376. This intersection has a mileage sign (10 miles to Buena Vista). |
| **8.4** | Stay on FSR 376, passing the intersection with FSR 376B on your right. |
| **9.3** | Turn left at the intersection with CR/FSR 315 (Shields Gulch). Enjoy the views. ***Note-*** *the* **Lenhardy Cutoff** *continues straight on FSR 376.* |
| **11.5** | Turn right at the intersection with TR 1450. There is a parking area and Fourmile signs designating the trailhead. |
| **14.2** | Continue straight on TR 1450. (TR 1450A, part of the Gentlemen's Loop, heads uphill on the right.) |
| **15.7** | Continue straight on FSR 376A. |
| **15.8** | Turn right onto CR 304. (**Hint-** *head toward the large "No Outlet" sign.*) Stay on CR 304 until you reach the intersection with the Barbara Whipple Trail on your left (2.1 miles). |
| **17.9** | Look left for the Barbara Whipple Trail. It's easy to pass this intersection; just watch left for the Midland Bike Trail sign. |
| **18.4** | Continue straight, passing a trail on the right. In another 100 yards, you'll pass sheltered benches at a scenic viewpoint. |
| **18.8** | Cross the bridge and call it a success! |

**Options:** one fun alternative in this ride is to take FSR 376 at mile 9.3. Continue on FSR 376 for approximately 0.2 miles, then turn left onto FSR 376A. Stay on 376A until you return to the Midland Bike Trail at mile 15.7 as documented in this ride.

## 100 • Arkansas Valley Mountain Biking
# Ride 25: Midland Railroad Grade

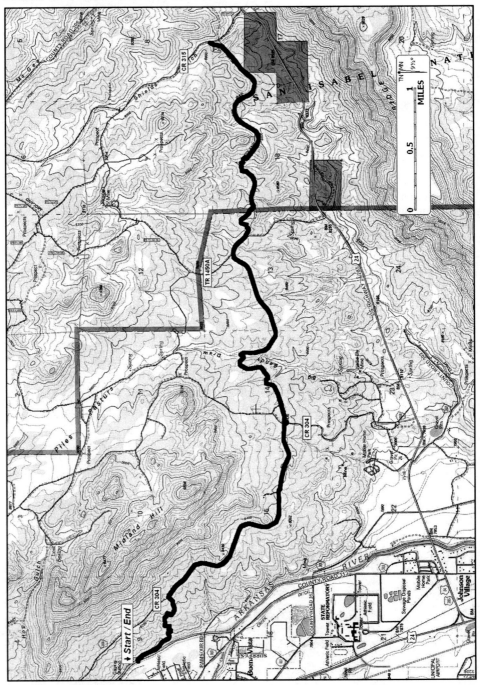

*Map 25: Midland Railroad Grade (© National Geographic)*

Okay. You've been to BV many times and you've ridden this one before. While easy to overlook, there is a great deal of charm to this route. Admit it: the Whipple Trail is nothing short of awesome and the "diversions" are a whole lot of fun. Nearly everyone loves this trail and it's a BV staple.

Start with a fun stretch of single-track along the Barbara Whipple Trail. After the climb, you reach spectacular views of Mount Princeton and the southern Arkansas Valley from the old Midland Railroad grade along CR 304. Once you turn east, the trail returns to single-track that slices through narrow stone cuts and drops into diversions that wind down through gullies once spanned by rail trestles.

**Ride length:** 14.6 miles
**Ride type:** out-and-back
**Riding time:** 2 hours
**Surface:** single-track (9.8 miles); dirt road (4.8 miles)
**Elevations:** start/end 7,960'; max 8,750'; min 7,960'
**Total climbing:** gain/loss 1,090'

**Aerobic level:** easy (the 0.9-mile climb at the start is moderate)
**Technical level:** 3 (the short technical sections are easily walked)
**Season:** April through November (year-round when dry)
**USGS Quadrangle:** Buena Vista East

**Trailhead GPS coordinates:** 38° 50.821' N; 106° 7.323' W

**Elevation profile:**

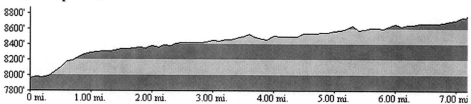

**Getting there:** from the stoplight at the intersection of US 24 and Main St. in Buena Vista, drive 0.5 miles east to the end of E. Main St. Bear left into the Buena Vista River Park parking lot. The ride starts at the west side (town side) of the footbridge over the river.

**Trailhead/trail amenities:** restrooms/water at trailhead; starts/ends in town.

**The ride:**
0.0   Cross the bridge and enjoy the Whipple single-track. Pure fun.
0.1   Stay right at the split. The trail drops down a few feet and parallels the river.
0.2   Pass the shaded bench area with 4 interpretive signs. If you have the time, stop to read the signs and enjoy the view.
0.3   Stay right at the split. *Note- bear left for an easier route to CR 304.*
0.9   Intersect CR 304 and turn right. (There are amazing views of Mt. Princeton here.) Stay on this road for the next 2 miles.

## 102 • Arkansas Valley Mountain Biking

**2.9** Turn left onto FSR 376A. The entrance is between the parking areas.

**3.3** Go straight onto TR 1450. (FSR 376A heads left.) Back on single-track.

**4.8** Continue straight along TR 1450. TR 1450 may not be marked at this intersection, but TR 1450A is the spur on the left.

**7.3** Bear left and drop down to the well-marked trailhead at the intersection with CR/FSR 315. Return the way you came.

**Options:** for an easier, primarily downhill ride, leave a vehicle at the River Park and start the ride at the eastern trailhead on CR 315. To get there, drive 2.4 miles south on US 24 from the intersection of Main St. and US 24 in Buena Vista. Turn left at the intersection with US 285/24 and drive 5.6 miles east to CR 315. Turn left onto CR 315 and drive 0.5 miles to the trailhead and parking area on the left.

*Mt. Princeton: Midland Bike Trail*

# Ride 26: Gentlemen's Loop

Buena Vista • 103

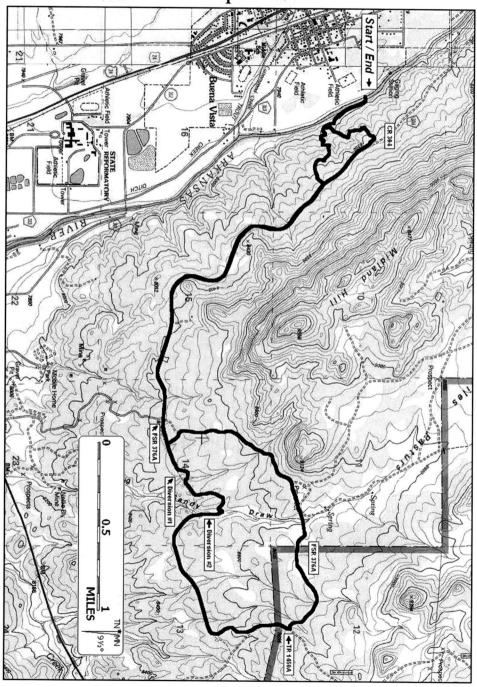

*Map 26: Gentlemen's Loop (© National Geographic)*

This is one of the most popular rides in Buena Vista and you are very likely to see locals out for quick workouts on the trail. Start by snaking your way up some tasty single-track from the Buena Vista River Park. The next section, a spin on the Midland Railroad Grade, is fast and easy, but a sustained climb awaits you on FSR 376A. From the highpoint of the route, make a lightning-fast descent back to the Midland Railroad Grade where two technical diversions will test your skills. The Whipple Trail back to town provides a perfect ending.

**Ride length:** 10.6 miles
**Ride type:** lollipop-loop (clockwise)
**Riding time:** 1-2 hours
**Surface:** single-track (3.4 miles); dirt roads (7.2 miles)
**Elevations:** start/end 7,960'; max 8,750'; min 7,960'
**Total climbing:** gain/loss 965'
**Aerobic level:** moderate (climbing)
**Technical level:** 3 (short technical sections are easily walked)
**Season:** April through November (can be ridden all year when dry)
**USGS Quadrangle:** Buena Vista East

**Trailhead GPS coordinates:** 38° 50.818' N; 106° 7.327' W

**Elevation profile:**

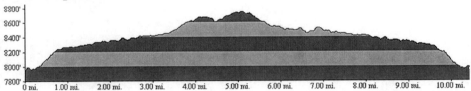

**Getting there:** from the stoplight at the intersection of US 24 and Main St. in Buena Vista, drive approximately 0.5 miles east to the end of E. Main St. Bear left into the Buena Vista River Park parking lot. The ride starts at the west side (town side) of the footbridge over the river.

**Trailhead/trail amenities:** restrooms/water at trailhead; starts/ends in town.

**The ride:**
0.0   Ride across the footbridge to start the ride. In a little over 100 yards you will pass a steep trail on your left. Continue riding parallel to the river.

0.3   Approximately 50 yards past the sun shelter, turn left to ascend along the Midland Stage Trail. *Note- the Midland Bike Trail route heads straight at this intersection. There isn't much difference in overall difficulty between these two trails and both lead to CR 304.*

0.5   Continue climbing straight past the intersection with the North Whipple Trail on your left.

0.8   Turn right onto CR 304.

1.2   Continue straight past the intersection with the Midland Bike Trail on your right. You'll descend this segment later.

3.2   Turn left onto FSR 376A. The entrance is between the parking areas.

| | |
|---|---|
| 3.3 | At the intersection with TR 1450, turn left to remain on FSR 376A. Get ready to climb. |
| 3.8 | Climb past a campsite on your left. |
| 4.0 | Pass a spur on the right. |
| 4.2 | Pass a gated, private drive on your left. |
| 4.6 | Pass a double track on your left. |
| 5.3 | Look right for the entrance to TR 1450A. Watch for this intersection as it is difficult to see from the approach. |
| 5.8 | Turn right at the "T" intersection with TR 1450. You are now on the Midland Railroad Grade and will soon be treated to some prime segments of single-track as you work your way back to Buena Vista. |
| 7.5 | Close the loop by riding straight onto FSR 376A. |
| 7.6 | Turn right onto CR 304 and ride toward the "No Outlet" sign. |
| 9.7 | Turn left to descend back to the start of the ride along the Midland Trail. *Note- use caution while descending and watch for other trail users around blind corners as you twist through several tight switchbacks.* |
| 10.2 | Continue straight and downhill past the Midland Stage Trail on your right. *Note- have some extra time? Turn right and add a loop on the Whipple Trail system.* |
| 10.6 | Finish at the bridge then pedal over to the Eddyline Restaurant and Brewery for a fine Colorado craft beer. |

*Midland Railroad Grade*

106 • *Arkansas Valley Mountain Biking*

# Ride 27: Fourmile Recreation Area Loop

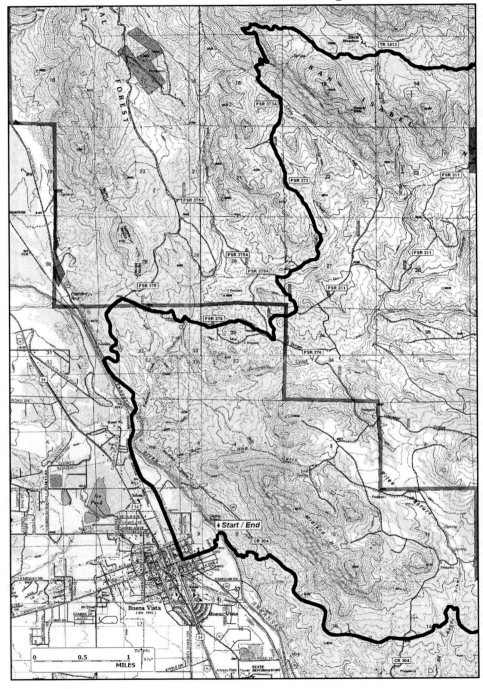

*Map 27a: Fourmile Recreation Area Loop - west (© National Geographic)*

# Fourmile Recreation Area Loop

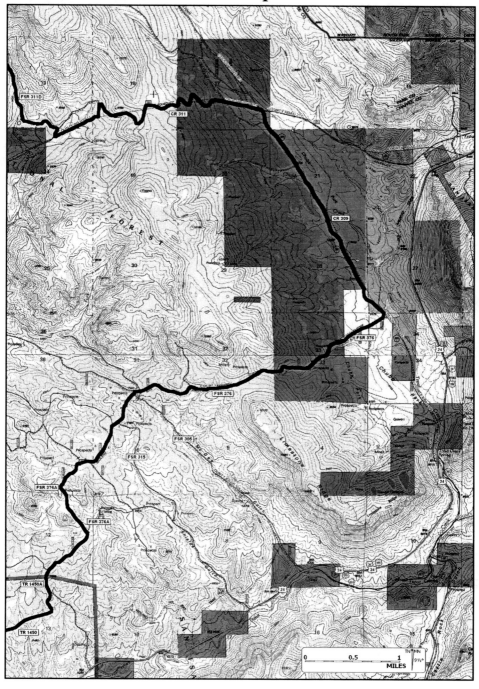

*Map 27b: Fourmile Recreation Area Loop - east (© National Geographic)*

### 108 • Arkansas Valley Mountain Biking

This is just one variation of an epic ride that captures the interest of many hearty locals. Touching nearly every popular riding area in the Fourmile Recreation Area east of Buena Vista, it's almost like a Fourmile Sampler for mountain bikers. Along this route you'll ride parts of the Midland Trail, the Gentleman's Loop, the Lenhardy Cutoff, the Davis Meadow Loop, the Natural Arch Loop, Fourmile Road, and the Buena Vista River Road.

No question, this is a long and tough ride. Bring plenty of water and food and brace for an epic.

**Ride length:** 31.3 miles
**Ride type:** loop
**Riding time:** 3-4 hours
**Surface:** dirt/jeep roads (24.4 miles); single-track (6.8 miles)
**Elevations:** start/end 7,960'; max 10,140'; min 7,960'
**Total climbing:** gain/loss 3,850'

**Aerobic level:** strenuous (long ride with lots of climbing)
**Technical level:** 4 (the descent from Davis Meadow is technical)
**Season:** May through October
**USGS Quadrangles:** Buena Vista East, Buena Vista West, Harvard Lakes, Marmot Peak

**Trailhead GPS coordinates:** 38° 50.795' N; 106° 7.342' W

**Elevation Profile:**

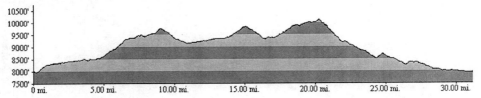

**Getting there:** from the stoplight at the intersection of US 24 and Main St. in Buena Vista, drive 0.5 miles east to the end of E. Main St. Bear left into the Buena Vista River Park parking lot. The ride starts at the west side (town side) of the footbridge over the river.

**Trailhead/trail amenities:** restrooms/water at trailhead; start/ends in town.

**The ride:**
- **0.0** Cross the footbridge to embark on your epic.
- **0.1** Continue straight past the trail on your left.
- **0.25** Pass the sun shelter on your right.
- **0.3** Pass a spur on your left. Follow the Midland Trail sign.
- **0.9** Turn right onto CR 304.
- **2.9** Turn left onto FSR 376A. The entrance is between the parking areas.
- **3.1** Continue straight on TR 1450 as FSR 376A splits away on your left.
- **4.7** Turn left to climb on TR 1450A. Look for a fiberglass trail marker.

## Buena Vista • 109

| | |
|---|---|
| 5.2 | Continue straight and uphill as TR 1450A ends at FSR 376A. |
| 5.5 | Continue climbing on FSR 376A past a campsite spur on the right. |
| 6.2 | Pass a campsite spur on left as you continue climbing on FSR 376A. |
| 6.5 | Pass a campsite spur on the right as you continue climbing on FSR 376A. |
| 6.6 | Pass yet another campsite spur on your right as you continue to climb. Stay on FSR 376A. |
| 6.8 | Turn right as FSR 376A ends at a "T" intersection with FSR 376. Continue riding east on FSR 376 past several campsite spurs. |
| 7.0 | Continue straight on FSR 376 as you pass the intersection with FSR 315 on your right. Follow the sign to Chubb Park. |
| 7.9 | Continue downhill on FSR 376 as you pass the intersection with FSR 376B on your left. |
| 8.0 | Continue straight on FSR 376 as you pass the intersection with FSR 305 on your right. Ride uphill through the seasonal closure gate on FSR 376 as you pass a campsite on the right. |
| 8.3 | Continue climbing on FSR 376 past a campsite on the right. |
| 8.4 | Pass another campsite spur on the right as you continue climbing on the main road. |
| 8.5 | Pass an intersection with an unmarked double-track on your left. |
| 9.9 | Pass another campsite spur on your left. |
| 10.0 | Continue straight on the main road past unmarked spurs on your right and left. |
| 10.9 | Turn left onto FSR 309 as FSR 376 ends at a "T" intersection. |
| 11.2 | Continue straight on the main road past a spur on the left then cross the cattle guard. |
| 11.7 | Pass an unmarked spur on the left and continue straight on FSR 309. |
| 13.5 | Turn left onto FSR 311 and ride toward Sevenmile Creek. Cross a cattle guard and continue riding on FSR 311 past the intersection with FSR 309 on the right. |
| 13.7 | Continue on FSR 311 past the intersection with FSR 309A on the right. |
| 14.8 | Ride straight on FSR 311 past a campsite spur on your left. |
| 15.0 | Continue straight past a spur on your right. Cross the cattle guard and start your descent back into the Fourmile Recreation Area. |
| 15.9 | Continue bombing the downhill on FSR 311 as you pass an unmarked double-track on your left. |
| 16.5 | Turn right onto FSR 311D. Look for a sign that reads "Fuelwood" to help you identify this intersection. Continue for 100 yards then bear left, passing a short spur on the right. |
| 17.2 | Enter the Davis Meadow trailhead (TR 1413). |

| | |
|---|---|
| 17.4 | Continue straight on the single-track; a sign marks the beginning of TR 1413. |
| 17.7 | Cross Sevenmile Creek. This area can get overgrown by late summer. Look for clues to help you follow the trail: cairns, cut branches, etc. |
| 18.8 | Enter a marshy area with several old cabins. Look directly across the marsh to an opening between the buildings; this is where the trail resumes on the other side. The trail is marked by a cairn once you pass the cabins. |
| 21.5 | Arrive at a jeep road (FSR 373A, unmarked) as TR 1413 ends. Pass the aqueduct vent and turn left for a fast descent. |
| 21.9 | Bear right as FSR 373A ends at a "T" intersection with FSR 373. |
| 24.3 | Enter a sandy wash and turn left to ride uphill on FSR 373. Look for a sign on your left. (Straight leads to FSR 375A.) |
| 24.9 | Turn right as FSR 373 ends at a "T" intersection with FSR 311. Ride downhill on FSR 311. |
| 25.3 | Turn right as FSR 311 ends at a "T" intersection with FSR 376. Ride for 100 yards then bear right to continue riding on FSR 376 past the fork with TR 6039. |
| 25.9 | Pass the intersections with TR 6039 and TR 6029 on your left as you glide downhill through the sand. |
| 26.4 | Cross Fourmile Creek. |
| 26.8 | Stay on FSR 376 as you pass intersections with OHV trails 1415 and 6037 on your right and left respectively. |
| 27.2 | Pass the intersection with TR 6038 on your left. |
| 27.3 | Turn left as FSR 376 ends at a "T" intersection with FSR/CR 375 (unmarked). Enjoy the easy downhill but watch for traffic. |
| 28.3 | Turn left as CR 375 ends at a "T" intersection with CR 371. |
| 30.8 | Turn left onto E. Main Street in Buena Vista. Not much further to go. Ride toward the River Park at the east end of E. Main Street. |
| 31.3 | The very end of the ride. Rehydrate at the water fountain at the boat house then get something decadent to eat! You earned it today! |

**Options:** this route has as many options as there are people willing to venture out to ride it. Grab a map and plan your own epic through this fantastic area.

# Ride 28: Buena Vista River Park

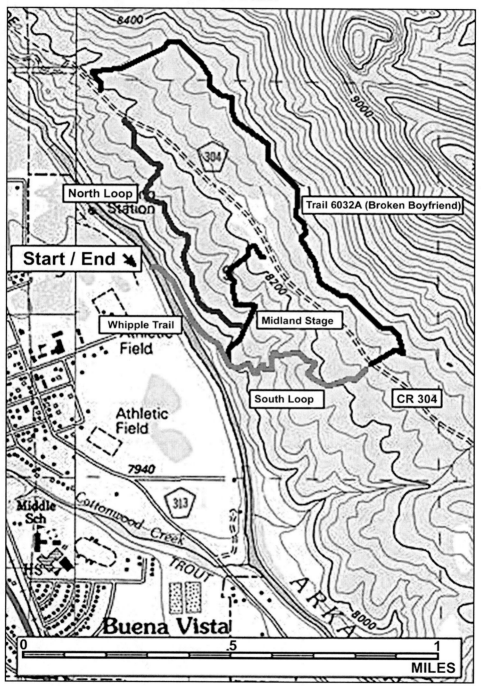

Map 28: Buena Vista River Park (© National Geographic)

## Arkansas Valley Mountain Biking

Just east of the Buena Vista River Park is a small network of single-track trails that thread the scrubby pinons at the base of Midland Hill. This little playground is a great place to sneak in a quick ride either after or before a raft trip. Explore the trails to create your own loops, but watch for hikers.

Special thanks for these trails must be extended to the Friends of Fourmile chapter of the Greater Arkansas River Nature Association and ArkValleyVelo. Volunteers from these organizations opened an additional 1.4 miles of technical single-track (TR 6032A) in 2008, making it possible to create several fun riding circuits within shouting distance from town.

For more information and current maps, please stop by Trailhead Cycle and Ski on US Highway 24 in Buena Vista.

**Ride length:** varies
**Ride type:** varies
**Riding time:** 1 hour (or more)
**Surface:** single-track
**Elevations:** start/end 7,960'; max 8,400'; min 7,960'
**Total climbing:** approx. 300' (from the trailhead to CR 304; highpoint is on TR 6032A)
**Aerobic level:** moderate
**Technical level:** 2+ to 4
**Season:** year round (snow permitting)
**USGS Quadrangles:** Buena Vista East

**Trailhead GPS coordinates:** 38° 50.821' N; 106° 7.323' W

**Elevation profile:** n/a

**Getting there:** from the stoplight at the intersection of US 24 and Main St. in Buena Vista, drive 0.5 miles east to the end of E. Main St. Bear left into the Buena Vista River Park parking lot. The rides start at the west side (town side) of the footbridge over the river.

**Trailhead/trail amenities:** restrooms and water at trailhead; starts/ends in town.

### Trail segments

**Midland Bike Trail (South Loop):** 0.9 miles; switchbacks; technical 3.

**Midland Stage Road:** 0.5 miles; moderate climb; technical 2.

**North Loop:** 0.8 miles; rocks; technical 4.

**TR 6032A (Broken Boyfriend):** 1.4 miles; rocks; technical 4.

Buena Vista • 113

# Ride 29: Trout Creek Pass to Buena Vista

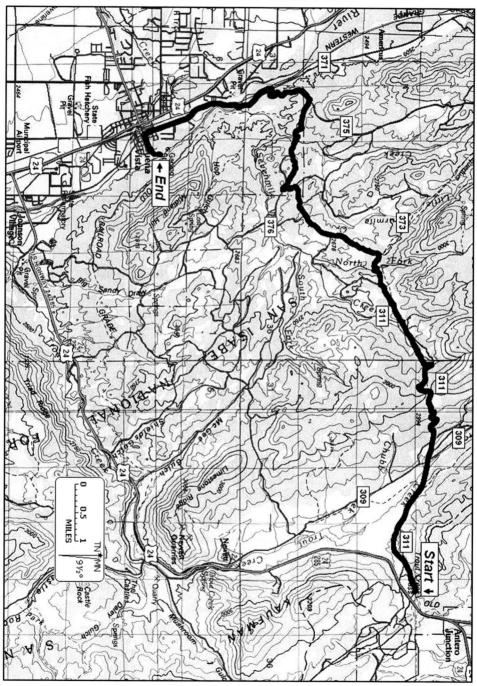

*Map 29: Trout Creek Pass to Buena Vista (© National Geographic)*

## Arkansas Valley Mountain Biking

This ride, connecting Trout Creek Pass to Buena Vista, is easier than the Midland Bike Trail and provides an excellent dirt alternative for touring off-road cyclists. With a little ingenuity, this route can be easily connected to routes extending north to Fairplay or south to Salida.

It's also a fun and easy ride on its own. The climb is gentle, and once you crest the ridge separating Chubb Park and the Fourmile Recreation Area, the expansive views of the Collegiate Peaks and Arkansas Valley are magnificent. The descent is fast and smooth, with just the right amount of ruts and steeps to keep it interesting. The route also passes through dense stands of aspen and mid-September is a perfect time to ride it.

**Ride length:** 15.8 miles
**Ride type:** one-way with shuttle
**Riding time:** 1.5-2 hours
**Surface:** dirt/jeep road (13.3 miles); paved road (2.5 miles)
**Elevations:** start 9,480'; end 7,960'; max 9,840'; min 7,960'
**Total climbing:** gain 730' – loss 2,300' = total -1,570'

**Aerobic level:** easy (some climbing and a few short steeps)
**Technical level:** 3 (some ruts, steeps, and a sandy section)
**Season:** April into November
**USGS Quadrangles:** Antero Reservoir, Marmot Peak, Harvard Lakes, Buena Vista East, Buena Vista West

**Trailhead GPS coordinates:** 38° 54.652' N; 105° 58.661' W

**Elevation profile:**

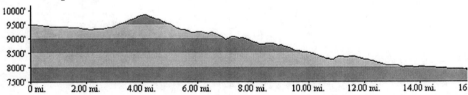

**Getting there:** leave a vehicle at the Buena Vista River Park. From the traffic light at the intersection of US 24 and Main St. in Buena Vista, drive 0.5 miles east to the end of E. Main St. Bear left into the Buena Vista River Park parking lot.

Take the other vehicle, riders, and bikes to the trailhead. From the intersection of US 24 and Main St. in Buena Vista, drive approximately 2.4 miles south to the intersection with US 24/285. Turn left and drive approximately 12.7 miles east/north on US 24/285 to CR 311. Turn left onto CR 311 and drive approximately 0.2 miles to the parking area and trailhead on the left. The ride starts at your vehicle.

**Trailhead/trail amenities:** restrooms/water at end; ends in town; seasonal porta-pot at mile 12.7.

**The ride:**
0.0   From the trailhead, turn left (west) onto CR 311. Remain on CR/FSR 311 for the next 9.8 miles.

## Buena Vista • 115

| | |
|---|---|
| 1.6 | Enter Chubb Park State Wildlife Management Area. Be sure to stay on the designated roads through this area. |
| 2.6 | Ride straight (west) on CR 311 toward Sevenmile Creek. Pass the intersection with CR 309 on the left. Continue for fifty yards and pass the second intersection with CR 309 on the right. (CR 311 becomes FSR 311 somewhere near this intersection.) |
| 2.8 | Continue straight on FSR 311 as you pass the intersection with CR 309A on the right. |
| 4.1 | Cross a cattle guard as you crest the summit of the route. Get ready for a fun descent into the Fourmile Recreation Area. |
| 5.5 | Stay on the main road as you pass FSR 311D on the right. |
| 6.6 | Continue straight on FSR 311 as you pass the intersection with FSR 311E on your right. |
| 6.7 | Stay on FSR 311 past the fenced entrance to TR 1414 on the left. |
| 7.0 | Try to keep your feet dry as you cross the creek. |
| 7.4 | Bear left at the fork, continuing on FSR 311 as you pass FSR 373 on the right. *Note-* FSR 373 *jug-handles and rejoins FSR 311 at mile 9.3 of this description. It's a fun diversion and offers views of a natural arch adjacent to the Davis Face. The road is steep and may not be suitable for novice riders.* |
| 8.4 | Stay on FSR 311 past TR 1414 on the left. |
| 8.7 | Continue straight on FSR 311 as you pass FSR 311F on the right. |
| 9.3 | Bear left to stay on FSR 311 as FSR 373 intersects on the right. |
| 9.8 | Turn right as FSR 311 ends at a "T" intersection with FSR 376. Ride 100 yards then bear right past TR 6039 on the left. |
| 10.3 | Enter some soupy sand. (Keep your weight slightly back and your front wheel straight. Pedal evenly and you will clean it.) You'll soon pass TR 6039 and TR 6029 on the left as you approach the creek. |
| 10.8 | The sand ends just before you cross Fourmile Creek. |
| 11.2 | Continue straight on FSR 376, past the intersections with TR 1415 and TR 6037 on the right and left respectively. |
| 11.6 | Pass TR 6038 on the left. |
| 11.7 | Turn left as FSR 376 ends at a "T" intersection with FSR/CR 375 (unmarked). Enjoy the easy downhill but watch for traffic. |
| 12.8 | Turn left as you intersect CR 371 at a stop sign. |
| 15.3 | Turn left onto E. Main St. |
| 15.8 | Enter the Buena Vista River Park. There are bathroom facilities and an outside spigot to refill water bottles. |

# 116 • *Arkansas Valley Mountain Biking*
# Ride 30: Fourmile Road – Buena Vista Overlook

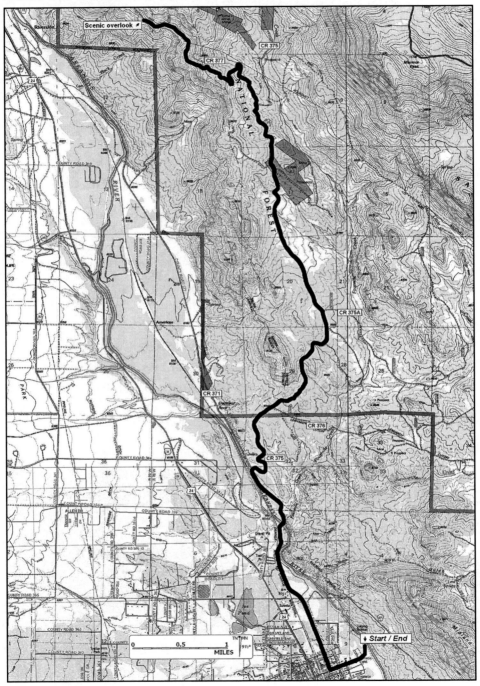

*Map 30: Fourmile Road – Buena Vista Overlook (© National Geographic)*

In addition to being a great aerobic/hill workout, this ride leads to one of the most spectacular vista points in the Arkansas Valley. From this lofty perch one will find panoramic views extending from Mt. Massive to the north all the way to the jagged summits of the Sangre de Cristo range south of Salida.

The heart of this route follows Fourmile Road (CR 375) from its start along the banks of the Arkansas River to its intersection with CR 377. Once on CR 377, the route climbs more than 500' in just over a mile to a ridge that separates the Fourmile Recreation Area from the Arkansas Valley. The last mile is a quick descent to a turnout that offers views that should be in everyone's photo album.

*This is a popular area for jeeps and ATVs; stay alert as you bomb downhill!*

**Ride length:** 20.6 miles
**Ride type:** out-and-back
**Riding time:** 2.5 hours
**Surface:** dirt roads
**Elevations:** start/end 7,960'; max 9,760'; min 7,960'
**Total climbing:** gain/loss 2,340'

**Aerobic level:** moderate/strenuous (climbing)
**Technical level:** 3 (some sand on a fast descent)
**Season:** April through October
**USGS Quadrangles:** Buena Vista East, Buena Vista West, Harvard Lakes

**Trailhead GPS coordinates:** 38° 50.795' N; 106° 7.342' W

**Elevation profile:**

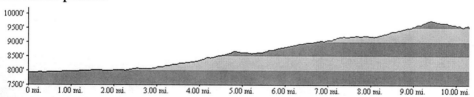

**Getting there:** from the intersection of US 24 and Main St. in Buena Vista, drive 0.5 miles east to the end of E. Main St. Bear left into the Buena Vista River Park parking lot.

**Trailhead/trail amenities:** restrooms/water at trailhead; start/ends in town; seasonal porta-pot at mile 3.1.

**The ride:**

0.0   From the parking lot at the Buena Vista River Park, ride west back onto Main Street.

0.5   Turn right onto N. Colorado Avenue. Once you leave Buena Vista city limits, this road becomes CR 371.

3.0   Turn right onto CR 375 (Fourmile Road) and start the climb. ***Note-*** *the intersection with CR 375 is just south of the tunnels on CR 371.*

3.4   Stay on CR 375 past the entrance to TR 6037 on the right.

3.8   Stay on CR 375 as you pass the Turtle Rock camping area on the left.

## 118 • Arkansas Valley Mountain Biking

| | |
|---|---|
| 3.9 | CR 375 becomes FSR 375 as you enter the San Isabel National Forest. |
| 4.0 | Stay on FSR 375 past the intersection with FSR 376 on your right. |
| 4.3 | Pass the Split Rock climbing area. |
| 5.1 | Descend on FSR 375 as it bends right. Pass the intersection with FSR 375E on the left. |
| 5.4 | Stay on FSR 375 past the intersection with FSR 375C on your right. |
| 5.6 | Stay on FSR 375 past the intersection with FSR 375A on the right. |
| 7.4 | Pass the seasonal closure gate on FSR 375. |
| 7.7 | Stay on FSR 375 around a bend and an unmarked spur on the right. |
| 8.2 | Continue straight and uphill on FSR 377. **Note-** *FSR 375 descends to your right and eventually dead-ends at the Buffalo Peaks Wilderness Area (no bikes) boundary.* |
| 9.5 | Crest the ridge and start a fast descent into the Arkansas Valley. *Need a little boost? Try some Vitamin B.* |
| 10.3 | Look left for a large pullout on the edge of the road. Break out the camera and let the shutter chatter. You won't find many photo-ops better than this. Return the way you came. ***Caution:*** *watch for traffic on the return trip. Your speed will be up and the road surface is sandy in sections.* |

**Options:** start this ride from the OHV parking area at the start of CR 375 at mile 3.0.

***Buena Vista scenic view***

# Ride 31: Buena Vista River Road

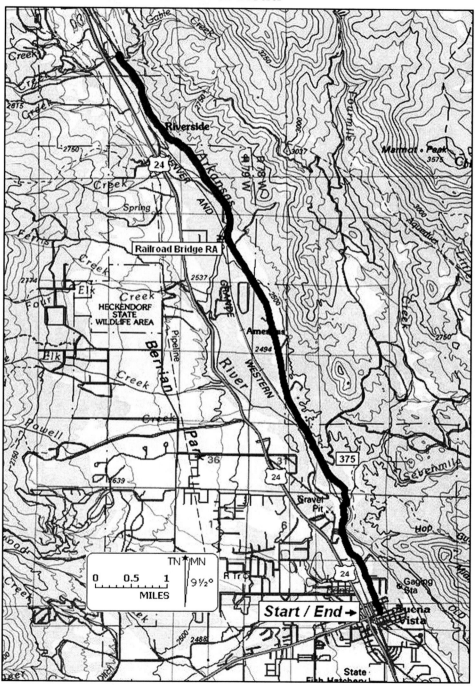

Map 31: Buena Vista River Road (© National Geographic)

# Arkansas Valley Mountain Biking

Want a fun ride for the entire family? This route follows the old Midland Railroad grade along the banks of the Arkansas River and parallels one of the most popular whitewater runs, the Narrows. There are no hills or technical obstacles; shorten the ride by turning around when the mood strikes.

During the summer you're likely to see intrepid boaters on the water and climbers on the rock outcroppings adjacent to the road. The real highlights of the ride, however, are the old railroad tunnels you'll pass through en route. (Though the tunnels are structurally safe, watch for cars; it's difficult for drivers to see bikers in the tunnels.)

**Ride length:** 18.6 miles
**Ride type:** out-and-back
**Riding time:** 1-4 hours
**Surface:** dirt road
**Elevations:** start/end 7,950'; max 8,520'; min 7,950'

**Total climbing:** gain/loss 550'
**Aerobic level:** easy
**Technical level:** 1
**Season:** all year
**USGS Quadrangles:** Harvard Lakes, Buena Vista West

**Trailhead GPS coordinates:** 38° 50.573' N; 106° 7.758' W

**Elevation profile:**

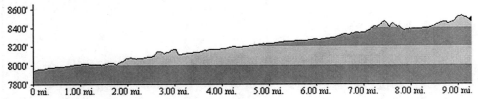

**Getting there:** park anywhere in downtown Buena Vista. The ride begins on N. Colorado Ave. at the intersection with E. Main St. (0.2 miles east of US 24).

**Trailhead/trail amenities:** start/ends in town; pit toilet at mile 6.2.

**The ride:**
- **0.0** Ride north on N. Colorado Ave. from the intersection with E. Main St.
- **0.3** Buena Vista city limits. N. Colorado Ave. is now CR 371.
- **1.8** Cross a bridge over the river. Stop to watch the boaters pass beneath you. The road surface turns to dirt just after the bridge.
- **2.5** Pass the intersection with CR 375 on your right.
- **2.6** Enter the first tunnel. Watch for traffic!
- **3.0** Pass by two popular rock climbing areas, one (Bob's Rock) immediately on your right, the other (Elephant Rock) just ahead on your left.
- **6.2** Pass the Railroad Bridge recreation area on your left (has restrooms).
- **9.3** The ride ends where CR 371 turns left and crosses the river. Return the way you came. The return trip is faster and just a little more fun.

# Nathrop

The main draw to Nathrop has always been the natural hot springs that bubble up along the banks of Chalk Creek. The most popular, Mt. Princeton Hot Springs, features two large developed pools with decks as well as several primitive pools right at the edge of the creek.

In addition to the hot springs, Nathrop is the gateway to two popular 14'ers: Mount Princeton (14,197') and Mount Antero (14,269'). Several US Forest Service campgrounds along the creek make it easy for you to get a pre-dawn start for attempts at their summits.

Nathrop is also home to Yeti RPM Developmental Racing, hosts of the Chalk Creek Stampede mountain bike race. This annual event held on Yeti RPM's private courses features dual slalom, mountain cross, and cross-country events. The race is a popular stage of the Mountain States Cup Championship race series and competitors are treated to first-rate, spectator-friendly courses designed specifically for racing.

Two of the Arkansas Valley's easiest rides are in this area. The Raspberry Gulch Loop is a short and smooth single-track loop that is ideal for beginners. The Cascade Railroad Grade is another easy route that is close to the hot springs and perfect for families.

Hammerheads will enjoy riding above the clouds on Mount Princeton Road. This strenuous route runs from Frontier Ranch to the hut above tree line in Bristlecone Park (elev. 12,120'). To add a little extra challenge, some hardcore locals will ride their bikes to the end of the road then hike to the summit of Mt. Princeton, a stiff endeavor for anyone.

Last, but certainly not least, the segment of the Colorado Trail between the Mount Princeton trailhead and South Cottonwood Creek is perhaps the best span of single-track in the central Valley. This route is easy to access and an absolute blast to ride, so if you only have time for one ride this should be it.

**122** • *Arkansas Valley Mountain Biking*

# Ride 32: Frontier Ranch to South Cottonwood Creek

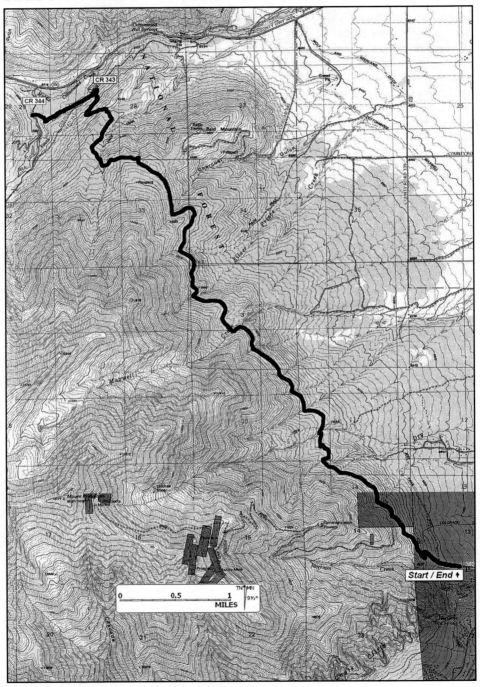

*Map 32: Frontier Ranch to South Cottonwood Creek (© National Geographic)*

# Nathrop • 123

What could be better than skimming across the forested flanks of Mount Princeton's east slopes? This route, another tasty segment of the Colorado Trail, is probably the best trail in the Nathrop/Buena Vista area.

With the exception of the downhill to South Cottonwood Creek, the route is technically moderate. There are some minor rock gardens and a few roots, but the toughest sections are the steep and sharp uphill/downhill transitions at the bottom of seasonal drainages.

While the downhill to South Cottonwood Creek is not as smooth as the rest of the trail, strong intermediate cyclists should be able to ride most of it. Conversely, climbing up from the trailhead at CR 344 is not bad; strong intermediates should be able to pedal up at least 75% of it.

Since the best of this ride is the return trip from about mile 6.1 to the parking area, some may elect to turn around early, skipping the technical descent to CR 344.

*Please be aware that FSR 345.2 connecting CR 345 to the trail is no longer open to bikes!*

**Ride length:** 16.8 miles
**Ride type:** out-and-back
**Riding time:** 3 hours
**Surface:** single-track (14.6 miles); jeep road (2.2 miles)
**Elevations:** start/end 8,910'; max 10,030'; min 8,890'

**Total climbing:** gain/loss 3,100'
**Aerobic level:** strenuous (climbing)
**Technical level:** 4 (overall 3 with one steep and technical section)
**Season:** May through October
**USGS Quadrangles:** Mt. Antero, Buena Vista West

**Trailhead GPS coordinates:** 38° 44.391' N; 106° 10.539' W

**Elevation profile:**

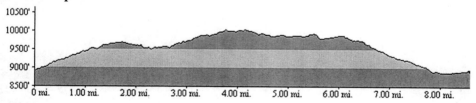

**Getting there:** from the stoplight at the intersection of US 24 and Main St. in Buena Vista, drive 0.8 miles west on W. Main (CR 306) to the intersection with CR 321 (Rodeo Road). Turn left onto CR 321 and drive 6.8 miles to the intersection with CR 322. Turn right, following the sign to Frontier Ranch, and drive 0.9 miles to the fork. Turn right into the Mt. Princeton parking area. The ride starts from the west end of this parking lot.

**Trailhead/trail amenities:** none.

## 124 • Arkansas Valley Mountain Biking

**The ride:**

0.0   Head west to ride out of the parking lot. Take the right fork and start pedaling uphill.

0.4   Stay right through the switchback to stay on the main road.

1.1   Turn right onto the Colorado Trail singe-track. Let the fun begin.

2.4   Stay on the main trail, passing between two cairns. (A faint line runs east-west across the main trail.)

6.1   Start the descent to Cottonwood Creek and CR 344. **Note-** *this is a good turn-around spot for those wishing to skip the climb back up from the creek and trailhead.*

8.0   Cross CR 343 to continue descending on the Colorado Trail.

8.3   Cross South Cottonwood Creek on a good bridge.

8.4   South Cottonwood Trailhead parking area and CR 344. Turn around and return the way you came.

**Options:** if you elect to ride this as a one-way with auto shuttles, starting at the South Cottonwood Trailhead and riding south to Frontier Ranch puts the bulk of the hard work at the start and rewards you with excellent single-track from the highpoint almost all the way to Frontier Ranch.

Leave a vehicle at Frontier Ranch and take the riders/bikes to the South Cottonwood Trailhead. From the intersection of US 24 and Main St. in Buena Vista, drive 6.8 miles west on W. Main (CR 306) to the intersection with CR 344. Turn left onto CR 344 and drive about 0.25 miles. Look for the small parking area and Colorado Trail markers on the left. Start the ride at the South Cottonwood Trail sign, about 30 yards southeast of the parking area.

*Above the clouds: Mt. Princeton Road*

# Ride 33: Mt. Princeton Road

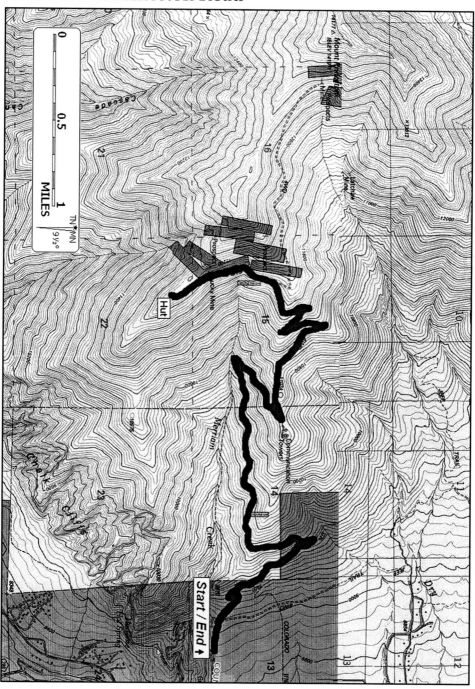

*Map 33: Mt. Princeton Road (© National Geographic)*

## 126 • Arkansas Valley Mountain Biking

You feel strong and relish the challenge of a tough climb. Here's a good one.

This demanding route will take you above the trees on one of Colorado's most striking 14'ers. Dominating Buena Vista's southwestern horizon, Mount Princeton (14,197') towers more than six thousand feet above the valley floor and serves as the chief iconic landmark of the area. Riding to the top of this road gives you an unrivaled appreciation of the sheer size of this commanding peak.

**Ride length:** 10.6 miles
**Ride type:** out-and-back
**Riding time:** 2 hours
**Surface:** jeep road
**Elevations:** start/end 8,910'; max 12,100'; min 8,910'
**Total climbing:** gain/loss 3,170'

**Aerobic level:** strenuous (climbing at altitude)
**Technical level:** 3+ (when you're sucking wind this hard, everything feels tough; fast descent over eroded, rocky terrain)
**Season:** June through October
**USGS Quadrangles:** Mt. Antero

**Trailhead GPS coordinates:** 38° 44.399' N; 106° 10.546' W

**Elevation profile:**

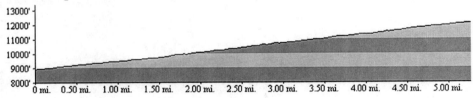

**Getting there:** from the traffic light at the intersection of US 24 and Main St. in Buena Vista, drive 0.8 miles west on W. Main (CR 306) to the intersection with CR 321 (Rodeo Road). Turn left onto CR 321 and drive 6.8 miles to the intersection with CR 322. Turn right onto CR 322, following the sign to Frontier Ranch, and drive 0.9 miles to the fork. Turn right into the Mt. Princeton parking area. The ride starts from the west side of the parking lot.

**Trailhead/trail amenities:** none.

**The ride:**
- 0.0  Head west to ride out of the parking lot. Take a right at the fork and start pedaling uphill.
- 0.4  Stay right through the switchback to remain on the main road.
- 1.1  Bear left, staying on the main road. (The Colorado Trail single-track heads right.)
- 3.1  Turn left onto FSR 322A. Communication towers are on your right.
- 4.6  The Mount Princeton summit trail is on the right. *Note- if you have some extra wind, why not summit the mountain? It's a 6-mile round-trip hike gaining/losing 3,200'. Stash your bikes and go for it.*

5.2    The road ends at a small parking lot. The Young Life hut is about 50 yards due south of the parking area. Scramble up the short hill to the Cross with great views of Mount Antero. Look east across the valley for great views of Ruby Mountain and the Fourmile Recreation Area. When your heart rate and breathing return to acceptable levels, head back down the way you came.

**Options:** persuasive hedonists may be able to find someone willing to shuttle them to the top. If that's you, breakout your favorite rig and let it rip. The first couple of miles of the descent are fast, chunky and loose, but those with the appropriate skills and nerve will eat it up. (*You'll want a high-clearance vehicle for the drive to the top!*)

*Ripping into Raspberry Gulch*

# 128 • *Arkansas Valley Mountain Biking*
# Ride 34: Raspberry Gulch Loop

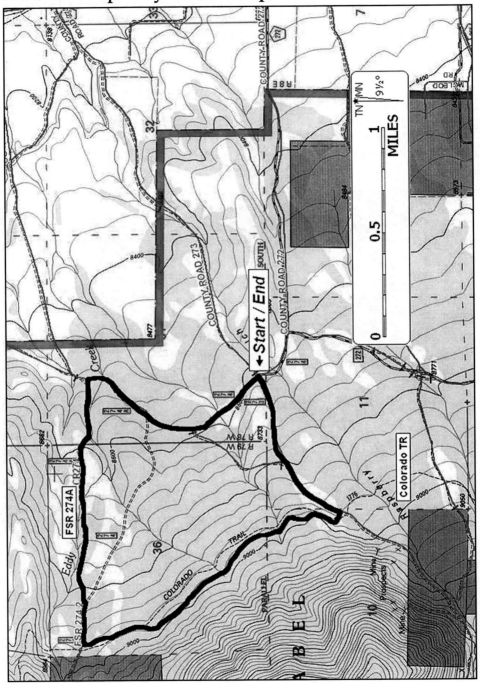

*Map 34: Raspberry Gulch Loop (© National Geographic)*

You are in the area with kids or someone new to riding and you want to introduce them to the joys of single-track. Where should you go?

This loop, incorporating a small, smooth section of the Colorado Trail in Raspberry Gulch, is the perfect place. The route provides a gentle, entry-level glimpse into the very best mountain biking has to offer: spectacular scenery on skinny single-track without any pain-inducing climbs, white-knuckled steeps, or brain-rattling rocks.

A gradual climb on a jeep road leads to a slightly steeper climb on single-track. Once at the top, the trail rolls through open meadows with sensational views of Mount Princeton's south slopes and the Chalk Cliffs. Once back on the road, you'll be treated to a fun downhill on a double-track jeep trail. A gentle climb (gaining only 150' in under 1 mile) returns you to your vehicle.

There are a few established primitive campsites (free/no facilities) in the area, making this an excellent ride to start or end your day.

**Ride length:** 4.5 miles
**Ride type:** loop (clockwise)
**Riding time:** 1 hour (or less)
**Surface:** single-track (1.5 miles); jeep trail/double-track (3.0 miles)
**Elevations:** start/end 8,625'; max 8,970'; min 8,480'

**Total climbing:** gain/loss 490'
**Aerobic level:** easy (two small climbs)
**Technical level:** 2 (a little sand and a few rocks on the downhill)
**Season:** May through October
**USGS Quadrangles:** Mount Antero

**Trailhead GPS coordinates:** 38° 41.684' N; 106° 9.528' W

**Elevation profile:**

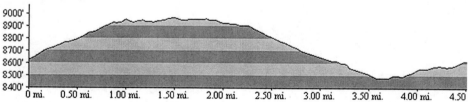

**Getting there:** from the junction of US 24/285 (2.4 miles south of Buena Vista), drive 8.9 miles south on US 285 to the intersection with CR 270. Turn right onto CR 270 and drive 1.6 miles west to the intersection with CR 272. Continue straight on CR 272 (dirt) and drive 2.0 miles west to the intersection with FSR 274. Continue straight (west/northwest) on FSR 274 until you reach the intersection with FSR 273 on your left in 0.3 miles. Park in the pullout across from FSR 273. The ride starts at your vehicle.

**Trailhead/trail amenities:** none; primitive campsites near the trailhead.

**The ride:**

| | |
|---|---|
| 0.0 | Ride uphill (southwest) on FSR 273. |
| 0.8 | Turn right onto the Colorado Trail single-track. The trail crosses the road just after you pass a small clearing and campsite on your right. Several trail markers on both sides of the road help you find this intersection. |
| 0.9 | Reach the top of the toughest climb of the ride. |
| 1.2 | The transition at the bottom of the downhill is a little tricky. |
| 2.3 | Turn right onto FSR 274. Watch your speed as you approach FSR 274A in just over 0.1 miles! |
| 2.4 | Bear left at the fork with FSR 274A. You might encounter a little sand. |
| 3.2 | A slightly tricky section ahead! The route descends and twists over some ruts and rocks. |
| 4.0 | Turn left at the "T" intersection with FSR 274. A small climb awaits you. |
| 4.5 | Arrive back at your vehicle. |

**Options:** extend your ride by exploring the Colorado Trail south of FSR 273 and north of FSR 274. Heading south, the trail gets somewhat technical and strenuous beginning about 1.6 miles south of FSR 273. From that point, you'll encounter more than 1.5 miles of steady climbing through rocky terrain before the trail settles into a smooth groove south of Brown's Creek.

North of FSR 274, the trail climbs moderately for 2.0 miles to the top of a very steep and extremely technical downhill leading to the Chalk Creek Trailhead.

**Raspberry Gulch**

# Ride 35: Cascade Railroad Grade

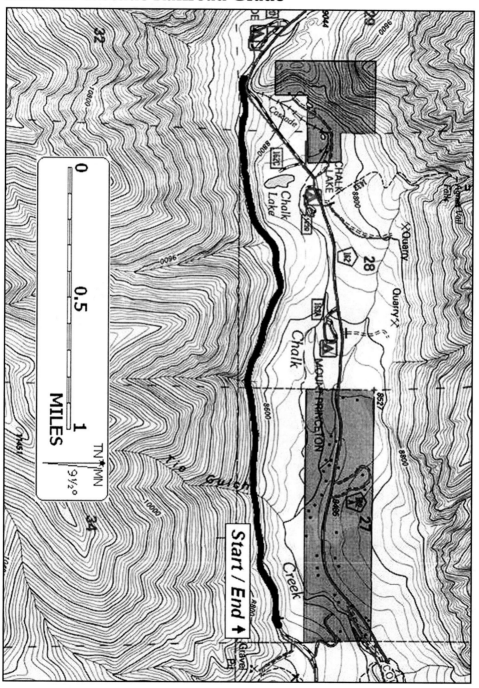

*Map 35: Cascade Railroad Grade (© National Geographic)*

## Arkansas Valley Mountain Biking

This gentle path, a former stretch of the Denver, South Park and Pacific Railroad grade, is an easy and scenic outing through the valley separating two massive mountains: Mount Princeton (north) and Mount Antero (south). Suitable for riders of all abilities, this is a perfect ride for the whole family.

*It may not be possible to get a kid carrier/trailer past the gates at either end of the trail. In addition, you'll need to lift your bike over a small barrier at the entrance gate.*

**Ride length:** 4.4 miles
**Ride type:** out-and-back
**Riding time:** 1 hour
**Surface:** wide dirt path
**Elevations:** start 8,600'; end 9,010'; max 9,030'; min 8,590'

**Total climbing:** gain/loss 490'
**Aerobic level:** easy
**Technical level:** 2- (some sand and brief rocky sections)
**Season:** May through October
**USGS Quadrangles:** Mount Antero

**Trailhead GPS coordinates:** 38° 42.671' N; 106° 12.168' W

**Elevation profile:**

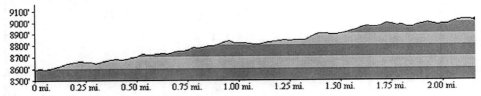

**Getting there:** from the junction of US 24/285 (2.4 miles south of Buena Vista), drive 5.5 miles south on US 285 to the intersection with CR 162. Turn right and drive 5.6 miles west on CR 162 to the intersection with CR 289/290. Turn left onto CR 289/290 and drive 0.2 miles to where CR 289 forks left from CR 290. Stay right on CR 290 and drive another 1.4 miles to the parking area at the end of the road. The ride starts at your vehicle.

**Trailhead/trail amenities:** none.

**The ride:**

0.0     From your vehicle, ride west 50 yards to the gate at the trailhead. You'll have to lift your bicycle over a low bar at the gate.

0.3     Look right at the Chalk Cliffs. Observe the eroded sections where wind and water have hollowed shallow caves in the rock face. One interesting fact about this formation is that the cliffs are not comprised of chalk but of clay hardened by geothermic water.

1.1     Encounter a rocky obstacle that may require you to dismount and push. Look up and to the right to catch a glimpse of Mount Princeton's false summit. The actual summit is still a fair distance beyond this prominent feature.

1.3     Pedal hard as you ride through approximately 10 yards of shallow sand. Dismount and push if you are uncomfortable riding through it.

| | |
|---|---|
| 1.4 | Cross an old wooden bridge. Will it hold? Continue for another 50 yards and cross a stream. **Hint-** *look left for a footbridge if you don't want to get your feet wet.* |
| 1.6 | Cross a short rocky section of trail. Dismount if you have any doubts. |
| 1.7 | Look down. That's Chalk Lake, a popular fishing area, at the bottom of a steep talus slope. |
| 2.0 | Dismount to push your bike across about 50 feet of avalanche debris. Look around and take note of the broken trees and rocks that fill the gulch both above and below the trail. Imagine the power it took to sweep this much junk down the mountain. |
| 2.1 | Look across at the Cascade Falls of Chalk Creek. |
| 2.2 | Beyond the gate, the trail ends at CR 162. Turn around and enjoy an easy coast almost all the way back to the start of this ride. |

**Options:** there are many ways to extend this ride. Use your imagination to add miles using CR 162, CR 289, or CR 290. Watch for traffic on these roads, especially on weekends. Please be aware that much of the land along these county roads is private. Respect area residents by parking only in designated public parking areas.

**Colorado Trail**

# St. Elmo

Widely considered the best-preserved ghost town in Colorado, St. Elmo was founded as an outpost for the Mary Murphy and other mines in the area. Even though the founders strove to enforce unusually high moral standards among town residents, the effort collapsed as the population swelled with young, single men drawn to the mines. The once orderly settlement quickly devolved into a place bustling with saloons, dance halls, and shady dens of an unsavory trade.

St. Elmo is unique because most of the buildings were well preserved and have not undergone major restoration efforts. In 2002, the St. Elmo schoolhouse and the site of the old town hall were donated to the Buena Vista Heritage Museum. The recently renovated Schoolhouse Museum is open for viewing during the summer.

The Alpine Tunnel, the first railroad tunnel built through the Continental Divide, opened rail passage between Denver and Gunnison via the Denver, South Park and Pacific Railroads. Taking almost eighteen months longer to construct than originally planned, this marvel of 19th century engineering eventually opened in 1882. Unfortunately, a collapse in 1910 permanently closed it; but by then the mining yields ebbed and the line was deemed irrelevant because it didn't extend beyond Gunnison.

Today, the old railroad grade and ghost town provide an excellent setting for mountain bike adventures. Moreover, the section of the Continental Divide Trail leading to the tunnel's East Portal is one of the most scenic and popular rides in the area. Interpretive signs along the route provide interesting historical facts about the rail line and the workers who built it.

# Ride 36: Alpine Tunnel

St. Elmo • 135

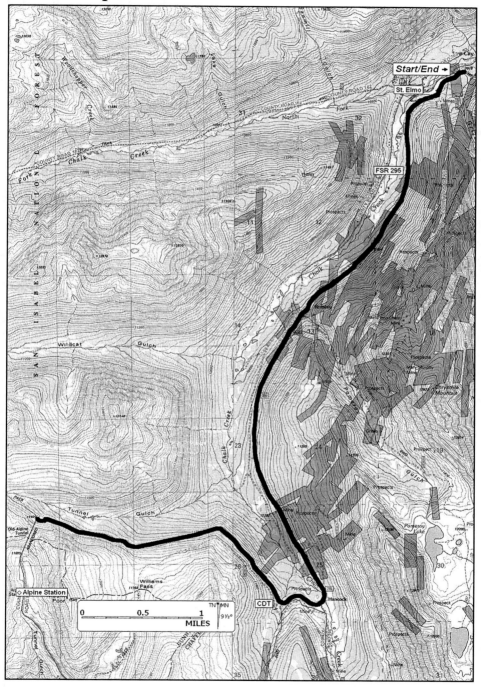

Map 36: Alpine Tunnel (© National Geographic)

## Arkansas Valley Mountain Biking

This classic, suitable for most cyclists, starts with a steady climb on FSR 295. Along the way, you'll pass several mine sites as you work your way toward the Hancock site. From there, you'll hop on the stretch of the Continental Divide Trail (CDT) that leads to the Alpine Tunnel East Portal. Some sections of the CDT are a bit bumpy as you roll over old railroad ties, but most novice riders should be able to pedal the lumps. The alpine valley of Tunnel Gulch is so spectacular that even the most hardened hammerhead will stop to take notice.

*This is a popular area for ATVs, jeeps, and motorcycles. Be prepared to share the road on the way to the CDT, especially on the weekends.*

**Ride length:** 16.6 miles
**Ride type:** out-and-back
**Riding time:** 2-3 hours
**Surface:** jeep road (10.6 miles); wide trail (6.0 miles)
**Elevations:** start/end 9,980'; max 11,630'; min 9,980'
**Total climbing:** gain/loss 1,650'

**Aerobic level:** easy (mostly mid-ring; drop into the granny if altitude leaves you winded)
**Technical level:** 2+ (a few bumps and rocks; be careful on the downhill)
**Season:** July into October
**USGS Quadrangles:** St. Elmo, Cumberland Pass

**Trailhead GPS coordinates:** 38° 42.352' N; 106° 20.404' W

**Elevation profile:**

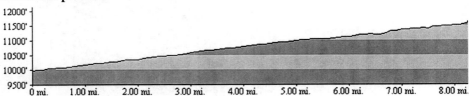

**Getting there:** from the intersection of US 285/24 (2.4 miles south of Buena Vista), drive 5.5 miles south on US 285 to the intersection with CR 162. Turn right onto CR 162 and drive 15.4 miles west to the parking area on the left, just east of FSR 295. If this area is full, continue driving 0.5 miles west on CR 162 to St. Elmo where parking is usually abundant. The ride starts at the intersection of CR 162 and FSR 295.

**Trailhead/trail amenities:** general store and restrooms in St. Elmo.

**The ride:**
0.0   At the intersection of CR 162 and FSR 295, ride up (southwest) FSR 295. Follow the sign to the Alpine Tunnel TR.
2.4   Bear right, staying on FSR 295.
2.6   After a slightly rough uphill, continue straight on FSR 295 past FSR 297.1 on the right.
4.3   Pass the Allie Belle Mine. The structure closest to the road appears to defy the laws of physics as it sits suspended over the road. Don't sneeze!

St. Elmo • 137

5.0 Enter the Hancock town site.
5.1 Cross a bridge and bear right, following the signs to the Alpine Tunnel trailhead. (Left leads to Hancock Pass.)
5.2 Continue straight and ride around the gate.
5.3 Stop and sign the trail register on the right. You are now riding on the Continental Divide Trail (CDT).
5.5 Arrive at the interpretive history sign for the infamous Sawmill Curve. After riding through the tricky drop, stay right on the trail past Williams Pass Road.
6.1 Another interpretive sign. *Note- if you stop to read the sign, look across the valley for the mine sites you passed on your approach to Hancock.*
8.3 Leave the bike at the trail intersection and hike to the Alpine Tunnel East Portal. The tunnel entrance collapsed long ago, but a little imagination is all it takes to see it as it once was. Turn around and return along the same route. *Note- the CDT continues climbing steeply on your left. It's possible to traverse the Divide to view the West Portal and restored historic buildings on the other side, but getting bikes up the formidable grade of the trail is a little tough.*

**Options:** skip the ride up FSR 295 and park at the trailhead in Hancock. It'll be a rough drive for a short ride, but you'll avoid the jeep and ATV traffic on FSR 295.

*Alpine Tunnel East Portal 1882-1910*

# Ride 37: Alpine Tunnel to Tin Cup Pass Road Loop

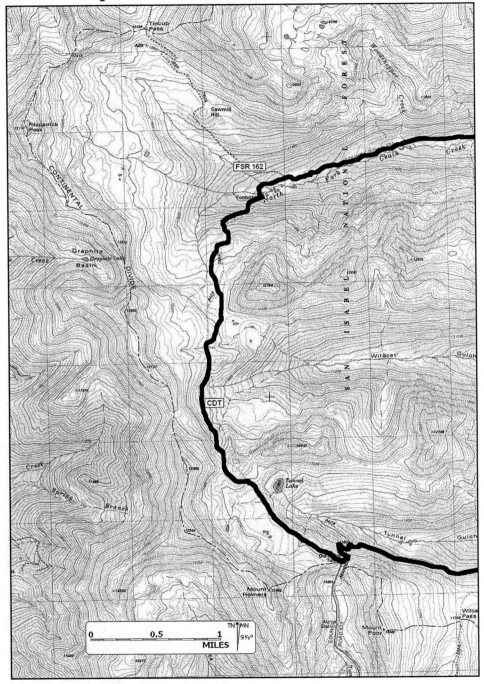

Map 37a: Alpine Tunnel to Tin Cup Pass Road - west (© National Geographic)

## St. Elmo • 139

# Alpine Tunnel to Tin Cup Pass Road Loop

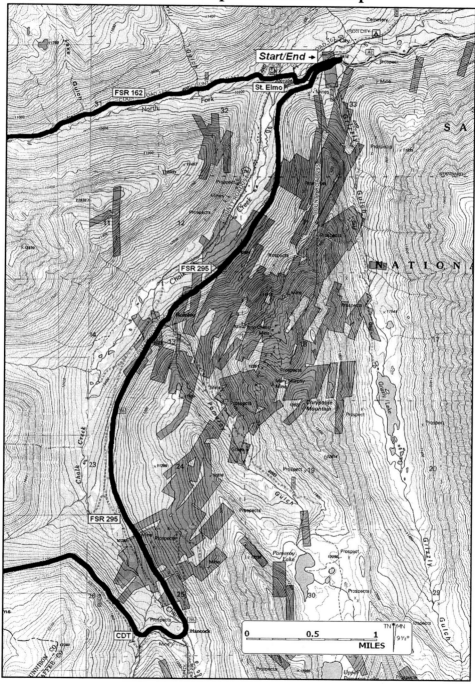

*Map 37b: Alpine Tunnel to Tin Cup Pass Road - east (© National Geographic)*

## 140 • Arkansas Valley Mountain Biking

To appreciate this ride more, think of it as two-thirds mountain biking and one-third adventure. Though there might be more hike-a-bike than you like, traversing the seldom-accessed span of the Continental Divide Trail to Tunnel Lake is a unique experience that few will know.

Start with an easy, scenic pedal up to the Alpine Tunnel. Along the way, you'll pass historic mining sites, interpretive signs, and stunning views of Tunnel Gulch. As you start the climb above the tunnel, however, the fun really begins. The next few miles will be a mix of hike-a-bike, route finding, and classic singletrack riding. Once you pass the last ridge, the downhill is pure bliss. End by zipping back to St. Elmo along the Tin Cup Pass Road, a rough jeep track with fast lines between the rocks.

*This is a popular area for ATVs, jeeps, and motorcycles. Be prepared to share the road.*

**Ride length:** 17.3 miles
**Ride type:** loop (clockwise)
**Riding time:** 3 hours
**Surface:** jeep road (9.9 miles); singletrack (4.4 miles); wide trail (3.0 miles)
**Elevations:** start/end 9,980'; max 12,340'; min 9,980'
**Total climbing:** gain/loss 2,500'

**Aerobic level:** strenuous (if you clean these steeps, then everything is easy for you!)
**Technical level:** 4 (some rocks, ruts, and roots; expect some walking)
**Season:** July into October
**USGS Quadrangles:** St. Elmo, Cumberland Pass

**Trailhead GPS coordinates:** 38° 42.352' N; 106° 20.404' W

**Elevation profile:**

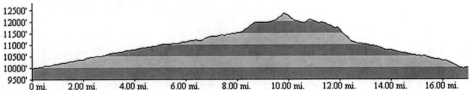

**Getting there:** from the intersection of US 285/24 (2.4 miles south of Buena Vista), drive 5.5 miles south on US 285 to the intersection with CR 162. Turn right onto CR 162 and drive 15.4 miles west to the parking area on the left, just east of FSR 295. If this area is full, continue driving 0.5 miles west on CR 162 to St. Elmo, where parking is usually abundant. The ride starts at the intersection of CR 162 and FSR 295.

**Trailhead/trail amenities:** general store and restrooms in St. Elmo.

**The ride:**
0.0   At the intersection of CR 162 and FSR 295, ride up (southwest) FSR 295. Follow the sign to the Alpine Tunnel TR.
2.4   Bear right and stay on FSR 295.
2.6   After a rough uphill, continue straight on FSR 295 past FSR 297.1.

## St. Elmo • 141

| | |
|---|---|
| 4.3 | Pass the Allie Belle Mine. The structure closest to the road appears to defy the laws of physics as it sits suspended over the road. Don't sneeze! |
| 5.0 | Enter the Hancock town site. |
| 5.1 | Cross a bridge and bear right, following the signs to the Alpine Tunnel trailhead. (Left leads to Hancock Pass.) |
| 5.2 | Continue straight and ride around the gate. |
| 5.3 | Stop and sign the trail register on the right. You are now riding on the Continental Divide Trail (CDT). |
| 5.5 | Arrive at the interpretive history sign for the infamous Sawmill Curve. After riding the tricky dip at the curve site, stay right, passing Williams Pass Road on your left. |
| 7.4 | Enjoy the picture-perfect alpine and sub-alpine valley to the right. *Note-this route eventually crosses the ridge at the northwestern end of the valley.* |
| 8.3 | Turn left and climb the burly grade of the CDT. A sign marks the way. If you can ride it, consider turning pro. Do your best and walk the rest. |
| 8.6 | Turn right at the sign, following the CDT to Tunnel Lake. (Straight leads to the Alpine Tunnel West Portal.) |
| 9.4 | Arrive at Tunnel Lake. This portion of the trail sees little use and route finding may prove difficult. Watch for cairns and follow the sometimes-faint line that meanders toward the ridge to the north. |
| 9.8 | Top-out on the big ridge. The trail is now very faint. Look for cairns and take your time. |
| 10.8 | Top-out on the next ridge. |
| 11.3 | The quality of the trail improves dramatically from this point forward. Get ready to let it rip! Single-track doesn't get much better than this! (Tin Cup Pass Road is now visible in the distance.) |
| 11.8 | Enter the pines. |
| 12.4 | Wow! Was that excellent or what? Cross some cool little bridges. |
| 12.5 | Stay right, passing small single-track spurs on the left. |
| 12.7 | Merge onto the Tin Cup Pass Road. Turn right and stay on this road until you reach St. Elmo. Fast and fun here, but watch for traffic. |
| 16.7 | Pass the Poplar Gulch trailhead on your left. |
| 16.8 | Enter St. Elmo. Continue straight. |
| 16.9 | Turn right and cross the bridge. Turn left onto the main street of St. Elmo and ride east. |
| 17.3 | Arrive back at your car. A long hot spring soak would be nice. |

# Poncha Springs

Often referred to as the "Crossroads of the Rockies," Poncha Springs is the gateway to some of the Arkansas Valley's hottest mountain biking. While known to most as simply a shuttle point for the Monarch Crest rides, its proximity to both the Rainbow Trail and Colorado Trail makes it a noteworthy mountain biking destination of its own.

Originally called Poncho Springs, Poncho being the Spanish word for "cape," the town acquired its name from the local hot springs. While historians debate whether Kit Carson or Zebulon Pike was the first US citizen to bathe in those springs, Chief Shavano discovered the healing powers of the waters long before any white men set foot in the region.

In an interesting turn of events, a 1935 WPA project capped the town's namesake hot springs and diverted the water to Salida. You can access the site of the former hot springs by riding up CR 115 from the center of town. The area is now a Scout Camp, but the ride is an interesting diversion to a few historic buildings that serve as a reminder of the site's former glory.

As for riding, the Rainbow Trail intersects US 285 about five miles south of town. West of the highway, the trail is fast and smooth with at least two primary riding options. (A little exploration and imagination always yields more!) On the east side, the trail climbs aggressively and is probably more fun ridden from east to west.

The Colorado Trail intersects US 50 less than nine miles west of town and offers an amazing twenty-mile stretch of single-track that runs north all the way to Nathrop. The south side is a fun out-and-back through lush forest.

## Ride 38: Colorado Trail: US 50 to Chalk Creek

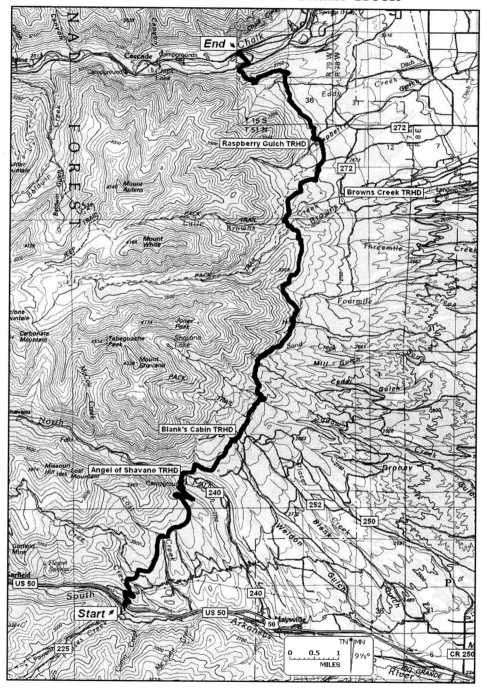

*Map 38: Colorado Trail: US 50 to Chalk Creek (© National Geographic)*

## 144 • Arkansas Valley Mountain Biking

Well, if you are going to go, go big. After a couple months of recon riding this segment of the Colorado Trail, I feel the best way to access these somewhat remote, yet very sweet single-track lines is to sweep the whole thing from south to north. You will work a little for it, but the reward is one of the valley's longest stretches of continuous single-track.

The ride begins with a stiff climb up from US 50 and ends with an insanely steep, technical descent to the Chalk Creek Trailhead. In between is an endless roller coaster of sometimes smooth/sometimes technical trail through deep stands of aspen and pine.

So, pack a lunch, bring plenty of water, and go for it!

*Please be aware that this ride is physically strenuous with few bailout points.*

**Ride length:** 20.1 miles
**Ride type:** one-way with shuttle
**Riding time:** 4 hours
**Surface:** single-track
**Elevations:** start 8,870'; max 10,160'; min 8,390'; end 8,390'
**Total climbing:** gain 3,130' - loss 3,600' = total -470'

**Aerobic level:** strenuous (long ride with lots of ups and downs)
**Technical level:** 4 (steeps with rocks; the final descent is a 5)
**Season:** June through October
**USGS Quadrangles:** Maysville, Mount Antero

**Trailhead GPS coordinates:** 38° 32.625' N; 106° 14.573' W

**Elevation profile:**

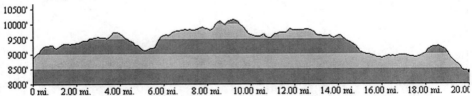

**Getting there:** leave a drop vehicle at the Chalk Creek Trailhead. From the intersection of US 24/285 (2.4 miles south of Buena Vista), drive 5.5 miles south on US 285 to the intersection with CR 162. Turn right and drive 6.8 miles west on CR 162 to the intersection with CR 291. Turn left onto CR 291 and drive about 50 yards to the trailhead and parking area.

Take the riders and bikes to the trailhead on US 50. From the intersection of US 50 and US 285 (where US 285 joins US 50 from the north), drive 9.2 miles west on US 50 to the intersection with CR 225. There is a large pullout on the left (south) side of the highway at the intersection. Park there. The ride begins at your vehicle.

**Trailhead/trail amenities:** pit toilets at miles 5.4 (Angel of Shavano CG) and 7.3 (Blank's Cabin trailhead).

**The ride:**

| | |
|---|---|
| 0.0 | Carefully cross the highway and look for the Colorado Trail marker at the start of the single-track. Start climbing. In about 100 yards, the trail crosses a double-track and continues climbing. |
| 0.5 | Turn right (east) and continue climbing up on the double-track. |
| 0.8 | Pass under the steel power tower and continue riding straight along the single-track into the pines. (A double-track spur heads east.) |
| 1.4 | Cross a dirt road and continue riding the trail on the other side. |
| 1.5 | After riding clockwise around a meadow, join a double track and ride east for about 20 yards. Look left for the single-track and the Colorado Trail marker about eight feet up on a pine tree. Head left on the single-track. |
| 2.4 | Cross an old jeep track and continue along the single-track through the aspen. |
| 3.8 | Nice downhill. Watch for lateral erosion, rocks, and downed trees. |
| 5.1 | Cross a stream on a good bridge, then head left on the main trail along the fence line. (A small single-track line scoots right.) |
| 5.3 | Cross CR 240 and continue on the single-track. The intersection is signed and well marked. |
| 5.4 | Arrive at the Angel of Shavano Trailhead. Continue riding along the trail as it skirts the parking area. Please register at the trailhead. Brace for a steep climb. ***Note-*** *to avoid the steep climb up from US 50, you may want to start the ride here. Maysville and US 50 are approximately four miles downhill on CR 240.* |
| 6.0 | The trail levels a bit and the crux of this climb is now history. |
| 6.9 | Cross a jeep track and continue on the single-track. |
| 7.3 | Continue straight as you pass a single-track spur on your right. Ride parallel to the timber fence. ***Note-*** *this spur leads to the Shavano/Tabeguache trailhead at Blank's Cabin, another possible shuttle point for this ride.* |
| 7.7 | Continue straight on the Colorado trail as the Shavano/Tabeguache hiking trail departs left (west). |
| 8.0 | A Colorado Trail sign provides useful info. Ride ahead for another fifty yards then sign the trail register. |
| 8.6 | Yet another steep climb is now behind you. |
| 10.5 | Stay on the single-track as you pass a jeep trail on the right. |
| 13.2 | Continue straight on the Colorado Trail as the Wagon Loop Trail intersects and joins this route from the right. |
| 13.5 | Cross Browns Creek on a nice bridge. |
| 13.7 | Turn right at the "T", following the Colorado Trail. (The Browns Creek trail heads left.) |

| | |
|---|---|
| 13.9 | Head left and uphill at the fork. The trail is very rocky here. |
| 14.2 | Turn right at the "T"; the Little Browns Creek Trail (#1430) heads left. |
| 15.5 | Cross the double-track. This is fun! |
| 16.1 | Cross FSR 273 (unmarked). Continue on the single-track as it begins to climb a ridge. *Note-* *this is an alternate place to end to this ride if you want to avoid the gnarly downhill to Chalk Creek. Leave your shuttle at the bottom of FSR 273.* |
| 17.6 | Cross FSR 274 and continue on the single-track. |
| 17.9 | Stay left on the main trail. Look for the Colorado Trail marker. |
| 18.6 | Here it is… are you ready? Hold on through a steep, loose, and extremely technical downhill. If in doubt, walk. |
| 19.7 | Turn right (east) on CR 290. Ride about 30 yards and look left for the Colorado Trail single-track just shy of gated CR 290A. Look for the Colorado Trail marker. |
| 20.0 | Pass the Bootleg Campsite spur on your right. |
| 20.1 | Cross the bridge and arrive at the Chalk Creek Trailhead. |

**Options:** there are two additional starting points for this ride. The first, avoiding the strenuous climb up from US 50, starts at the Angel of Shavano Trailhead. To get there: from the intersection of US 285 and US 50 (from US 285 north), drive 6.2 miles west on US 50 to CR 240. Turn right onto CR 240 and drive 3.8 miles to the trailhead.

To start from the Blank's Cabin Trailhead: from the intersection of US 285 and US 50 (from US 285), drive approximately 2.3 miles west on US 50 to the intersection with CR 250. Turn right onto CR 250 and drive 4.7 miles on CR 250 to the intersection with CR 252. Bear left, following the sign to the Shavano/Tabeguache trailhead, and drive 2.9 miles to the trailhead parking area. Start the ride on the Shavano/Tabeguache trail; it joins the Colorado Trail in about 0.1 miles.

Riding the final descent to Chalk Creek is strictly for experts. To avoid this section, end the ride at Raspberry Gulch. To leave a car there: drive to the intersection of CR 270 and US 285 (about 3 miles south of Nathrop). Drive 1.5 miles west on CR 270 to the intersection with CR 272. Drive 2.1 miles west on CR 272 to the intersection with CR/FSR 274. Drive 0.4 miles northwest on CR/FSR 274 to the intersection with FSR 273. Park on the right side of the intersection. The Colorado Trail crosses FSR 273 about 0.8 miles southwest (uphill) from this point.

# Ride 39: Marshall Pass to Silver Creek Loop

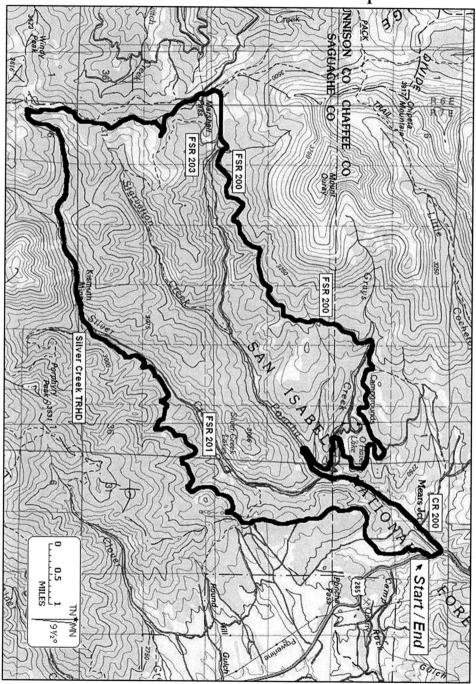

*Map 39: Marshall Pass to Silver Creek Loop (© National Geographic)*

### 148 • Arkansas Valley Mountain Biking

This is an ambitious ride with an abundance of everything mountain bikers love: lots of sweet single-track, high elevations, sweeping vistas, and a healthy climb.

Before setting out on this one, be sure you have plenty of water, food, some extra clothing layers, and good weather. You will be out for a while, far from your car, and retreat will not be easy or fast.

**Ride length:** 32.5 miles
**Ride type:** loop (counter-clockwise)
**Riding time:** 5 hours
**Surface:** paved road (0.2 miles); dirt road (14.9 miles); single-track (17.4 miles)
**Elevations:** start/end 8,550'; max 11,300'; min 8,440'
**Total climbing:** gain/loss 4,890'

**Aerobic level:** strenuous (it's a long ride)
**Technical level:** 4+ (steeps with loose rocks; laterally eroded side-cuts; tight vertical transitions on single-track)
**Season:** July through October
**USGS Quadrangles:** Poncha Pass, Mount Ouray, Bonanza

**Trailhead GPS coordinates:** 38° 26.748' N; 106° 6.328' W

**Elevation profile:**

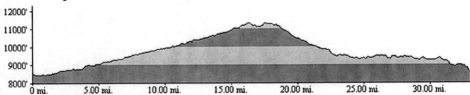

**Getting there:** from the intersection of US 50 and US 285 (5 miles west of Salida on US 50), turn left onto US 285. Drive 5.2 miles south on US 285 to the large parking turnout adjacent to the Rainbow Trail sign on the right. Park there. *Note- this area is approximately 0.2 miles south of the intersection of CR 200 and US 285 (designated by signs to O'Haver Lake and Marshall Pass).*

**Trailhead/trail amenities:** pit toilets at miles 2.7 and 14.6.

**The ride:**
0.0 From your car, ride north (downhill) on US 285.
0.2 Turn left (west/southwest) onto CR 200.
2.5 Continue straight on FSR 200, passing a turn-off for the O'Haver Lake Campground on your right.
2.7 Turn right and continue on FSR 200 at the intersection with FSR 201. Follow the signs to Marshall Pass and Poncha Creek. *Note- the Shirley Site is on your left, distinguished by a large parking area with pit toilets.*
3.2 Cross the bridge over Poncha Creek then turn right at the "T" intersection to continue on FSR 200 (Marshall Pass Road).
3.4 Continue straight on FSR 200, passing a spur on the left.

## Poncha Springs • 149

| | |
|---|---|
| 4.3 | Continue straight on FSR 200 through the intersection with FSR 202. (Note the sign: Marshall Pass 10 Miles.) |
| 6.2 | Continue on FSR 200 past the intersection with FSR 204 on your right; follow the sign to Marshall Pass. |
| 7.0 | Stay on the main road. |
| 11.4 | Pass over Tent Creek. Is this a long climb or what? |
| 13.6 | Pass over Ouray Creek. Yes, it's a long climb. |
| 14.5 | Stay on the main road. You're almost there! |
| 14.6 | Pass the entrance to the Monarch Crest Trail on the right. Pedal a little more and you will arrive at the top of Marshall Pass... finally! (Pit toilets are available at the parking area on the left.) |
| 14.7 | Continue on FSR 200 past the meadow on the left. |
| 14.8 | Bear left onto FSR 203 and ride toward a small rise. Continue until you reach a 4-way split. From there, take the route that's about 45 degrees right of your front wheel. This is poorly marked and slightly confusing. The left-most spur is FSR 203 (this leads to the intersection of FSR 200 and 203 below O'Haver Lake). The next option on the left is unmarked and leads to a campsite. The third option, the Colorado Trail, is about 45 degrees right of your front wheel; take this one. The fourth option, a hard right, is unmarked and leads back to FSR 200. |
| 14.9 | Depart left from the road and ride toward the single-track, the Colorado Trail/Continental Divide Trail (TR 486). A large message board marks the entrance to the trail. Follow the sign to Silver Creek (3 miles). (Do not ride on TR 243.3H!) |
| 15.9 | Ignore the Colorado Trail marker and broken sign at the switchback. Stay on the main trail, following the switchback right. |
| 17.0 | Turn left at the intersection marked by the sign "Silver Creek 1." Climb. |
| 17.3 | Stay on the main trail. Look for the Colorado Trail/Continental Divide Trail marker. |
| 17.5 | Stay straight on the main trail past all the zigzagging tracks. Follow the orange blazes on the trees. |
| 18.0 | Turn left onto the Silver Creek Trail (#1407). The downhill begins in earnest. (The Colorado Trail continues straight to Saguache.) |
| 22.1 | Cross Silver Creek on a bridge. Prepare for wet feet as the trail becomes the creek for the next 150 yards. |
| 22.2 | Stay left on FSR 201. Do not climb up Toll Road Gulch. |
| 22.4 | Leave FSR 201 to enter the Rainbow Trail at the Silver Creek Trailhead on your right. There is a prominent sign about 20 yards from the trail entrance. Be sure to sign the trail register. **Note-** *if you've had enough, descend on FSR 201 and return to FSR 200 at the Shirley Angler Site. US 285 is an easy 7.6 miles ahead on this route. The descent is gentle, but you should anticipate a couple wet stream crossings.* |

## 150 • *Arkansas Valley Mountain Biking*

**22.5** Stream crossing and some mud. You won't get wet feet, but each little stream crossing ahead comes with a tight downhill/uphill transition. There are several more.

**28.7** Cross an unmarked road and continue straight on the trail through the opening in the fence.

**31.2** Continue straight on the single-track through a meadow.

**32.5** After a steep descent to US 285, you are finished. And so is the ride. Crawl into your car and take a nap.

**Options:** there are several options for decreasing the intensity of this ride. First, you can use a shuttle to start from Marshall Pass.

The next option is to descend FSR 203/Starvation Creek Trail from Marshall Pass. This amazing single-track rivals the Silver Creek Trail and, as some claim, may even be better. See the Monarch Crest section of this book or *www.arkvalleymtb.com* for more info.

Finally, you can opt out of the final 9 miles of Rainbow Trail single-track by descending along FSR 201. This option is much easier and faster than the single-track.

***Starvation Creek Trail***

# Ride 40: Silver Creek Loop

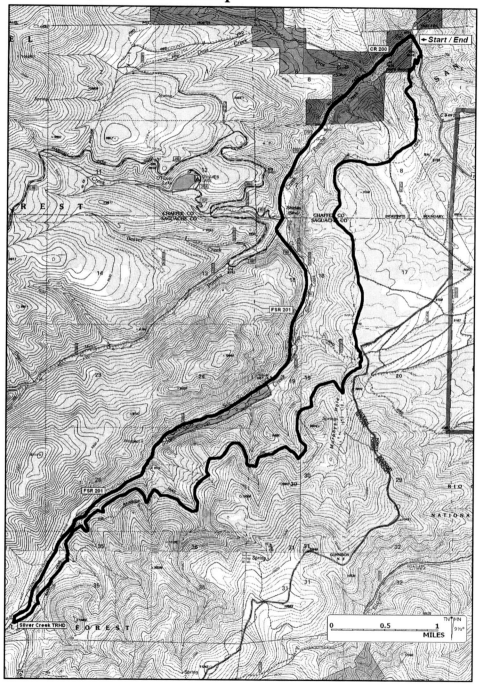

*Map 40: Silver Creek Loop (© National Geographic)*

# 152 • Arkansas Valley Mountain Biking

Friends who know me well will say that I claim every great trail as one of the best I've ever ridden. If that's true, here I go again.

The climb out is on an easy yet extremely scenic road. The single-track that comes next is some of the best in the Valley: the narrow dirt vein ahead of you just keeps going and going and going, and the bliss seems to never end. Moreover, the views of nearby Mount Ouray and distant Mount Shavano will make you leap out of your shoes.

**Ride length:** 17.9 miles
**Ride type:** loop (counter-clockwise)
**Riding time:** 2.5 hours
**Surface:** paved road (0.2 miles); dirt road (7.6 miles); single-track (10.1 miles)
**Elevations:** start/end 8,550'; max 9,550'; min 8,440'
**Total climbing:** gain/loss 2,660'

**Aerobic level:** moderate (moderate climbing throughout the route)
**Technical level:** 3+ (rocks and laterally eroded side-cuts; the descent to US 285 is steep)
**Season:** May through October
**USGS Quadrangles:** Poncha Pass, Mount Ouray, Bonanza

**Trailhead GPS coordinates:** 38° 26.721' N; 106° 6.318' W

**Elevation profile:**

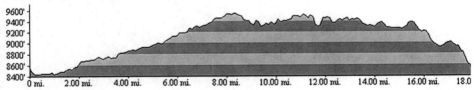

**Getting there:** from the intersection of US 50 and US 285 (5 miles west of Salida on US 50), turn left onto US 285. Drive 5.2 miles south on US 285 to the large parking turnout adjacent to a Rainbow Trail sign on the right. Park there. *Note-this area is approximately 0.2 miles south of the intersection of CR 200 and US 285 (designated by signs to O'Haver Lake and Marshall Pass).*

**Trailhead/trail amenities:** pit toilet at mile 2.7.

**The ride:**
0.0    From your car, ride north (downhill) on US 285.
0.2    Turn left onto CR 200.
2.5    Continue straight on FSR 200 past the turn-off for O'Haver Lake Campground on your right.
2.7    Continue straight on FSR 201. (Do not turn right onto FSR 200 to Marshall Pass and Poncha Creek.) Unless you need a bio-break, pass the parking lot for the Shirley Site on the left.
4.4    Stay right, climbing on FSR 201. You will soon see lakes on your left.
5.7    Continue straight on the main road, passing a road on the left.

## Poncha Springs • 153

**5.8** Break out the waders and make your way upstream. Enthusiastic beavers at it again. (A few eager rodents diverted Silver Creek so that during high flows, the road serves as the creek's channel for about 100 yards; this "feature" may change in the future.)

**7.8** Leave FSR 201 to enter the Rainbow Trail at the Silver Creek Trailhead on your left. There is a prominent sign about 20 yards from the trail entrance. Be sure to sign the trail register.

**7.9** Stream crossing and some mud. You won't get wet feet, but each crossing comes with a tight downhill/uphill transition. Several more of these await you.

**14.1** Cross an unmarked road and continue straight on the trail through the opening in the fence.

**16.6** Stay on the Rainbow Trail as you ride through a meadow.

**17.9** An intense, technical downhill brings you down to US 285. That's it. Now go get a football-sized burrito in Salida.

*Monarch Crest*

# Monarch Crest

Hands-down, this is the best the Arkansas Valley has to offer. Not only is it critically acclaimed as one of the finest trails in all of Colorado, it's also regarded as one of the best trails in the United States. The quality of the ride and unsurpassed views just can't be beat. Officially, the Monarch Crest Trail is a stretch of the Continental Divide Trail from Monarch Pass to Marshall Pass. Unofficially, the ride also includes any of several descent routes, accessed either from Marshall Pass or from one of the intersecting trails along the way.

One popular myth is the misconception that these rides are entirely downhill. As you will see from the elevation profiles, there will be some climbing, especially on the classic Silver Creek descent route. Don't let that discourage you: the net loss in elevation is much greater than the net gains on every route option except the out-and-back on the Crest and the optional looping of the Agate Creek and South Fooses Creek trails.

Because of this area's popularity, it is especially important to obey the rules of the trail. Please yield to hikers and ride within the trail boundaries. Our behavior here has a great impact on the status of this treasured area.

Also, since much of the Crest trail is above tree line, you'll want to get an early start to avoid getting caught in afternoon storms.

**Note-** *the High Valley Center in Poncha Springs (just south of the intersection of US 50/US 285) shuttles bikes and riders to the top of Monarch Pass for a very reasonable rate. Shuttles leave daily at regularly scheduled intervals, or by reserved, special arrangements. Please call for more information. (719)539-6089 / (800)871-5145*

# Ride 41: Monarch Crest Trail

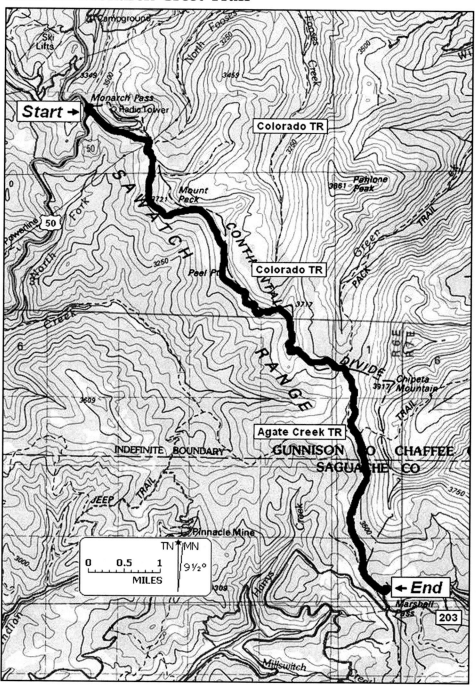

Map 41: Monarch Crest Trail (© National Geographic)

# 156 • *Arkansas Valley Mountain Biking*

This route description is for an out-and-back ride between Monarch and Marshall Passes. Included elsewhere in this guide are descriptions for some of the more popular descent routes.

**Ride length:** 20.8 miles
**Ride type:** out-and-back
**Riding time:** 3 hours
**Surface:** jeep road (4.8 miles); single-track (16.0 miles)
**Elevations:** start/end 11,300'; max 11,960'; min 10,830'
**Total climbing:** gain/loss 2,610'

**Aerobic level:** moderate (the climbs are easy, but the altitude can make them feel tough)
**Technical level:** 3 (some rocks and roots, but the overall line is clean and built for speed)
**Season:** July through October
**USGS Quadrangles:** Pahlone Peak, Mount Ouray

**Trailhead GPS coordinates:** 38° 29.784' N; 106° 19.541' W

**Elevation profile:**

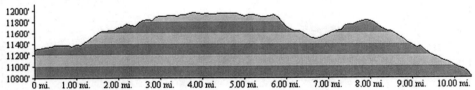

**Getting there:** from the intersection of US 50 and US 285 (5 miles west of Salida on US 50), turn right (north/west) on US 285/US 50. Drive 18.0 miles west on US 50 to the summit of Monarch Pass. Park in the large lot by the Scenic Ride.

*Note-* you can avoid riding against the flow on the return trip by leaving a shuttle at Marshall Pass. The dirt road leading to the pass (CR/FSR 200) is mellow-graded and suitable for passenger vehicles. To get there, drive 5.0 miles south from the intersection of US 50/US 285 in Poncha Springs. Turn right onto CR 200 and follow it to the summit of Marshall Pass. The road is well marked, but you may wish to consult a map.

**Trailhead/trail amenities:** gift shop with restrooms at trailhead; pit toilet at mile 10.4.

**The ride:**
0.0    From your car, ride up the paved drive leading to the Scenic Ride. The surface quickly turns to dirt. Continue climbing.

0.3    Bear right onto the Continental Divide Trail. The single-track looks awesome, but don't forget to sign the trail register!

1.0    Pass under some power lines then bear right onto the jeep track leading uphill.

1.5    Bear right and leave the jeep track for another helping of single-track. Trail markers and a map board show the way.

2.8    Pass the sign marking Middle Fooses Creek on your left.

## Monarch Crest • 157

**4.7** Round a big bend and check out that view.

**5.0** Continue straight past the intersection with the South Fooses Creek Trail (Colorado Trail) on your left. From this point forward, the Colorado Trail overlaps the Continental Divide Trail.

**5.7** Get ready for some speed.

**6.6** Pass the Greens Creek spur and the backpackers' shelter on your left.

**7.7** Continue straight past the Little Cochetopa trail on the left.

**7.8** Stay on the main trail past the Agate Creek Trail (TR 484) on your right.

**8.8** The single-track becomes a fast jeep trail. Let it rip, but watch for hikers and other traffic.

**10.2** Pop-out onto Marshall Pass Road (FSR 200). Turn right and ride toward the parking lot and pit toilet.

**10.4** That was excellent, but now what? If you are riding without a shuttle, turn back and return to Monarch Pass along the same route. If you have a shuttle vehicle at Marshall Pass, you are done.

**Monarch Crest**

158 • *Arkansas Valley Mountain Biking*

# Ride 42: Descending Marshall Pass Road

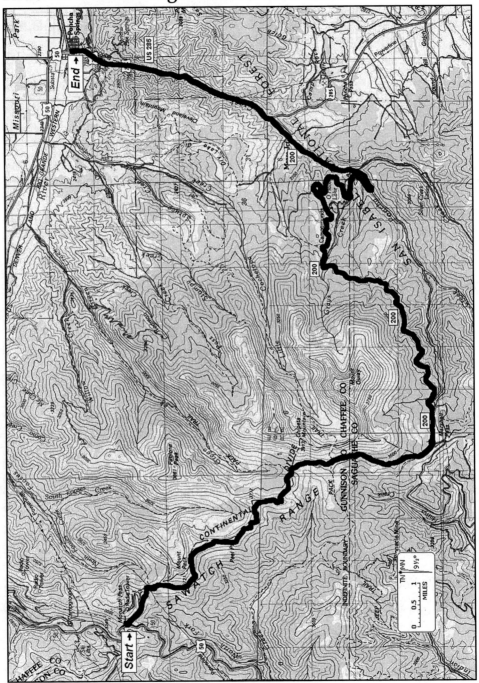

*Map 42: Monarch Crest descending Marshall Pass Road (© National Geographic)*

## Monarch Crest • 159

This is the least technical descent from Marshall Pass. After riding the amazing Crest line, some may want to finish with an easy glide back to Poncha Springs. Better yet, take the first shuttle from the High Valley Center, hustle down this route, eat lunch, and then catch another shuttle for a second run on a different descent line.

**Ride length:** 29.7 miles
**Ride type:** one-way with shuttle
**Riding time:** 3 hours
**Surface:** single-track (8.0 miles); dirt road (16.7 miles); paved road (5.0 miles)
**Elevations:** start 11,300'; end 7,480'; max 11,960'; min 7,480'
**Total climbing:** gain 1,200' – loss 5,020' = total -3,820'

**Aerobic level:** moderate (easy climbs, but altitude might make them feel tough)
**Technical level:** 3 (some rocks and roots)
**Season:** July through October
**USGS Quadrangles:** Pahlone Peak, Mount Ouray, Poncha Pass, Salida West

**Trailhead GPS coordinates:** 38° 29.784' N; 106° 19.541' W

**Elevation profile:**

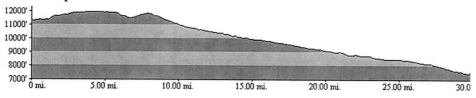

**Getting there:** from the intersection of US 50 and US 285 (5 miles west of Salida on US 50), turn left onto US 285 and drive about 0.25 miles south. Leave a vehicle in the open parking area on the left, just north of the High Valley Center in Poncha Springs.

Take the bikes and riders to the top of Monarch Pass. From the parking area in Poncha Springs, turn right (north) on US 285/US 50 and drive approximately 18.2 miles west on US 50 to the summit of Monarch Pass. Park in the large lot by the Scenic Ride.

**Trailhead/trail amenities:** gift shop with restrooms at trailhead; pit toilets near mile 10.2 and mile 22.1.

**The ride:**
0.0 From your car, ride up the paved drive leading to the Scenic Ride. The surface quickly turns to dirt. Continue climbing.
0.3 Bear right onto the Continental Divide Trail. The single-track looks awesome, but don't forget to sign the trail register!
1.0 Pass under some power lines then bear right onto the jeep track leading uphill.

| | |
|---|---|
| 1.5 | Bear right and leave the jeep track for another helping of single-track. Trail markers and a map board show the way. |
| 2.8 | Pass the sign marking Middle Fooses Creek on your left. |
| 5.0 | Continue straight past the intersection with the South Fooses Creek Trail (Colorado Trail) on your left. |
| 6.6 | Pass the Greens Creek spur and the backpackers' shelter on your left. |
| 7.7 | Continue straight past the Little Cochetopa trail on the left. |
| 7.8 | Stay on the main trail past the Agate Creek Trail (TR 484) on your right. |
| 8.8 | The single-track becomes a fast jeep trail. Let it rip, but watch for traffic and hikers. |
| 10.2 | Intersect Marshall Pass Road (FSR 200). Turn left to start the descent. *Note- if you need a pit toilet break, turn right and ride to the Marshall Pass summit parking lot.* |
| 10.3 | Stay on the main road, FSR 200. |
| 17.8 | Stay on the main road. |
| 18.6 | Pass the intersection with FSR 204 on your left. Stay on FSR 200. |
| 20.5 | Continue straight on FSR 200 past the intersection with FSR 202. |
| 21.4 | Continue straight on FSR 200, passing a spur on the right. |
| 21.6 | Turn left at the "T" intersection, staying on FSR 200 (Marshall Pass Road), then cross the bridge over Poncha Creek. |
| 22.1 | Turn left at the intersection with FSR 200 and FSR 201. The Shirley Site is on your right, distinguished by a large parking area with pit toilets. Continue rolling down FSR/CR 200. |
| 22.3 | Continue straight past the turn-off for O'Haver Lake Campground on your left. |
| 24.8 | Intersect US 285. Carefully cross then turn left (north) on US 285. |
| 29.9 | Arrive at the car. Awesome! Go get a cold drink and something to eat at the High Valley Center. |

## Ride 43: Descending Starvation Creek Trail

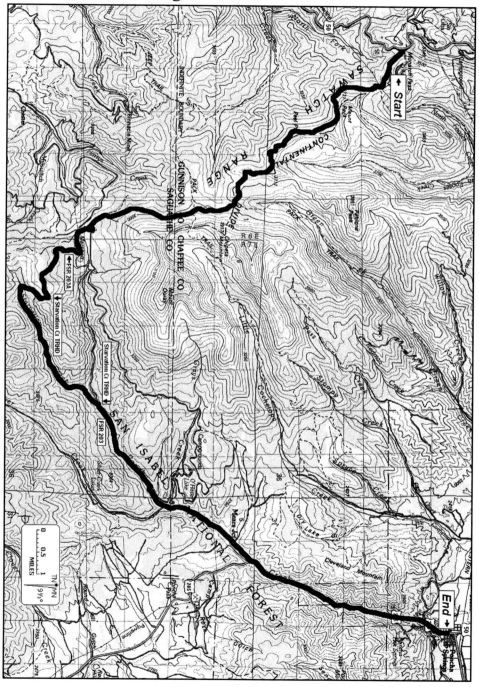

*Map 43: Monarch Crest descending Starvation Creek Trail (© National Geographic)*

## 162 • Arkansas Valley Mountain Biking

This is quickly becoming one of the most popular descent routes from Marshall Pass. The Starvation Creek Trail is extremely fast, flowy and fun. The only complaint you could possibly have is that it ends too soon.

**Ride length:** 28.0 miles
**Ride type:** one-way with shuttle
**Riding time:** 2.5-3.5 hours
**Surface:** single-track (10.1 miles); dirt road (12.8 miles); paved road (5.1 miles)
**Elevations:** start 11,300'; end 7,480'; max 11,960'; min 7,480'
**Total climbing:** gain 1,615' – loss 5,440' = total -3,825'

**Aerobic level:** moderate (easy climbs, but altitude can make them feel tough)
**Technical level:** 4 (roots and rocks at high speed)
**Season:** July through October
**USGS Quadrangles:** Pahlone Peak, Mount Ouray, Poncha Pass, Salida West

**Trailhead GPS coordinates:** 38° 29.784' N; 106° 19.541' W

**Elevation profile:**

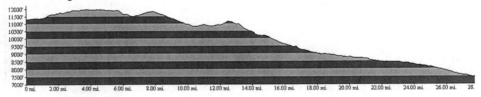

**Getting there:** from the intersection of US 50 and US 285 (5 miles west of Salida on US 50), turn left onto US 285 and drive about 0.25 miles south. Leave a vehicle in the open parking area on the left, just north of the High Valley Center in Poncha Springs.

Take the bikes and riders to the top of Monarch Pass. From the parking area in Poncha Springs, turn right (north) on US 285/US 50 and drive approximately 18.2 miles west on US 50 to the summit of Monarch Pass. Park in the large lot by the Scenic Ride.

**Trailhead/trail amenities:** gift shop with restrooms at trailhead; pit toilets near mile 10.5 and mile 20.6.

**The ride:**
0.0   From your car, ride up the paved drive leading to the Scenic Ride. The surface quickly turns to dirt. Continue climbing.
0.3   Bear right onto the Continental Divide Trail. The single-track looks awesome, but don't forget to sign the trail register!
1.0   Pass under some power lines then bear right onto the jeep track leading uphill.
1.5   Bear right and leave the jeep track for another helping of single-track. Trail markers and a map board show the way.

## Monarch Crest • 163

**2.8** Pass the sign marking Middle Fooses Creek on your left.

**5.0** Continue straight past the intersection with the South Fooses Creek Trail (Colorado Trail) on your left.

**6.6** Pass the Greens Creek spur and the backpackers' shelter on your left.

**7.7** Continue straight past the Little Cochetopa trail on the left.

**7.8** Stay on the main trail past the Agate Creek Trail (TR 484) on your right.

**8.8** The single-track becomes a fast jeep trail. Let it rip, but watch for hikers and other traffic.

**10.5** Intersect Marshall Pass Road (FSR 200). Turn right and ride toward the parking lot and pit toilet. If you don't need to stop, continue south on FSR 200 past an open meadow.

**10.6** Bear left onto FSR 203. This road is slightly rougher and climbs a bit.

**10.7** Approach a 4-way intersection. Take the left-most option, Poncha Creek Road (FSR 203).

**11.3** Turn right onto Starvation Creek Road (FSR 203A). Prepare for a fairly stiff climb.

**12.9** Following the climb you will descend into a large, open meadow. Look right for a sign marking the Starvation Creek trailhead. *(This intersection is very easy to miss, so keep your eyes open.)* Turn right onto the Starvation Creek Trail to begin a long, continuous downhill on superb single-track.

**17.7** After crossing a small bridge, turn right onto Poncha Creek Road (FSR 203). This next section is very fast and you will be tempted to open it up, but stay alert and please ***watch for motorized vehicles!***

**20.0** Turn right onto FSR 200 (Marshall Pass Road) and continue descending.

**20.6** Turn left at the intersection with FSR 201 at the Shirley Site and continue downhill on FSR/CR 200. ***Note-*** *to ride the Rainbow Trail to US 285, turn right and climb a little over 5 miles to the trailhead on FSR 201.*

**18.6** Continue downhill on FSR/CR 200, passing a road leading to O'Haver Lake on your left.

**20.9** Cross US 285 (be careful!) then turn left (downhill) on the pavement toward Poncha Springs.

**26.0** Find your car, pack your bikes, and plan your next adventure.

# 164 • *Arkansas Valley Mountain Biking*
# Ride 44: Descending Silver Creek Trail

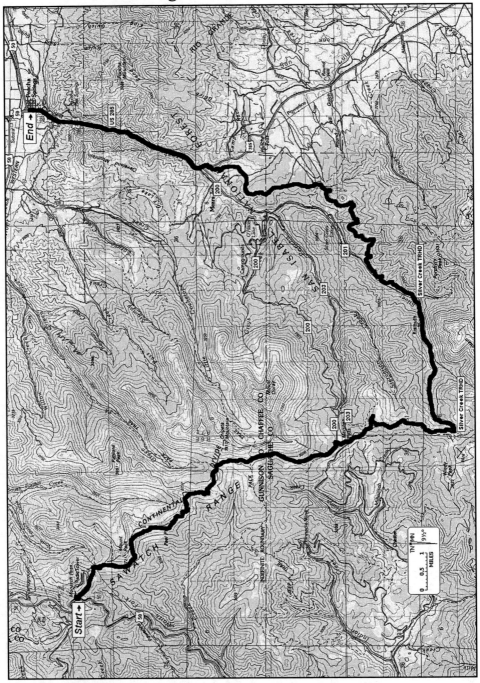

*Map 44: Monarch Crest descending Silver Creek Trail (© National Geographic)*

# Monarch Crest

You've seen it: your friends just got back from riding the "Monarch Crest" and they rave on-and-on about endless single-track and epic scenery. That's a typical reaction to this route. This is the one, the classic ride Front Range mountain bikers return to each summer like disciples on a pilgrimage. Few rides anywhere offer as much.

Please bear in mind that this is a strenuous and technically demanding route. The stretch from Marshall Pass to US 285 is much tougher than the initial ride to Marshall Pass, and some intermediate riders will find it above their skill level. Also, be prepared for many short, strenuous climbs on the Rainbow Trail between the Silver Creek trailhead and the highway.

**Ride length:** 33.2 miles
**Ride type:** one-way with shuttle
**Riding time:** 4-5 hours
**Surface:** dirt/jeep road (2.8 miles); single-track (26.4 miles); paved road (5.0 miles)
**Elevations:** start 11,300'; end 7,480'; max 11,960'; min 7,480'
**Total climbing:** gain 3,260' – loss 7,080' = total -3,820'

**Aerobic level:** strenuous (lots of ups and downs)
**Technical level:** 4+ (roots, rocks, and steeps)
**Season:** July through October
**USGS Quadrangles:** Pahlone Peak, Mount Ouray, Bonanza, Poncha Pass, Salida West

**Trailhead GPS coordinates:** 38° 29.784' N; 106° 19.541' W

**Elevation profile:**

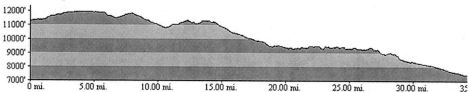

**Getting there:** from the intersection of US 50 and US 285 (5 miles west of Salida on US 50), turn left onto US 285 and drive about 0.25 miles south. Leave a vehicle in the open parking area on the left, just north of the High Valley Center in Poncha Springs.

Take the bikes and riders to the top of Monarch Pass. From the parking area in Poncha Springs, turn right (north) on US 285/US 50 and drive approximately 18.2 miles west on US 50 to the summit of Monarch Pass. Park in the large lot by the Scenic Ride.

**Trailhead/trail amenities:** gift shop with restrooms at trailhead; pit toilets near mile 10.2.

**The ride:**

0.0  From your car, ride up the paved drive leading to the Scenic Ride. The surface quickly turns to dirt. Continue climbing.

| | |
|---|---|
| 0.3 | Bear right onto the Continental Divide Trail. The single-track looks awesome, but don't forget to sign the trail register! |
| 1.0 | Pass under some power lines then bear right onto the jeep track leading uphill. |
| 1.5 | Bear right and leave the jeep track for another helping of single-track. Trail markers and a map board show the way. |
| 2.8 | Pass the sign marking Middle Fooses Creek on your left. |
| 5.0 | Continue straight past the intersection with the South Fooses Creek Trail (Colorado Trail) on your left. |
| 6.6 | Pass the Greens Creek spur and the backpackers' shelter on your left. |
| 7.7 | Continue straight past the Little Cochetopa trail on the left. |
| 7.8 | Stay on the main trail past the Agate Creek Trail (TR 484) on your right. |
| 8.8 | The single-track becomes a fast jeep trail. Let it rip, but watch for hikers and other traffic. |
| 10.2 | Intersect Marshall Pass Road (FSR 200). Turn right and ride toward the parking lot and pit toilet. If you don't need to stop, continue south on FSR 200 past the open meadow. |
| 10.4 | Bear left onto FSR 203 and ride toward a small rise. Continue until you reach a 4-way split. From there, take the route that's about 45 degrees right of your front wheel. This is poorly marked and slightly confusing. The left-most spur is FSR 203. The next option on the left is unmarked and leads to a campsite. The third option, the Colorado Trail, is about 45 degrees right of your front wheel; take this one. The fourth option, a hard right, is unmarked and leads back to FSR 200. |
| 10.6 | Depart left from the road and ride toward the single-track, the Colorado Trail/Continental Divide Trail (TR 486). A large message board marks the entrance to the trail. Follow the sign to Silver Creek (3 miles). (Do not ride on TR 243.3H!) |
| 11.6 | Ignore the Colorado Trail marker and broken sign at the switchback. Stay on the main trail and take the switchback right. |
| 12.7 | Turn left at the intersection marked by the sign "Silver Creek 1." Climb. |
| 13.0 | Stay on the main trail. Look for the Colorado Trail/Continental Divide Trail marker. |
| 13.2 | Continue straight on the main trail, passing various zigzagging tracks. Use the orange blazes on trees to guide you. |
| 13.7 | Turn left onto the Silver Creek Trail (#1407). The downhill begins in earnest. (The Colorado Trail continues straight to Saguache.) |
| 17.5 | Enter private property and prepare for lots of loose rocks ahead. |
| 17.8 | Cross Silver Creek on a bridge. Prepare for wet feet as the trail becomes the creek for the next 150 yards. |
| 17.9 | Stay left on FSR 201. Do not climb up Toll Road Gulch. |

**18.1** Turn right to enter the Silver Creek Trailhead of the Rainbow Trail. There is a prominent Silver Creek Trailhead sign about 20 yards from the trail entrance. Don't forget to register your party. **Note-** *if you've had enough, descend on FSR 201 to FSR 200; US 285 is an easy 7.6 miles ahead along this route, but a couple stream crossings will refresh your drying shoes.*

**18.2** Stream crossing and some mud. You won't get wet feet, but each little stream crossing comes with a tight downhill/uphill transition. There are several more ahead.

**24.4** Cross an unmarked road and continue straight on the trail through the opening in the fence.

**26.9** Continue straight on the single-track through the meadow.

**28.2** After a steep, technical descent, carefully cross US 285 and turn left to coast into Poncha Springs.

**33.2** Arrive back at your car. Yes!!!

**South Fooses Creek Trail**

## Ride 45: Descending South Fooses Creek Trail

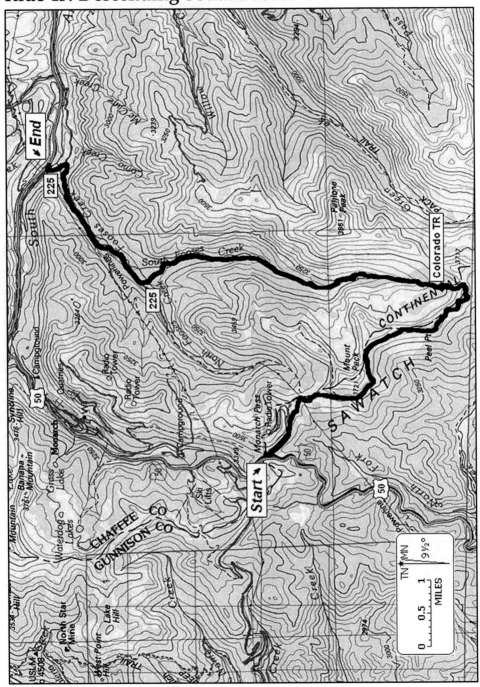

*Map 45: Monarch Crest descending South Fooses Creek Trail (© National Geographic)*

This is an excellent ride combining tasty portions of two area classics: the Monarch Crest section of the Continental Divide Trail and the South Fooses section of the Colorado Trail.

The descent on the South Fooses Trail starts with a hairy, technical drop from the Divide. You'll want to break out the camera and capture it forever. Clean that section and you'll have something to brag about when you get home. The rest of the ride is a classic romp over some amazing single-track. As miles fly under your wheels, you will remember why you started mountain biking all those years ago.

**Ride length:** 13.3 miles
**Ride type:** one-way with shuttle
**Riding time:** 2 hours
**Surface:** jeep road (4.0 miles); single-track (9.3 miles)
**Elevations:** start 11,300'; end 8,870'; max 11,960'; min 8,800'
**Total climbing:** gain 715' – loss 3,180' = total -2,465'

**Aerobic level:** moderate (easy climbing, but altitude might make it feel tough)
**Technical level:** 4 (one hairy steep, some rocks/roots)
**Season:** July through October
**USGS Quadrangles:** Pahlone Peak, Garfield, Maysville

**Trailhead GPS coordinates:** 38° 29.784' N; 106° 19.541' W

**Elevation profile:**

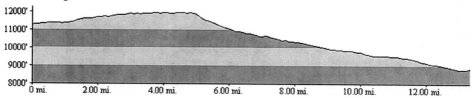

**Getting there:** from the intersection of US 50 and US 285 (from US 50), drive approximately 9.7 miles west on US 50 to the intersection with CR 225. There is a large pullout on the left (south) side of the highway at the intersection. Leave the drop vehicle here.

Take riders and bikes to Monarch Pass. Continue west on US 50 for about 8.4 miles to the summit. The ride starts from the large parking lot by the Scenic Ride.

**Trailhead/trail amenities:** gift shop with restrooms at trailhead; pit toilet at mile 12.5.

**The ride:**
0.0  From your car, ride up the paved drive leading to the Scenic Ride. The surface quickly turns to dirt. Continue climbing.
0.3  Bear right onto the Continental Divide Trail. The single-track looks awesome but don't forget to sign the trail register!

### 170 • *Arkansas Valley Mountain Biking*

| | |
|---|---|
| **1.0** | Pass under some power lines then bear right onto the jeep track leading uphill. |
| **1.5** | Bear right and leave the jeep track for another helping of single-track. Trail markers and a map board show the way. |
| **2.8** | Pass the sign for Middle Fooses Creek on your left. |
| **5.0** | Turn left and ride over the grassy knoll at the intersection with the Colorado Trail/South Fooses Creek. Whether the initial descent looks awesome or terrifying is a matter of perspective. The surface is rocky and loose, and excessive braking is the best way to eat dirt. If you aren't up to the challenge, walk to the bottom; the rest of the trail is nowhere near as steep or technical. |
| **5.2** | The steep is over. |
| **7.2** | Nice! Let it rip as the rocky section ends and the trail gets soft and loamy. Watch for roots! |
| **10.3** | Guess what: another bridge. Continue 50 feet to the trailhead. Another 100 feet and you'll intersect a road. Turn right and ride the road downhill. |
| **10.6** | Turn right at the intersection with FSR 225. From this point, you'll intersect US 50 in approximately 3 miles. Stay on the main road throughout the descent as spurs cut in-and-out under the power lines. |
| **12.5** | Continue straight on the main road. You'll pass a pit toilet on your right in another 50 yards and Fooses Lake on the left. |
| **13.2** | Turn right at the "T" intersection. Look for a blue diamond trail marker on the tree to your right for reassurance. Make the short climb to the highway. |
| **13.3** | Arrive at the intersection with US 50. Some rides end too soon. |

**Options:** if shuttles aren't your thing, start the ride at the intersection of US 50 and CR 225. It's an easy 8.4 miles to the summit of Monarch Pass, but use extreme caution when riding along the highway. Expect to spin some of those miles on a sandy, soft shoulder and be prepared to dodge wide-load trucks and RVs.

# Ride 46: Descending Agate Creek Trail

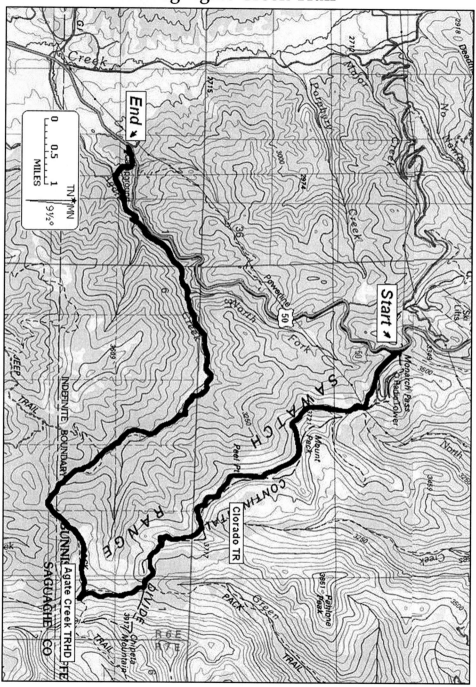

*Map 46: Monarch Crest descending Agate Creek Trail (© National Geographic)*

## 172 • Arkansas Valley Mountain Biking

Question: Which trail has more water crossings, Moab's Onion Creek or Monarch's Agate Creek Trail?

Answer: Who cares! The upper portions of the Agate Creek Trail offers one of the best single-track descent lines to be found anywhere. Steep and fast, you can really test your skills on this one. There is, however, a small price to pay for all this bliss: the last few miles of the trail are tough and you may end up paying your share of bike pushing dues.

Oh, yeah, and don't forget: there are more water crossings than you will be able to count.

**Ride length:** 17.6 miles
**Ride type:** one-way with shuttle
**Riding time:** 3-4 hours
**Surface:** single-track (16.8 miles); double-track (0.8 miles)
**Elevations:** start 11,300'; end 9,150'; max 11,960'; min 8,925'
**Total climbing:** gain 1,485' – loss 3,630' = total -2,145'

**Aerobic level:** strenuous (altitude and tough, technical steeps)
**Technical level:** 5 (rocks, roots, and steeps)
**Season:** July through October
**USGS Quadrangles:** Pahlone Peak, Sargents

**Trailhead GPS coordinates:** 38° 29.784' N; 106° 19.541' W

**Elevation profile:**

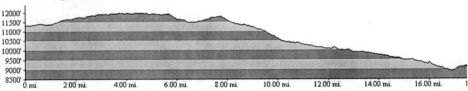

**Getting there:** leave a car at the trailhead at the old Agate Creek Campground. From the summit of Monarch Pass on US 50, drive 6.9 miles west on US 50. Look on the south side of the highway for a driveway with a stop sign. Turn left and find a good parking spot within the old campground. The trailhead is at the eastern edge of the campground, about 0.1 miles from the entrance.

Take riders and bikes to the summit of Monarch Pass. The ride starts in the parking lot adjacent to the Scenic Ride.

**Trailhead/trail amenities:** gift shop with restrooms at trailhead.

**The ride:**
0.0 From your car, ride up the paved drive leading to the Scenic Ride. The surface quickly turns to dirt. Continue climbing.

0.3 Bear right onto the Continental Divide Trail. The single-track looks awesome, but don't forget to sign the trail register!

## Monarch Crest • 173

| | |
|---|---|
| 1.0 | Pass under some power lines then turn right onto the jeep track leading uphill. |
| 1.5 | Turn right and leave the jeep track for another helping of single-track. Trail markers and a map board show the way. |
| 2.8 | Pass the sign marking Middle Fooses Creek on your left. |
| 5.0 | Continue straight past the intersection with the South Fooses Creek Trail (Colorado Trail) on your left. |
| 6.6 | Pass the Greens Creek spur and the backpackers' shelter on your left. |
| 7.7 | Continue straight past the Little Cochetopa trail on the left. |
| 7.8 | Turn right onto the Agate Creek Trail (TR 484). Fast riding awaits you. |
| 10.1 | The first of many water crossings. There's a bench on the downhill side of the creek if you need to stop to change your socks. Hope you brought a lot of socks. |
| 10.7 | Continue straight on the Agate Creek Trail (TR 484) as you pass the intersection with the Lime Creek Trail (TR 485) on the left. |
| 13.8 | Bear left, staying on the Agate Creek Trail as you pass the intersection with the Agate Spur Trail (TR 484.2A) on your right. |
| 16.8 | Turn right at the fork and drop down to another water crossing. After the water crossing, the trail is a tight single-track that climbs steeply to the campground. You should be able to hear highway traffic to reassure you that you are on course. *Note- this intersection may not be well marked, but continuing straight eventually leads to a dead end.* |
| 17.6 | Arrive at the campground. As grandma would say: get out of those wet shoes before you catch a cold! |

**Options:** ride it as a loop. Why not? It's just 7 miles from the trailhead to the summit of Monarch Pass. Save gas by parking at the closest trailhead (Monarch Pass if you are driving from Salida and the east; the old Agate Creek Campground if you are arriving from Gunnison and the west). Be sure to use caution when riding along US 50.

# Salida

There's a reason Salida made Outside magazine's 2004 list of best towns in the United States. The town's proximity to so many world class recreational areas combined with its laid back vibe and unpretentious atmosphere make it an outdoor paradise. Unlike so many other mountain towns with similar claims, Salida is a place of genuine soul.

Originally founded as a rail center, Salida is now the largest town in Chaffee County and serves as its county seat. In addition to a wide variety of retail stores and other amenities, there are two great bicycle shops in town that can satisfy your every need. Check them out for up-to-date trail conditions and other information.

A group of dedicated local riders are working hard to establish Salida as a national mountain biking destination that, in my opinion, will soon rival Crested Butte and Fruita. The superb new single-track around Tenderfoot Mountain is one example of their work. Look for new trails in the Methodist Mountain area in the near future as another proposed trail network is already in the works. Visit *http://salidamountaintrails.org* for more information and to learn how you can get involved.

*Arkansas Hills Trails: Burn Pile*

# Ride 47: Bear Creek to Methodist Mountain Loop

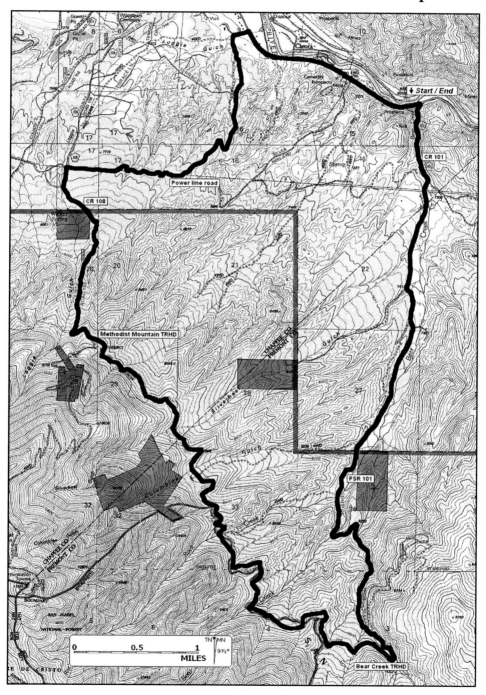

*Map 47: Bear Creek to Methodist Mountain Loop (© National Geographic)*

# Arkansas Valley Mountain Biking

Do you want to know why local riders regard Salida as one of Colorado's best mountain biking towns? Do this ride.

This section of the Rainbow Trail is a local single-track staple and there are many well-documented variations of the route. This version, a clockwise loop incorporating fun sections of the Methodist Mountain BLM area east of CR 108, serves as a sampler for two popular riding areas.

The first area, the Rainbow Trail single-track between Bear Creek and Methodist Mountain, is first rate. The trail is fast with excellent transitions and flow. The terrain and scenery, if you slow down long enough to look around, are spectacular. It's a cross-country rider's dream.

The second area, along the power line road, is a popular early and late season playground and a fine alternate when snow covers higher trails. Single-track spurs opened in 2009 now provide legal technical alternatives to riding on the jeep road. Find a local to take you out and show you some of the prime circuits, but please ride only on legal, established routes.

**Ride length:** 17.2 miles
**Ride type:** loop (clockwise)
**Riding time:** 2-3 hours
**Surface:** paved roads (1.8 miles); dirt road/jeep track (9.9 miles); single-track (5.5 miles)
**Elevations:** start/end 6,995'; max 9,020'; min 6,995'
**Total climbing:** gain/loss 3,345'

**Aerobic level:** strenuous (climbing-more than 3,000' of it)
**Technical level:** 3 (some tricky rocks and loose sections; some laterally eroded side-cuts)
**Season:** May through October
**USGS Quadrangles:** Salida East, Wellsville, Poncha Pass

**Trailhead GPS coordinates:** 38° 30.422' N; 105° 57.646' W

**Elevation profile:**

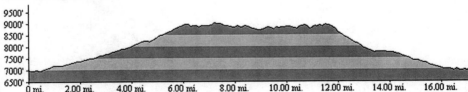

**Getting there:** from the intersection of 1st St. (CO 291) and F St. in downtown Salida, drive 1.0 miles east on 1st St. to the intersection with US 50. Turn left onto US 50 and drive 1.9 miles east to the Salida East river access area on the left. Turn into the area and drive about 0.2 miles west to the day use/boat launch parking area. Ride bikes back out to the highway where the ride starts.

**Trailhead/trail amenities:** pit toilet at trailhead.

## Salida • 177

**The ride:**

| | |
|---|---|
| 0.0 | From the entrance of the Salida East area, cross US 50 and ride east (left). The shoulder is wide and comfortable. |
| 0.5 | Turn right at the intersection with CR 101. Be aware that this public road crosses private land; please stay on the road! |
| 1.4 | Cross into Fremont County. The road you are on is now CR 49. Continue climbing. |
| 3.6 | Pass a parking area on the right and cross a cattle guard at the National Forest boundary. The road, now FSR 101, is considerably rougher and steeper. |
| 3.8 | Pass an unmarked spur on your left. |
| 4.1 | Pass an unmarked spur on the right. |
| 5.7 | Continue straight up FSR 101 as you pass the intersection with FSR 101A on your left. |
| 6.0 | Stream crossing. Continue uphill. After 100 yards, you'll intersect the Rainbow Trail (TR 1336). Turn right to ride toward Methodist Mountain (6 miles). At the trail entrance, sign the trail register. The next 6 miles are fantastic. |
| 7.0 | Stunning views here. Now, this is Colorado! |
| 11.5 | Arrive at the Methodist Mountain trailhead. Turn right and brace for a rigorous downhill. |
| 11.7 | Pass the Rainbow Trail entrance on the left. Continue downhill on the main road. ***Note-*** *from this intersection it's about 9 (not 6, as the sign reads) stiff, mostly single-track miles to US 285.* |
| 13.0 | Pass a gated spur on your left at the forest boundary. Continue straight downhill. |
| 13.2 | Pavement. Continue downhill. |
| 13.4 | Turn right (east) and ride the undulating, rugged dirt road (#5670) under the power lines. *Note- there are 3 new single-track options ahead: Lost Trail (T5670A) is very steep and technically challenging; Racetrack (T5672A) is much less technical but has amazing views; and Dead Bird (T5672B) is another alternative. All three will drop you back on the road (#5672) leading to US 50.* |
| 14.2 | Look for Lost Trail (T5670A) on the left. It's steep and loose, but really fun if you still feel fresh. Stay on the road if you are beat. |
| 14.7 | You have three choices here: 1.) Stay on the main road, now road #5672, for the quickest route down. 2.) Take Racetrack (T5672A) on your right for extremely scenic, moderate single-track. Or, 3.) turn left onto Dead Bird (T5672B) single-track. *In my opinion, Racetrack is your best bet!* |
| 15.3 | Continue straight on the main road. *Note- if you are riding Racetrack, look right to re-enter the single-track after it merges with Road 5672.* |

### 178 • Arkansas Valley Mountain Biking

15.9   Stay on the main road past a deep, rutted climb on your right. This used to be an ugly, illegal dump site, but was reclaimed and cleaned in 2009. *Note- if you are on Racetrack, search for the single-track line on the right that parallels the road; it may not be obvious, but it's there.*

16.0   Continue straight on the main road past the spur on the left. *Note- this is where Lost Trail and Racetrack rejoin the main route.* Pass through the signed exit from the BLM area. Ride downhill and turn right onto the well-maintained dirt road. Continue to the highway.

16.1   Turn right onto US 50.

17.2   Arrive back at the entrance to the parking/camping area. Cross US 50 and find your vehicle. Had enough?

**Options:** there are many ways to ride this trail. Some people prefer riding just the single-track as an out-and-back. Drive CR/FSR 101 to the parking area at the trailhead; you'll want a high-clearance 4WD vehicle if this is your plan. For a more vehicle-friendly alternate, drive CR 101/49 to the parking area at the San Isabel National Forest boundary (approximately 3.6 miles from the highway).

You can also do this as a one-way with a shuttle. Leave a drop car at the top of the paved section of CR 108 and start wherever you like. If you fancy something epic, leave the drop car at the intersection of US 285 and The Rainbow Trail (5.2 miles south of the intersection of US 285 and US 50).

For more information and other potential ride options in this area, see *www.arkvalleymtb.com*.

*Epic views from Racetrack (T5672A)*

## Ride 48: Spiral Drive/Arkansas Hills Trails

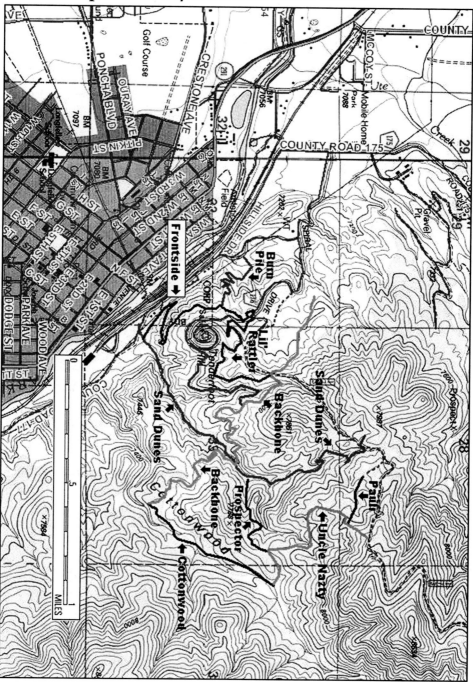

Map 48: Spiral Drive/Arkansas Hills Trails (© National Geographic)

# Arkansas Valley Mountain Biking

The Arkansas Hills trail system is one of the best mountain biking additions to Salida in recent years. Built and maintained by local riders, this stacked loop system is quickly becoming one of the "must-do" rides in the area.

With something for everyone, these trails are typically dry throughout winter and provide an excellent place to get dirty after a day of boarding or skiing at nearby Monarch Mountain. This is also a great early spring/late fall fat tire destination when snow covers high country single-track in Summit and Eagle counties.

Expect this system to get bigger and better over time. Trail crews are out there right now, cutting new tread and extending existing lines. Stop by Absolute Bikes in Salida for the latest info, better maps, and riding suggestions.

**Ride length:** various
**Ride type:** stacked loop system
**Riding time:** 1-? hours
**Surface:** single-track
**Elevations:** start/end 7,020';
**Total climbing:** it's up to you
**Aerobic level:** moderate
**Technical level:** various
**Season:** all year (when dry)
**USGS Quadrangle:** Salida East

**Trailhead GPS coordinates:** 38° 32.28' N; 105° 59.39' W

**Getting there:** from the intersection of 1st St. (CO 291) and F St. in downtown Salida (the only traffic light downtown), drive northeast on F St. until you reach the parking area past the bridge at the end of the road. The ride starts at your vehicle.

Additional parking is available in several other downtown locations.

**Trailhead/trail amenities:** ride starts/ends in town.

## Trail segments

*Hint-* the trails listed as Most Difficult are typically more fun when ridden downhill toward town.

**Backbone:** Easiest (great way to connect other segments)
**Burn Pile:** More difficult
**Cottonwood:** More difficult (excellent, fast downhill)
**Frontside:** Easiest (more fun to climb than Spiral Drive)
**Lil' Rattler:** Easiest (wild, painted trees to ponder as you ride)
**Pauli:** Most difficult (access the top from CR 173/T5677)
**Prospector:** Most difficult (downhill from Uncle Nazty to Sand Dunes)
**Sand Dunes:** Most difficult (this one is a blast ridden downhill from the top)
**Tenderfoot:** More difficult
**Uncle Nazty:** Most difficult (take Pauli to access this one)

**Trail system access:**

0.0  The easiest way to begin your first exploration of the Arkansas Hills trails is to ride to the trailhead on Spiral Drive. To get there, ride through the gate at the northeast corner of the parking lot. Cross the railroad tracks and turn left when you reach the road (CR 177).

0.3  Turn right onto CR 177 (unmarked) and start to climb.

0.8  Pass the colorful water tank on your left then turn right onto CR 176 (Spiral Drive).

0.9  Continue straight on the main road.

1.4  Just shy of the gate, stop to consult the Arkansas Trails map. Use your imagination to create loops suitable to your skill level.

**Options:** There are as many ways to ride this as there are mountain bikers in Colorado.

*Arkansas Hills*

# Ride 49: Ute Trail Loop

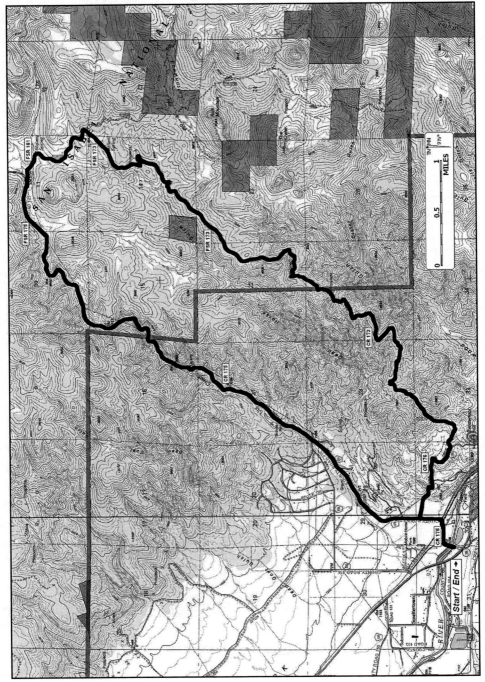

*Map 49: Ute Trail Loop (© National Geographic)*

This ride packs a lot of punch and offers great views of the southern Arkansas Valley. The big, technical descent on CR/FSR 273 is one of the best in the Arkansas Valley; it's not single-track, but line selection is so critical that it may as well be.

Start with a climb that, if you push hard enough, is guaranteed to purge your body of nasty toxins and negative thoughts. The mellow climbing/traverse across CR 181 is just long enough to allow the sweat to dry from your jersey. A few quick climbs will protect you from dangerous pleasure overloads on the long technical descent that brings you back to town.

**Ride length:** 15.9 miles
**Ride type:** lollipop-loop (clockwise)
**Riding time:** 2 hours
**Surface:** paved road (2.5 miles) dirt road (6.4 miles); jeep trail (6.5 miles)
**Elevations:** start/end 7,060'; max 8.990'; min 7,060'
**Total climbing:** gain/loss 2,630'

**Aerobic level:** moderate (for the most part, the climb is a long middle-ring grind)
**Technical level:** 4 (steep, loose, and rocky descent)
**Season:** April into November (snow may linger into April on CR 273)
**USGS Quadrangles:** Salida West, Salida East

**Trailhead GPS coordinates:** 38° 32.65' N; 106° 0.377' W

**Elevation profile:**

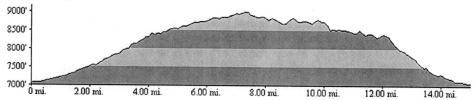

**Getting there:** from the intersection of 1st St. (CO 291) and F St. in downtown Salida (the only traffic light downtown), drive northeast on F St. until you reach the parking area past the F Street Bridge at the end of the road. The ride starts at your vehicle. Additional parking is available in several other downtown locations.

**Trailhead/trail amenities:** none.

**The ride:**

0.0   Ride through the opening in the fence at the northeast corner of the parking area. Cross the railroad tracks then turn left (west) and ride along the paved road that parallels the tracks.

0.3   Pass CR 177 on the right. Stay on the pavement.

0.9   Turn right (north) on CR 175.

1.1   Continue straight on CR 175 past CR 176 (Spiral Drive) on the right.

1.2   Continue straight on CR 175 as you pass CR 178 on the right.

### 184 • *Arkansas Valley Mountain Biking*

**1.7** Continue straight on CR 175 as you pass another intersection with CR 178 on your right.

**2.5** Continue on CR 175 as it turns to dirt. Pass CR 156 on your left.

**2.9** Continue straight on CR 175.

**4.5** Pass the US Forest Service signs. The road is now FSR 175.

**6.0** Continue straight on FSR 175 past an unmarked road on the left.

**7.0** Turn right onto FSR 181. An ATV sign marks the entrance.

**7.5** Pass a spur on the right. Stay on the main road.

**7.9** Follow the main road left, passing an unmarked spur on the right.

**8.0** Turn right onto FSR 173.

**8.9** Stay right on the main trail past a double-track spur on the left.

**9.3** Bear left to stay on FSR 173, passing a spur on the right.

**9.7** Stay on the main road.

**13.0** Continue straight, passing an unmarked spur on the left.

**14.2** Stay on the main road as you work your way down to the backside of Tenderfoot Mountain and Spiral Drive (CR 176). ***Note-*** *you'll pass a couple single-track spurs on your left. Explore them if you like. Most lead to CR 177 along the river.*

**14.3** Pass a few uphill spurs as you blast down hill. Many jeep spurs intersect the route as you approach Spiral Drive (CR 176). Your ultimate destination for this section is the graffiti-covered water tank on Spiral Drive. (See it to your right in the distance?) Just take the most obvious descent line and don't worry about making a "wrong" turn. Most of these tracks eventually intersect Spiral Drive.

**14.4** Follow the main track down to the left.

**14.5** Intersect CR 176 (Spiral Drive), a well-maintained, gently descending dirt road. Turn right and ride downhill toward the water tank.

**15.0** Turn left onto CR 177 (at the water tank) and descend.

**15.5** Turn left onto the paved road at the bottom of the hill.

**15.8** Look right for the path over the tracks and the opening in the fence at the parking area.

**15.9** Arrive at the F St. parking area. Another ride under your jersey.

**Options:** if you want to extend the ride, climb another 1.5 miles to the top of Tenderfoot Mountain. Turn left onto CR 176 at mile 14.5 and wind your way to the top. Explore the single-track descent routes from the top.

# Ride 50: The Crater

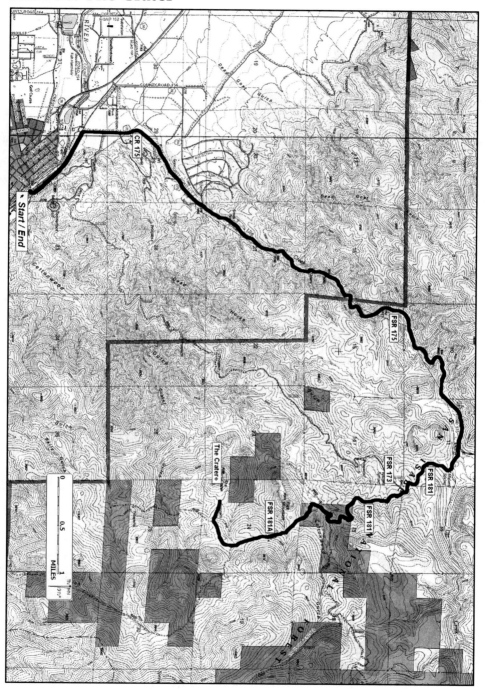

Map 50: The Crater (© National Geographic)

## Arkansas Valley Mountain Biking

This ride takes you to the brim of The Crater, one of Chaffee County's many natural wonders. While not an actual crater created by volcanic activity or a meteor strike, the Crater is actually a rock outcropping exposed by erosion.

The ride itself is tough. While the majority of the climb is a steady grind up well-maintained roads, the last two miles get steeper as the road surface deteriorates. Strong riders will have no problem pedaling the entire route, but some less experienced riders may encounter a little hike-a-bike. As with every ride in the Salida area, the sweeping vistas of the lower Arkansas Valley and Sangre de Cristo range are spectacular.

**Ride length:** 22.2 miles
**Ride type:** out-and-back
**Riding time:** 3-4 hours
**Surface:** paved road (5.0 miles); dirt/jeep roads (17.2 miles)
**Elevations:** start/end 7,020'; max 9,250'; min 7,020'

**Total climbing:** gain/loss 3,110'
**Aerobic level:** strenuous (climbing)
**Technical level:** 3 (some rocky sections)
**Season:** April through October
**USGS Quadrangles:** Salida East, Salida West

**Trailhead GPS coordinates:** 38° 32.28' N; 105° 59.39' W

**Elevation profile:**

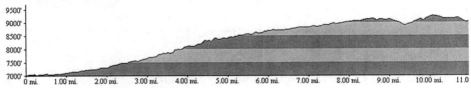

**Getting there:** from the intersection of 1st St. (CO 291) and F St. in downtown Salida (the only traffic light downtown), drive northeast on F St. until you reach the parking area past the F Street Bridge at the end of the road. The ride starts at your vehicle. Additional parking is available in several other downtown locations.

**Trailhead/trail amenities:** ride starts/ends in town.

**The ride:**
- **0.0** Ride through the opening in the fence at the northeast corner of the parking area. Cross the railroad tracks then turn left (west) and ride along the paved road that parallels the tracks.
- **0.3** Pass CR 177 on the right. Stay on the pavement.
- **0.9** Turn right (north) on CR 175.
- **1.1** Continue straight on CR 175 past the intersection with CR 176 (Spiral Drive) on your right.
- **1.2** Continue on CR 175 past the intersection with CR 178 on your right.

| | |
|---|---|
| 1.7 | Continue on CR 175 past the second intersection with CR 178 on your right. |
| 2.5 | Continue straight on CR 175 past CR 156 on your left. CR 175 turns to dirt just past this intersection. |
| 2.9 | Continue climbing on the main road as you pass an unmarked spur on the right and a driveway on the left. |
| 4.5 | Enter the San Isabel National Forest. The road is now FSR 175. |
| 5.1 | Pass a turnout on the right as you continue climbing on FSR 175. |
| 5.2 | Pass a campsite on the left as you continue climbing on FSR 175. |
| 6.0 | Pass an unmarked spur on the left as you keep climbing on FSR 175. |
| 7.0 | Turn right onto FSR 181. (The ATV sign just past the intersection will help you identify this intersection.) |
| 7.5 | Stay on FSR 181 past an unmarked spur that peels off to your right. |
| 7.9 | Stay left on the main road past a double-track spur on your right. |
| 8.0 | Continue straight on FSR 181 as you pass the intersection with FSR 173 on your right. *Note-* returning to Salida along FSR 173 is an awesome, technical finish to this ride; please refer to the ***Ute Trail Loop*** in this guide for more information. |
| 8.6 | Continue straight and cross a cattle guard as you pass an unmarked intersection on your left. |
| 8.7 | Enter private property. Please stay on the main road through here. |
| 9.2 | Look for the sign post and turn right onto FSR 181A. |
| 9.4 | Bear left at the fork to remain on FSR 181A. |
| 9.6 | Tough little climb as the road surface deteriorates. |
| 10.5 | After a nice downhill break, turn right at a sandy intersection. |
| 10.9 | Make a hard right turn at an unmarked intersection and continue riding toward the hill with the rock outcropping at the top. You are now on your final approach to The Crater. |
| 11.1 | Ditch your bike at the closure sign and hike the remaining way up to the edge of The Crater. You made it! After pondering the wonder of The Crater, return the way you arrived. |

**Options:** descend along FSR/CR 173 to combine the complete ***Ute Trail Loop*** within this ride. This descent option is fast, technical, and may not be suited for novice riders.

## 188 • *Arkansas Valley Mountain Biking*
# Ride 51: Upper Bighorn Sheep Canyon

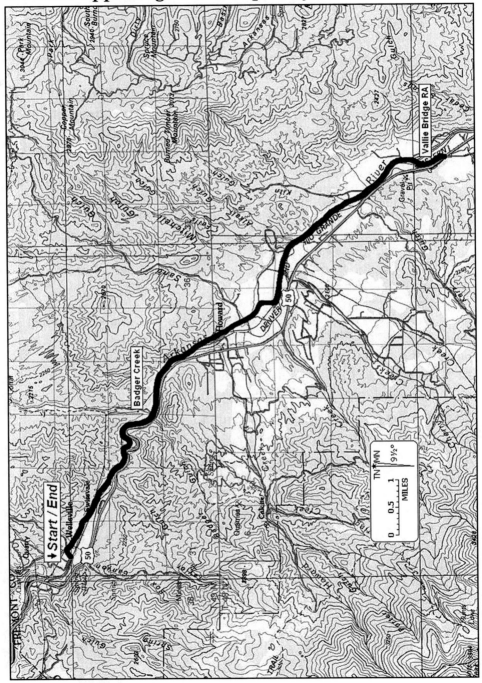

*Map 51: Upper Bighorn Sheep Canyon (© National Geographic)*

Gather the family for a ride on the "Pathway through History." This route, an easy outing through the Upper Bighorn Sheep Canyon, has twelve interpretive signs to give an historical perspective to your journey.

This is an easy ride, so take it at a relaxed pace and read the interpretive signs along the way. Keep a sharp eye out for a chance sighting of Colorado's official state animal, the bighorn sheep, grazing in the canyon. And, as the first sign suggests, try to let your imagination carry you back to the time when this road was a simple dirt path.

*Note-* *Badger Creek may be impossible when water levels are high and attempting to cross it in winter is hazardous. In addition, some parts of the road may flood during times of high water.* DO NOT ATTEMPT TO CROSS ANY FLOWING, FLOODED AREAS OF THE ROAD.

**Ride length:** 22.4 miles (or any length you choose by turning back before Vallie Bridge)
**Ride type:** Out-and-back
**Riding time:** 3-4 hours
**Surface:** dirt road
**Elevations:** start/end 6,900'; max 6,925'; min 6,515'
**Total climbing:** gain/loss 560'
**Aerobic level:** easy
**Technical level:** 2- (some beginners may struggle with the mile of rocky/sandy road adjacent to Badger Creek)
**Season:** April through November
**USGS Quadrangles:** Wellsville, Howard

**Trailhead GPS coordinates:** 38° 29.216' N; 105° 54.554' W

**Elevation profile:**

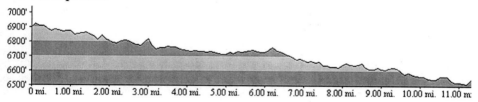

**Getting there:** from the intersection of 1st St. (CO 291) and F St. in downtown Salida, drive approximately 1.0 miles east on 1st St. to the intersection with US 50. Turn left onto US 50 and drive 4.9 miles east to the intersection with CR 7/45. Turn left onto CR 7/45. Drive over the bridge and continue for approximately 0.6 miles. Cross the railroad tracks and a cattle guard then park in the clearing on the right.

Additional parking is available at the pullout on the north side US 50 just east of CR 7/45 (this adds 1.2 miles to the ride).

**Trailhead/trail amenities:** pit toilets at mile 2.5 and at the Vallie Bridge recreation site.

**The ride:**

| | |
|---|---|
| 0.0 | From the parking area, turn right onto CR 45. The entire ride is on CR 45. |
| 0.2 | Pass a spur on the left. The first set of signs is on the right. |
| 1.8 | Pass under the railroad trestle and turn left. |
| 2.0 | Bear right at the fork and take the double-track to the next sign. |
| 2.5 | Turn right for the next sign and a toilet. |
| 2.6 | The next sign is on the right. |
| 3.4 | See the sign on the right? |
| 3.5 | Cross Badger Creek. If water levels are high, you may need to turn around here. Use good judgment and be cautious: water currents may be stronger than they appear. Turn left and ride toward the trestle; the trail continues right just before you cross under the tracks. |
| 3.6 | Another sign for you. |
| 5.2 | Look for the sign on your left. |
| 5.5 | Pass Howard Hall on your right. Look for the next sign on the right, at the intersection with CR 56. |
| 7.5 | Stop at the stop sign then continue straight on CR 45. |
| 8.6 | Look for the sign on the left. |
| 9.9 | Another sign on the right. |
| 11.2 | The Vallie Bridge recreation area is on the right. This concludes the ride and the interpretive sign tour. Turn around and return along the same route. ***Note-*** *if you use the picnic facilities at Vallie Bridge, please pay the daily use fee.* |

**Options:** ride out and turn back at anytime along the route. CR 45 crosses US 50 at mile 11.4; ambitious riders may want to continue for another 1.9 miles to Coaldale.

Or do this as a one-way ride with shuttles. Leave a drop vehicle at the Vallie Bridge Recreation area. From 1st and F Sts. in downtown Salida, drive 1.0 miles east on 1st St. to the intersection with US 50. Drive about 16 miles east on US 50 to the Vallie Bridge recreation area entrance. There is a fee to park and a self-service fee station.

For an interesting diversion, at mile 3.5 continue straight under the tracks and ride along a single-track spur that leads to the green BLM gate. Pass through the gate and follow the old jeep trail that parallels Badger Creek for approximately 4 miles. The route is technical, aerobically demanding, and route finding is extremely difficult. If you go, be sure to stay within your limits and don't get lost!

# South Park

No matter how many times you've driven it, the view while descending from Kenosha Pass on US 285 is impressive. Stretched out before you is a broad, rolling, grassland basin of nearly 900 square miles. Impressive, yes, but how many times when you reach the bottom do you punch the cruise control and grab the steering wheel without giving a thought to stopping?

If you are like me, and I'm ashamed to admit it here, the answer is many. As the popularity of the South Park animated television series grew, I might chuckle and point out Fairplay (the town that serves as the basis for the show) to my passengers. But stop? Not until I reached Buena Vista.

As I now know, that was a big mistake. Tucked discreetly into the rollers of the Mosquito Range, the mountains bounding the basin to the west, are incredible single-track and alpine pass routes. And it must be said that the towns of Fairplay, Alma, and Como are fascinating places to visit and explore.

Originally established as the Fair Play Diggings mining district in 1859, Fairplay became the Park County seat in 1867. The town's name came from its reputation that, unlike the nearby Tarryall Diggings near Como, every man would have a fair chance to stake a claim there. In the early years, Fairplay was also called Platte City, Fair Play and South Park City, but in 1874 "Fairplay" became the officially accepted name.

Today, Fairplay is Park County's most populous town. Mining still plays a part in the county's economy, but the roles of summer tourism and recreation are expanding. Major events include Burro Days, with its "Get Your Ass Up the Pass" annual burro race, and the South Park Music Tour. In addition, the South Park City museum and historical sites are a must-see for any western history buff.

What is burro racing? In the days of the Gold Rush, prospectors scouring the mountains in search of riches often used donkeys as pack animals to carry their mining tools. When they made a strike, the men ran to town with their burros in tow to be the first to file their claim at the assay office. Modern burro racing recreates the excitement of filing a claim as competitors run a course on Mosquito Pass leading a burro packed with mining tools. To be a strong competitor, runners must combine high levels of physical fitness with excellent burro handling skills.

# Ride 52: Salt Creek-McQuaid Loop

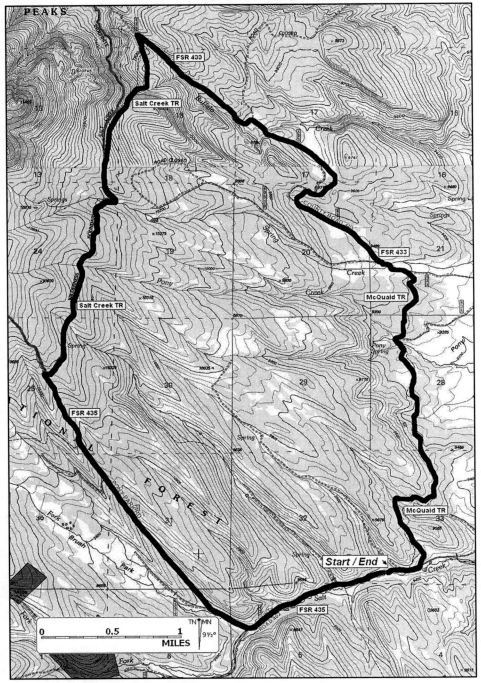

*Map 52: Salt Creek-McQuaid Loop (© National Geographic)*

This is a great little loop that doesn't see a lot of use. Start with a three-mile climb up FSR 435. Hit the single-track for about 0.7 miles of additional climbing to the highpoint of the route. Next, the trail roller-coasters until you reach FSR 433. Sail down FSR 433 until you intersect the McQuaid Trail single-track. The remainder is an easy glide on more pristine and skinny single-track.

The route traverses some dense stands of aspen and mid-September is an especially nice time to ride it. In addition, the trail passes through several open range areas, so please close and chain all gates after passing through them.

*Please be aware that this route is not well maintained and there may be a lot of downed trees and other trail hazards. But don't let that discourage you because it's still a lot of fun.*

**Ride length:** 12.8 miles
**Ride type:** loop (clockwise)
**Riding time:** 2-3 hours
**Surface:** dirt road (3.0 miles); single-track (6.4 miles); jeep track (3.4 miles)
**Elevations:** start/end 9,370'; max 10,570'; min 9,290'
**Total climbing:** gain/loss 1,950'

**Aerobic level:** moderate (some climbing and a few short steeps)
**Technical level:** 3+ (one steep littered with loose rocks)
**Season:** May through October
**USGS Quadrangles:** Marmot Peak, Jones Hill

**Trailhead GPS coordinates:** 38° 57.381' N; 106° 1.051' W

**Elevation profile:**

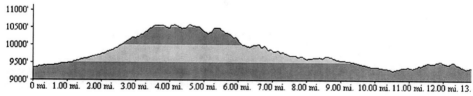

**Getting there:** from the intersection of US 24/285, (2.4 miles south of Buena Vista), drive approximately 15.7 miles north on US 285 to the intersection with FSR 435. This intersection is difficult to anticipate, but it's approximately 1.7 miles north of the split between US 285/24 at Antero Junction. Look left for an opening in the fence and a stop sign. Turn left onto FSR 435 and drive approximately 3.5 miles west to a parking area at a campsite adjacent to some beaver ponds on Salt Creek. FSR 435 is an open range area so drive with caution. **Note-** *look right for the McQuaid trailhead after driving 3.3 miles on FSR 435. The trailhead is very difficult to see as you drive west, but two fiberglass posts and a sign mark it.*

**Trailhead/trail amenities:** primitive camp sites near trailhead.

**The ride:**
0.0   From the campsite, turn left (west) on FSR 435.
1.2   Bear right at the fork to continue on FSR 435. Follow the sign to the Salt Creek Trail (2 miles). (FSR 436 heads left to Trout Creek Pass.)

| | |
|---|---|
| 1.5 | Continue straight on FSR 435 as FSR 435.2C forks to the left. |
| 2.7 | Continue on FSR 435 past the entrance to FSR 435B on your left. |
| 2.9 | Continue straight on the main road. |
| 3.0 | FSR 435 ends at the intersection with the Salt Creek Trail. Take the right, single-track entrance to TR 618. (This entrance may not be properly signed because someone uses it for target practice.) The trail continues climbing for approximately 0.7 miles to the highpoint of the ride. *Note- the left entrance climbs for 0.1 miles before descending into a valley along broad switchbacks.* |
| 3.5 | Turn right at the intersection, continuing up into a stand of pine. (Left heads into a stand of aspen.) |
| 3.7 | Crest the highpoint of the trail and enjoy a break in the climbing. |
| 4.7 | Get ready for a steep and technical downhill. |
| 4.8 | Stream crossing. Look left for the footbridge. |
| 4.9 | Bear left, staying on the Salt Creek Trail as it leads to Buffalo Peaks Road. |
| 5.6 | Pass through a gate. |
| 6.4 | Cross a small creek then turn right onto FSR 433. (The Salt Creek Trail continues left and uphill on FSR 433.) |
| 7.1 | **CAUTION!!!** Cross through a gate. You'll be sliced to ribbons if you hit this one at speed! |
| 9.6 | Cross a cattle guard then turn left, continuing downhill on FSR 433. (The road on the right is FSR 433.2B.) |
| 9.8 | Turn right onto the McQuaid Trail single-track. The entrance is faint, but there's a sign to help you find it. |
| 10.4 | Intersect FSR 434. Ride left about 20 yards and look for the entrance to the single-track. Once again, this intersection is faint, but there is a sign about 50 yards from the road to help you find it. |
| 10.6 | Cross a small footbridge. Ride 20 yards, then stay right past a very faint spur heading left. |
| 10.9 | Pass through another gate and continue straight as cattle trails intersect from the right and left. |
| 12.6 | After a nice and easy downhill, turn right onto FSR 435. |
| 12.8 | Arrive back at your vehicle. Watch for cow patties as you pack up the bikes. |

South Park • 195

# Ride 53: Tumble Creek Trail

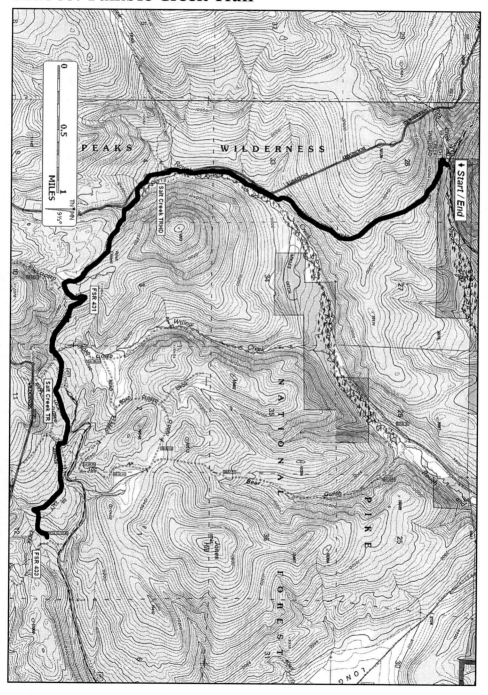

*Map 53: Tumble Creek Trail (© National Geographic)*

# Arkansas Valley Mountain Biking

Imagine riding tight, pristine single-track that skirts the edge of the Buffalo Peaks Wilderness Area. Imagine solitude and tranquility as you effortlessly sail down a trail deep under the cover of pine and aspen. Imagine the Tumble Creek Trail.

The ride out is a little physically demanding, but you'll fly on the return trip. Most of the route is over a bed of loamy pine needles with just enough technical obstacles to keep it interesting without slowing you down. You'll want to ride this one more than once.

The trailhead is a little far from the highway, but there are numerous primitive campsites in the area and a developed Forest Service campground (Weston Pass) is less than two miles west of the trailhead on CR 22.

**Ride length:** 13.2 miles
**Ride type:** out-and-back
**Riding time:** 2-3 hours
**Surface:** single-track (9.6 miles); dirt/jeep road (3.6 miles)
**Elevations:** start/end 9,950'; max 10,625'; min 9,935'

**Total climbing:** gain/loss 2,260'
**Aerobic level:** moderate (a few steeps)
**Technical level:** 3+ (some rocks)
**Season:** June through October
**USGS Quadrangles:** Jones Hill

**Trailhead GPS coordinates:** 39° 4.097' N; 106° 6.982'

**Elevation profile:**

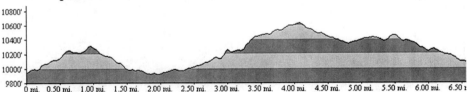

**Getting there:** from Fairplay, drive approximately 4.7 miles south on US 285 to the intersection with CR 5. Turn right (west) on CR 5 and drive about 6.9 miles to the intersection with CR 22. Turn right (west) on CR 22 and drive approximately 3.0 miles to the Tumble Creek Trailhead. Park here. The ride starts at your car.

From the Arkansas Valley: from the split of US 24/285 at Antero Junction, drive approximately 10.7 miles north on US 285 to the intersection with CR 22. Turn left (west) and drive approximately 9.9 miles on CR 22 to the Tumble Creek Trailhead. Park at the trailhead and the ride starts at your car.

**Trailhead/trail amenities:** none.

**The ride:**
0.0    After signing the trail register at the trailhead, cross the foot bridge and ride 100 feet. Turn right and ride another 100 feet along the South Platte River. Turn left and climb up to the Rich Creek Trail (no bikes). Turn left onto the Tumble Creek Trail (TR 617).

| | |
|---|---|
| 0.4 | The grade eases some, but more climbing and false summits await you! |
| 2.6 | Turn right to cross Tumbling Creek on a solid bridge. Continue through the wash until you reach a clearing. From the clearing, continue straight and uphill to ride on the Salt Creek Trail (TR 618) toward the Lynch Creek Trailhead. *Note-* from this intersection, the Tumble Creek Trail (TR 617) enters the Buffalo Peaks Wilderness Area (no bikes). |
| 3.0 | Potentially muddy water crossing. Do your best. |
| 3.2 | After a somewhat steep and rocky climb, look slightly left to find the trail. Continue for another couple hundred yards to arrive at the Lynch Creek Trailhead. Ride out to FSR 431 (unmarked) and turn right (east). |
| 3.7 | Stay on FSR 431 as you pass an unmarked double-track on your right. |
| 3.9 | Keep riding on FSR 431 past a campsite on the left. **Note-** *the Salt Creek Trail resumes from this campsite and weaves back-and-forth across FSR 431, but route finding is difficult and probably not worth the effort.* |
| 4.0 | Continue riding along FSR 431 past the intersection with FSR 431.2B on your right. |
| 4.1 | Stay on FSR 431 as you pass an unmarked intersection on your right. |
| 4.8 | Continue riding on FSR 431 past FSR 164 on the left and an unmarked road on your right. |
| 5.2 | Turn right and resume riding along TR 618 (Salt Creek Trail). You are back on single-track. |
| 5.8 | Continue straight on the main trail through the intersection with an unmarked single-track. |
| 6.4 | Turn left, passing the intersection with an unmarked single-track on the right. |
| 6.5 | Turn left to stay on the Salt Creek Trail as you pass the intersection with the Pony Park Trail on the right. |
| 6.6 | Arrive at the trailhead in a clearing adjacent to FSR 433. Turn around and go back the way you came. A good time awaits you. |

**Options:** to add about 13 more miles, continue riding along FSR 433 from the trailhead to incorporate the *Salt Creek-McQuaid Loop Trail* into this ride. You'll want to stay on FSR 433 until you reach the McQuaid Trail so that you can ride this loop clockwise (I think it's better that way).

## Ride 54: Weston Pass (east)

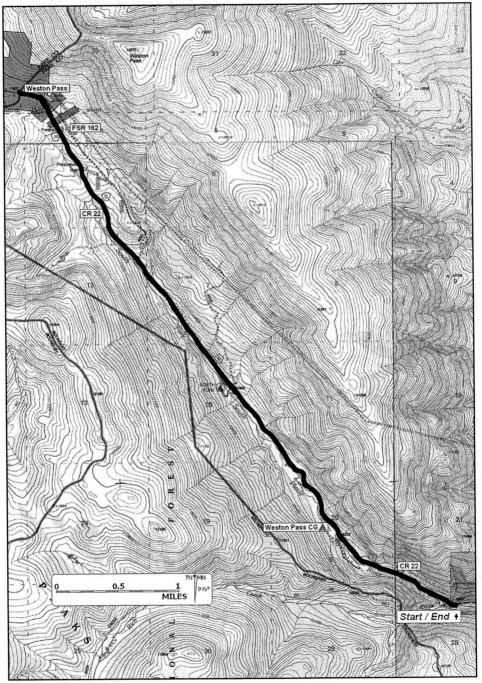

*Map 54: Weston Pass (east) (© National Geographic)*

The east side of Weston Pass is a little shorter, a little steeper, and just as beautiful (if not more so) than its western sibling. One key difference, however, is that this side provides an alternate descent route that is at once smoother yet more technical than the road leading to the top.

Along the way you'll pass numerous structures and sites that provide historically interesting perspective for you to ponder as you grind to the top. You'll also notice numbered wagon wheel signs along the route; free interpretive brochures for these markers are available online (*www.fs.fed.us/r2/psicc/sopa*) or at the South Park Forest Service office in Fairplay.

The trailhead is a little far from the highway, but there are numerous primitive campsites in the area and a developed Forest Service campground (Weston Pass) is less than two miles west of the trailhead on CR 22.

**Ride length:** 11.8 miles
**Ride type:** out-and-back
**Riding time:** 2-3 hours
**Surface:** dirt/jeep road
**Elevations:** start/end 9,950'; max 11,935'; min 9,950'
**Total climbing:** gain/loss 1,990'

**Aerobic level:** strenuous (it gets steeper the higher you go)
**Technical level:** 3+ (loose rocks on road); optional descent: 4 (steep and rutted)
**Season:** June through October
**USGS Quadrangles:** Jones Hill, South Peak, Mount Sherman

**Trailhead GPS coordinates:** 39° 4.097' N; 106° 6.982' W

**Elevation profile:**

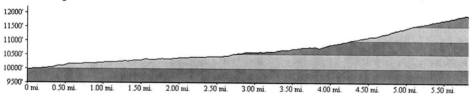

**Getting there:** from Fairplay, drive approximately 4.7 miles south on US 285 to the intersection with CR 5. Turn right (west) on CR 5 and drive about 6.9 miles to the intersection with CR 22. Turn right (west) on CR 22 and drive approximately 3.0 miles to the Tumble Creek Trailhead. Park here. The ride starts at your car.

From the Arkansas Valley: from the split of US 24/285 at Antero Junction, drive approximately 10.7 miles north on US 285 to the intersection with CR 22. Turn left (west) and drive approximately 9.9 miles on CR 22 to the Tumble Creek Trailhead. Park at the trailhead and the ride starts at your car.

**Trailhead/trail amenities:** none.

**The ride:**

| | |
|---|---|
| 0.0 | From the trailhead, turn left to ride west on CR 22. |
| 1.2 | Pass the Weston Pass Campground on your left. |
| 3.1 | Pass an unmarked campsite spur on your left. |
| 4.0 | Now that you are warmed-up, the grade gets steeper and road surface looser. |
| 4.1 | Continue on CR 22 past the intersection with FSR 162 on your right. |
| 5.0 | Continue on CR 22 as you pass FSR 161 on the right. |
| 5.7 | Continue climbing toward the Pass as you pass the intersection with the top of FSR 162 on the right. |
| 5.9 | Arrive at the Pass. See any bighorn sheep? Turn around and return along the same route, or: |

**This is a fun alternative to descending on CR 22, but it's steep and line selection gets critical toward the end of the spur.**

| | |
|---|---|
| 6.1 | Turn left onto FSR 162. The road enters a flowing groove as you sail past Ruby Lake. |
| 6.9 | Bear left to remain on FSR 162 as FSR 161 forks to the right. |
| 7.0 | Continue descending straight toward the trees on FSR 162 as you pass another fork with FSR 161 on the right. |
| 7.4 | Bear left past a campsite spur on the right. It gets steep and fast here. |
| 7.7 | Continue descending past an unmarked double-track on the left. |
| 7.8 | Turn left onto CR 22 as FSR 162 ends. Return to your car along CR 22. |

**Options:** ride down the west side as far as you like. The return trip isn't as steep and you are more likely to have a tail wind on the way back up to the top. Just don't dip lower than you are able climb back.

*Sheep Creek Trail*

# Ride 55: Sheep Creek Trail

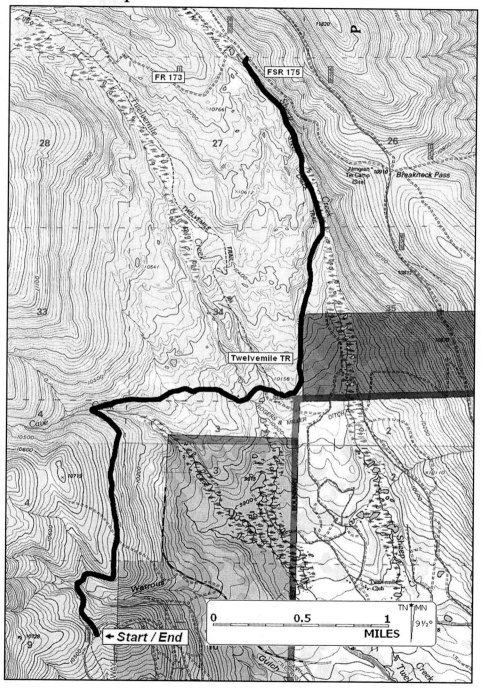

Map 55: Sheep Creek Trail (© National Geographic)

# 202 • Arkansas Valley Mountain Biking

This little traveled, 100% single-track trail is a gem. The single-track is super skinny and winds through deep stands of aspen, far from the all-too-familiar rumble of ATVs and motorcycles. Though the trail is relatively close to developed lands, the route winds deep into isolated wilderness and you are very likely to see wildlife not encountered on more popular trails.

Because of the route's remote nature, your group should stick together and DO NOT ride this one alone. While exploring the Twelvemile Creek Trail, a mountain lion crossed the trail about 150 feet ahead of me. I also happened upon fresh bear scat on the trail. More evidence than I needed to remind me this is bear and lion habitat.

The trailhead is a little far from the highway, but there are numerous primitive campsites at the trailhead and a developed Forest Service campground (Weston Pass) a few miles farther west on CR 22.

**Ride length:** 10.2 miles
**Ride type:** out-and-back
**Riding time:** 2-3 hours
**Surface:** single-track
**Elevations:** start/end 10,450'; max 10,705'; min 10,000'
**Total climbing:** gain/loss 1,420'

**Aerobic level:** moderate (sustained climbs)
**Technical level:** 3+ (some rocks; abundant side growth)
**Season:** June through October
**USGS Quadrangles:** Jones Hill, Fairplay West

**Trailhead GPS coordinates:** 39° 6.521' N; 106° 6.533' W

**Elevation profile:**

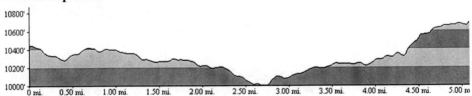

**Getting there:** from Fairplay, drive approximately 4.7 miles south on US 285 to the intersection with CR 5. Turn right (west) on CR 5 and drive about 6.9 miles to the intersection with CR 22. Turn right (west) on CR 22 and drive approximately 0.6 miles to CR 455. Turn right onto CR 455 and drive 1.1 miles to the National Forest boundary.

From Buena Vista: from the split of US 24/285 at Antero Junction, drive approximately 10.7 miles north on US 285 to the intersection with CR 22. Turn left (west) and drive approximately 7.4 miles on CR 22 to CR 455. Turn right onto CR 455 and drive 1.1 miles to the National Forest boundary.

If you do not have a high-clearance vehicle, park in the grassy pullout inside the forest boundary on the left and ride your bikes 0.6 miles further on CR 455 to the trailhead. If you have a truck, continue up the steep and deeply rutted road to the trailhead. The trailhead is adjacent to a campsite and clearly marked.

**Trailhead/trail amenities:** primitive campsites at trailhead.

**The ride:**

0.0   Start at the trailhead.

1.6   Cross a high plank bridge over Cave Creek. This is no place to test your bravado (even if you do have a COSAR card).

2.5   Cross Twelvemile Creek. Beavers can make this one tough. Look left for a plank bridge and follow the zigzagging line of logs across the water. If beavers extended their dam up to the bulky plank of the first section, use caution when crossing (the stagnant water gets a little stinky).

2.7   Continue straight on the Sheep Creek Trail as you pass the intersection with the Twelvemile Creek Trail (#684) on your left.

4.4   Cross Sheep Creek.

5.1   The trail ends at FSR 175. Turn around and return the way you came—the views and ride are better on the return trip. Or, turn right onto FSR 175 and ride an additional 1.0 miles to Breakneck Pass (10,910') for excellent views of the Buffalo Peaks to the south. Then turn around and return the way you came; just be aware that the Sheep Creek trailhead is extremely difficult to see from the road.

**Options:** loop the Twelvemile Creek Trail into this ride. This is an interesting but challenging spur that eventually joins FSR 173.

Turn left onto the Twelvemile Creek Trail at mile 2.7. After reaching the trailhead at FSR 173, ride southeast on FSR 173 for about 1.5 miles until it ends at FSR 175. Turn right onto FSR 175 and ride about 0.1 miles to the concealed and hard-to-find Sheep Creek trailhead. Route finding might be very tough and the surface is rocky in spots.

*Early homestead*

## 204 • *Arkansas Valley Mountain Biking*
## Ride 56: Mosquito Pass (east)

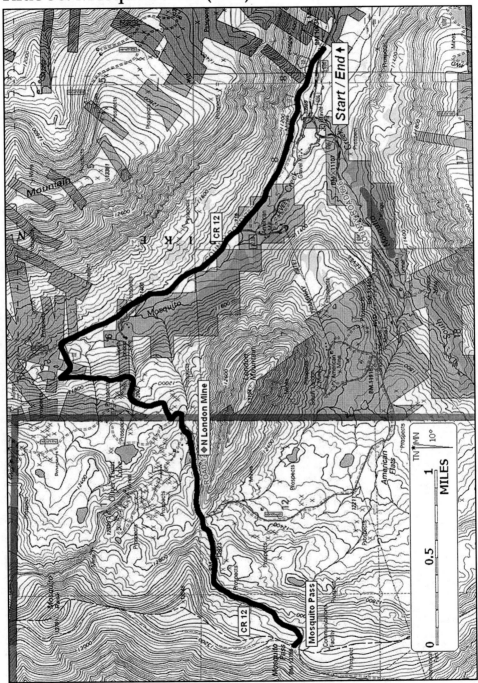

*Map 56: Mosquito Pass (east) (© National Geographic)*

Just like its western sibling, this is an epic climb. Unlike the Leadville side, however, all of the east side can be ridden by most strong cyclists. But you must be mighty strong to pull it off and don't feel bad if you find yourself hopping off for a little pushing.

These high passes may prove to be more a test of mettle than great rides. As a result, they won't appeal to everyone. If you relish the challenge of a very difficult grind and you are determined to show all the jeepers and ATV riders that you are truly tough (and maybe a little crazy), then go for it.

**Ride length:** 10.5 miles
**Ride type:** out-and-back
**Riding time:** 2-3 hours
**Surface:** dirt/jeep road
**Elevations:** start/end 10,930'; max 13,185'; min 10,930'

**Total climbing:** gain/loss 2,225'
**Aerobic level:** strenuous (high and steep)
**Technical level:** 5 (rocky road)
**Season:** July through October
**USGS Quadrangles:** Alma, Climax

**Trailhead GPS coordinates:** 39° 16.691' N; 106° 7.315' W

**Elevation profile:**

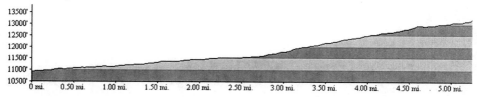

**Getting there:** from the intersection of CO 9 and US 285 in Fairplay, drive approximately 4.75 miles west (toward Alma/Breckenridge) on CO 9 to the intersection with CR 12. Turn left (west) on CR 12 and drive about 4.5 miles to the forked intersection with FSR 696 (unmarked- look for the large "Mosquito Pass 5.5 miles" sign). There are a couple turnouts appropriate for parking on the south side of the road before the fork. Park here and the ride starts at your car.

**Trailhead/trail amenities:** none.

**The ride:**
0.0    From your car, ride west and bear right at the fork to climb on CR 12 toward Mosquito Pass. (The road is passable for most high clearance vehicles for approximately 2.7 miles.)
1.2    Stay right and continue climbing on the main road as you pass an unmarked spur on the left.
1.9    Stay right on the main road as you pass an unmarked spur that leads to an old mine site on your left.
2.4    Bear left to stay on CR 12 as you pass an unmarked spur on the right.
2.7    The road gets seriously steep and rough after a switchback.

## 206 • Arkansas Valley Mountain Biking

3.5 Turn left and pass an unmarked spur on the right in a switchback. You might (or might not) see flagging and signs for the annual burro race to help guide you.

3.7 Pass the North London Mine then stay left and continue to climb past an unmarked spur on the right.

4.2 Stay on the main road past the unmarked intersection with FSR 696 on the left. (This intersection may not be obvious as you huff by it.) Keep climbing toward the pass.

5.3 Arrive at the summit. Wow!! The return trip along the same route is much easier than the climb and experienced riders will have no problem riding the steeps.

**View from Mosquito Pass**

# Ride 57: Boreas Pass-Gold Dust Trail

South Park • 207

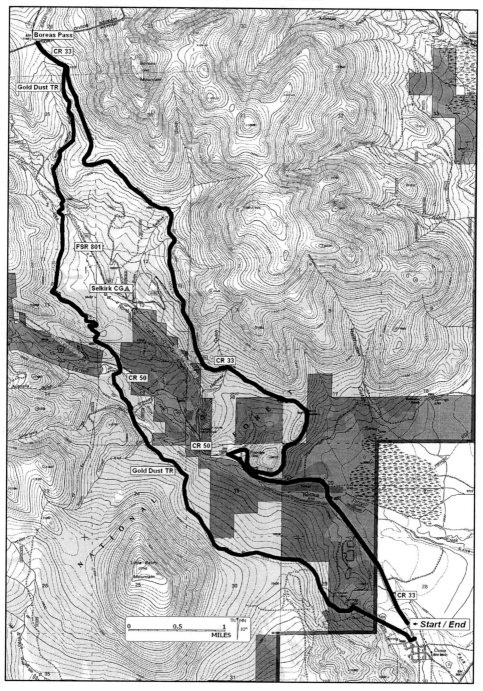

*Map 57: Boreas Pass-Gold Dust Trail (© National Geographic)*

## 208 • Arkansas Valley Mountain Biking

Sometimes it's tough deciding which rides to include in this guide. I spent the better part of two years riding and researching so many routes in the area that if you combined all my GPS files you'd get a pretty good map of the back country. But it would be a lousy guide.

One of my main criteria is simple: would someone from the Front Range want to drive two or more hours to ride it? Too often, the answer is no. In this case, however, the answer is yes. Definitely, YES! The pass is cool, easy to reach, and the single-track descent is simply amazing. You won't want to miss this one.

**Ride length:** 19.7 miles
**Ride type:** loop
**Riding time:** 3-4 hours
**Surface:** dirt/jeep road (11.3 miles); single-track (8.4 miles)
**Elevations:** start/end 9,820'; max 11,485'; min 9,820'
**Total climbing:** gain/loss 2,350'

**Aerobic level:** moderate (easy climbing; last few miles may be strenuous)
**Technical level:** 4 (rocks, especially a big rock garden)
**Season:** July through October
**USGS Quadrangles:** Boreas Pass, Como

**Trailhead GPS coordinates:** 39° 19.216' N; 105° 53.748' W

**Elevation profile:**

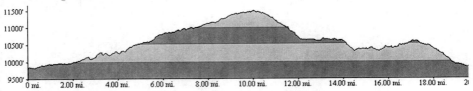

**Getting there:** from the traffic light at the intersection of CO 9 and US 285 in Fairplay, drive approximately 9.3 miles north on US 285 to the intersection with CR 33. Turn left (west) on CR 33 and drive about 1 mile to the town of Como. Once in Como, find a legal place to park in town; please respect property owners by parking only in legal parking areas. If in doubt, park on the street near the Mercantile. Ride your bike back onto CR 33 and ride northwest to the cattle guard at the western edge of town. The ride starts where CR 33 turns to dirt at the cattle guard.

**Trailhead/trail amenities:** pit toilets at miles 2.8 and 10.1.

**The ride:**
0.0   From the cattle guard, ride northwest on CR 33.
2.8   Pass Robert's Cabin on your right. There are pit toilets here. *Note- Robert's cabin can be rented from the Forest Service in summer; for more info call (719)836-2031.*
2.9   Turn right to stay on CR 33 at the intersection with CR 50. Follow the sign to Boreas Pass. The next mile is the steepest climb of the route.
3.0   Continue straight on the main road past a jeep track on the left.

## South Park • 209

**4.4** Pass the Davis Overlook on your right. Stop to take a look.

**5.6** Pass the Rocky Point Trail on your left. This is a cool little spur that leads to Rocky Point, a nice overlook of Tarryall Creek and the Fortune Placer Mine workings.

**6.2** Continue climbing on the main road as you pass FSR 33.3A (unmarked- leads to the Selkirk Campground) on the left.

**8.6** Keep climbing on CR 33 past Windy Point on the left. Check out the view. Very nice.

**9.7** Pass the unmarked entrance to the Gold Dust Trail on the left. You could turn left here to start the descent, but the pass is pretty cool and worth the few extra minutes it takes to get there.

**10.1** Arrive at the pass. Take some time to explore the Section House, Ken's Cabin, and other restored buildings. (There is a pit toilet here.) When ready, turn around and ride back down to the Gold Dust Trail.

**10.5** Just after passing a parking pullout on your right, you will arrive at the single-track trailhead (unmarked). Look for a post with a blue diamond marker and a fiberglass trail marker. The initial drop is steep and littered with lots of loose rock, but the trail improves dramatically in no time. *Note- this trail was once TR 653, but the current system number is TR 698; the trail is still listed as #653 on some maps and in the old South Park Mountain Bike Guide (copyright 1995).*

**12.1** The trail bends right before intersecting FSR 801 (unmarked). Cross the road and look right for the single-track and trail marker for the Gold Dust Trail (TR 698). The trail now follows an old water flume for more than 2 miles.

**14.5** Cross CR 50 to continue riding on the Gold Dust Trail (TR 698) back to Como. *Note- the next section is a little more strenuous and technical than the previous stretch. If you are beat, consider turning left and returning to Como via CR 50 and CR 33.*

**15.3** Continue straight on TR 698 as you pass the very, very faint intersection with TR 194 on your right. *Note- this was once a cool spur leading to Fairplay, but it is not maintained and no longer a reasonable route for bikes. Explore it only if you have the route-finding skills of an Eagle Scout and the patient, good nature of a Buddhist monk.*

**16.3** The rock garden. Ugh. Ride it or push the bike. It will be over before you know it.

**17.5** For whatever reason, the trail blazes on the trees change from blue to orange.

**18.2** Enter a clearing with amazing views before intersecting an unmarked jeep track (FSR 838). Turn left onto the jeep track and sail downhill for about 0.1 miles.

**18.3** Bear right to resume riding on single-track. This section is great.

**18.6** Pass through a gate.

**18.9** Turn right at the entrance to Camp Como and sail down FSR 838 (unmarked) toward town.

**19.6** Follow the road and make your way back into town.

**19.7** Intersect CR 33. Find your car and support the Mercantile.

**Options:** There are several ways to loop this route. For an easier ride, start at Robert's Cabin, climb to the pass then descend on the trail to CR 50. Return to your car via CR 50.

For an even shorter loop, start at the Selkirk Campground, climb to the pass, descend on the trail, and return to your car via FSR 801.

***Boreas Pass***

# One more ride...
## Ride 58: River Park to River Park- Buena Vista to Salida

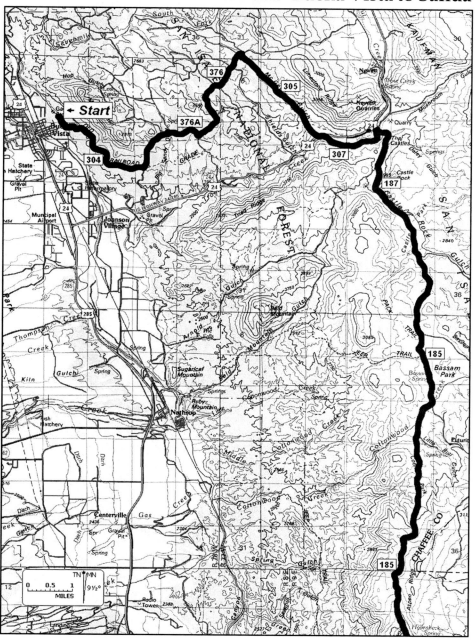

*Map 58a: River Park to River Park - north (© National Geographic)*

# River Park to River Park

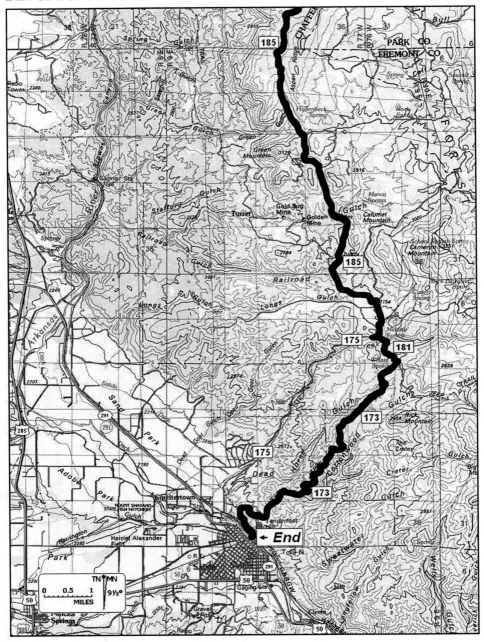

Map 58b: River Park to River Park - south (copyright National Geographic)

Ever wondered about an all-dirt route between Buena Vista and Salida? Wonder no more. This long ride takes you from Buena Vista's River Park to the F Street Bridge in Salida's historic downtown.

As epics go, this one is fairly easy. I say "fairly" because the spaghetti single-track climbing from Buena Vista gets slightly challenging and the descent to Salida along CR 173 is downright tough (a less technical descent option is included in the mileage log). In between, however, are many miles of pleasant rolling.

If you enjoy traveling the back roads of Colorado, you will love this ride.

**Ride length:** 40.1 miles
**Ride type:** one-way with shuttle
**Riding time:** 4-5 hours
**Surface:** single-track (0.9 miles); dirt road (32.8 miles); jeep trail (6.4 miles)
**Elevations:** start 7,960'; end 7,020'; max 10,300'; min 7,020'
**Total climbing:** gain 4,950' – loss 5,880' = total -930'

**Aerobic level:** strenuous (this is a very long ride with lots of climbing)
**Technical level:** 4 (the final descent on FSR/CR 173 is steep and technical)
**Season:** May into November
**USGS Quadrangles:** Buena Vista West, Castle Rock Gulch, Cameron Mountain, Salida East

**Trailhead GPS coordinates:** 38° 50.822' N; 106° 7.328' W

**Elevation profile:**

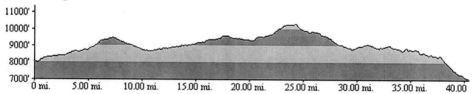

**Getting there:** leave your drop car at the parking area just north of the F St. Bridge in Salida. From the intersection of 1st St. (CO 291) and F St. in downtown Salida (the only traffic light downtown), drive northeast on F St. until you reach the parking area past the bridge at the end of the road.

The ride starts at the Buena Vista River Park. From the stoplight at the intersection of US 24 and Main St. in Buena Vista, drive east approximately 0.5 miles to the end of E. Main St. Bear left into the Buena Vista River Park parking lot.

**Trailhead/trail amenities:** restrooms and water at the start; ends in Salida.

**The ride:**
0.0    From the west side of the river, cross the footbridge to begin your journey.
0.1    Stay right at the split.
0.3    Stay right at the fork.
0.9    Turn right at the intersection with CR 304.

| | |
|---|---|
| 2.9 | Take the left-most fork at the 3-way intersection. This sandy spur is a shortcut that feeds into FSR 376A. (The middle fork is the Midland Bike Trail and right is CR 304.) |
| 3.0 | Merge with FSR 376A and continue left, riding uphill. |
| 3.3 | Stay on the main road past a spur. |
| 3.4 | Stay on the main road past another spur. |
| 3.9 | Turn right, passing a large, gated drive on the left. |
| 4.3 | Bear right, staying on the main road as you pass a double-track on your left. Keep climbing. |
| 5.0 | Continue climbing on the main road past TR 1450A on the right. FSR 376A is now rutted and moderately technical. |
| 5.3 | Continue climbing on FSR 376A past a campsite spur on the right. |
| 5.6 | Continue climbing, passing the double-track spur on your right. |
| 6.0 | Continue climbing on the main road as you pass a spur leading to an awesome campsite on your left. |
| 6.3 | Stay left on the main road, passing a spur on your right. |
| 6.5 | Turn right as FSR 376A ends at a "T" intersection with FSR 376 (**Lenhardy Cutoff**). Continue straight on FSR 376 as numerous campsite spurs intersect the main road over the next 0.2 miles. |
| 6.7 | Continue straight on FSR 376 as you pass the intersection with CR/FSR 315 (Shields Gulch) on the right. (The route now overlaps both the **Lenhardy Cutoff** and the **Midland Bike Trail**.) |
| 7.6 | Continue downhill on FSR 376 past the intersection with FSR 376B on the left. |
| 7.7 | Turn right onto CR/FSR 305 to descend McGee Gulch. |
| 10.5 | Cross US 24/285 as CR 305 ends at the highway. Turn left, ride 50 yards, then turn right onto CR 307, following the sign to Castle Rock Gulch. |
| 12.1 | Turn right onto CR 187. (CR 307 continues to Trout Creek Pass.) |
| 13.2 | Stay on CR 187 past the intersection with FSR 300 on the right. |
| 15.9 | Continue on CR 187 past the intersection with FSR 188 on the left. |
| 17.9 | Turn right onto FSR 185, following the sign to Aspen Ridge (5 miles). |
| 18.0 | Continue on FSR 185 past a spur on the right. |
| 18.5 | Continue descending straight on the main road. |
| 19.6 | Stay right on FSR 185 past the intersection with FSR 185C on the left. |
| 20.4 | Bear right onto FSR 185 as the main road becomes FSR 185B and leads to Elk Mountain Ranch. Continue climbing and look right for some nice views. The road gets rougher for about the next 9 miles. |
| 21.0 | Continue straight on FSR 185 as you pass a spur on the right. |

| | |
|---|---|
| 21.6 | Stay on the main road as you pass a double-track on the right. |
| 22.1 | Cross a cattle guard and pass through the seasonal closure gate as you enter the Aspen Ridge State/Trust Wildlife Management Area. Stay on the main road. |
| 22.7 | Continue straight on the main road, passing 2 double-track spurs on the right. Continue climbing. |
| 23.3 | Stay left in a clearing as an unmarked spur heads right. Check out the big view on the right. |
| 23.7 | Stay on FSR 185 as you pass spurs, first on the left then on the right. |
| 24.5 | Cross through a fence and over a cattle guard. From this point, you will see the northern peaks of the Sangre de Cristo Range to the south. |
| 26.1 | Stay right as you pass through a seasonal closure gate. You are now leaving the Aspen Ridge State/Trust Wildlife Management Area. |
| 26.2 | Stay right as a double-track departs left. |
| 26.8 | Turn left at an unmarked intersection and continue riding downhill. |
| 27.1 | Stay right on the main road and continue descending. (An unmarked road heads uphill on your left.) |
| 29.4 | Pass the intersection with FSR 184A on your right and continue descending on FSR 185. **Note-** *FSR 184A leads to the ghost town of Turret in approximately 2.5 miles.* |
| 29.8 | Continue on the main road and begin a short climb as you pass a spur on the right. |
| 31.2 | Intersect and merge right onto FSR 175. The road surface improves. |
| 31.8 | Continue descending on FSR 175 past an unmarked road on your left. |
| 32.2 | Take a sharp left onto FSR 181. The route now overlaps the **Ute Trail Loop** and leads to a very technical descent. **Note-** *for a less demanding descent, continue riding down FSR/CR 175 until it intersects CO 291. Turn left onto CO 291 and ride approximately 1 mile to the intersection of 1st St. (CO 291) and F St. in downtown Salida. Turn left at the traffic light and ride 2 blocks north to the F St. Bridge and the parking area.* |
| 32.8 | Stay left on the main road, passing a spur on the right. |
| 33.2 | Stay left on the main road as you pass a double-track on the right. |
| 33.3 | Turn right onto FSR 173. |
| 34.1 | Stay on the main road as it wraps around an exaggerated switchback. You'll pass an unmarked spur at the start of the big bend. |
| 34.5 | Stay left on FSR 173 as an unmarked spur heads right. |
| 36.0 | The downhill begins to get serious. |

| | |
|---|---|
| 38.1 | Although you have great views of Salida here, you are not down yet! This may be the most technically formidable portion of the descent. You've already ridden many miles, so dismount and walk if you are tired or not comfortable on the terrain. |
| 39.4 | Stay on the main road as you work your way down to the backside of Tenderfoot Mountain and Spiral Drive. *Note-* *you'll pass a couple single-track spurs on your left. Explore them if you like; most lead to CR 177 along the river.* |
| 39.5 | Pass a few uphill spurs as you descend like a rock in water. Many jeep spurs intersect the route as you approach CR 176 (Spiral Drive). Your ultimate destination for this section is the graffiti-covered water tank on Spiral Drive. (See it to the right in the distance?) Just take the most obvious descent line and don't worry about making a "wrong" turn. Most of these tracks eventually intersect Spiral Drive. |
| 39.7 | Intersect CR 176 (Spiral Drive), a well maintained, gently descending dirt road. Turn right and ride downhill toward the water tank. *Note-* *turning left will take you to the top of Tenderfoot Mountain. Check it out if you still have something left in your legs.* |
| 40.2 | Turn left at the intersection with CR 177 to descend past the colorful, graffiti-covered tank on the right. |
| 40.7 | Turn left onto the paved road. |
| 41.0 | Look right for the path over the tracks and the opening in the fence at the parking lot. Ride that way, but you might have to carry your bike over at least two sets of the tracks. |
| 41.1 | Arrive at the F St. Bridge and the Salida whitewater park. What? You left your kayak back in Buena Vista? |

*It was steeper than it looks (yeah... right)*

# Local resources

## Bike shops

**Cycles of Life**
309 Harrison Ave.
Leadville, CO 80461
(719)486-5533
www.pbbicycles.com

**The Trailhead** *(bikes & gear)*
707 N Hwy 24
Buena Vista, CO 81211
(719)395-8001
www.thetrailheadco.com

**Absolute Bikes**
330 W Sackett Ave.
Salida, CO 81201
(719)539-9295/(888)539-9295
www.absolutebikes.com

**Subculture Cyclery**
246 1/2 E 1st St.
Salida, CO 81201
(719)539-5329
www.subculturecyclery.com

**High Valley Bike Shuttle**
6250 Hwy 285
Poncha Springs, CO 81242
(800)871-5145/(719)539-6089
www.monarchcrest.com

## Agencies

**Colorado Division of Wildlife**
7405 Hwy 50
Salida, CO 81201
(719) 530-5520
www.wildlife.state.co.us

**Greater Arkansas River Nature Association**
www.garna.org

**Arkansas Headwaters Recreation Area**
307 W Sackett Ave.
Salida, CO 81201
(719)539-7289
www.parks.state.co.us/Parks/ArkansasHeadwaters

**Salida Ranger District**
325 W Hwy 50
Salida, CO 81201
(719) 539-3591
www.fs.fed.us/r2/psicc/sal

**Leadville Ranger District**
810 Front St.
Leadville, CO 80461
(719)486-0749
www.fs.fed.us/r2/psicc/leadvile

**South Park Ranger District**
320 Hwy 285
Fairplay, CO 80440
(719)836-2031
www.fs.fed.us/r2/psicc/sopa

**USFS Campground reservations:**
www.recreation.gov

## Hospitals

**Heart of the Rockies Medical Center**
1000 Rush Dr.
Salida, Colorado 81201
(719) 530-2200

**St. Vincent's Hospital**
822 West 4th St.
Leadville, CO 80461
(719)486-0230

## Other info

www.leadvilleusa.com
www.coloradoheadwaters.com

LaVergne, TN USA
07 January 2011
211370LV00004B/32/P